Compromise in an Age
of Party Polarization

Compromise in an Age of Party Polarization

JENNIFER WOLAK

OXFORD
UNIVERSITY PRESS

OXFORD
UNIVERSITY PRESS

Oxford University Press is a department of the University of Oxford. It furthers
the University's objective of excellence in research, scholarship, and education
by publishing worldwide. Oxford is a registered trade mark of Oxford University
Press in the UK and certain other countries.

Published in the United States of America by Oxford University Press
198 Madison Avenue, New York, NY 10016, United States of America.

Library of Congress Cataloging-in-Publication Data
Names: Wolak, Jennifer, author.
Title: Compromise in an age of party polarization / Jennifer Wolak.
Description: New York, NY : Oxford University Press, 2020. |
Includes bibliographical references and index.
Identifiers: LCCN 2019052466 (print) | LCCN 2019052467 (ebook) |
ISBN 9780197510490 (hardback) | ISBN 9780197510506 (paperback) |
ISBN 9780197510520 (epub) | ISBN 9780197510537
Subjects: LCSH: Political ethics—United States. |
Compromise (Ethics)—Political aspects—United States. |
Polarization (Social sciences)—Political aspects—United States. |
Opposition (Political science)—United States. | Divided government—United States. |
Political culture—United States. | United States. Congress—Rules and practice. |
United States—Politics and government—Public opinion.
Classification: LCC JK468.E7 W65 2020 (print) |
LCC JK468.E7 (ebook) | DDC 306.20973—dc23
LC record available at https://lccn.loc.gov/2019052466
LC ebook record available at https://lccn.loc.gov/2019052467

1 3 5 7 9 8 6 4 2

Paperback printed by Marquis, Canada
Hardback printed by Bridgeport National Bindery, Inc., United States of America

CONTENTS

ACKNOWLEDGMENTS

I am very grateful to those who have helped me write this book.

Elizabeth Theiss-Morse was gracious enough to read the manuscript and share her feedback and advice, and I appreciate the time and care she invested into providing these suggestions. Along the way, Carew Boulding, Jennifer Fitzgerald, and Eric Gonzalez Juenke read chapters of the book and shared their advice. I am grateful for their help and encouragement. I would also like to thank David Doherty and Andrea McAtee for the advice and suggestions that they have shared with me. I have benefited from helpful conversations with Moonhawk Kim, Samara Klar, and Anand Sokhey. I appreciate the comments and suggestions that I have received at a number of conferences over the years as well as at talks at the University of North Carolina, the University of Texas, and Texas A&M University. I am grateful to Scott Adler for his advice about writing books and publishing them.

I would also like to thank Mike MacKuen, David Lowery, and Jim Stimson for their mentoring in graduate school. So much of how I think about political science can be traced back to what they have taught me.

I am grateful to my parents Tom and Mary Wolak for their love and support. I am also deeply indebted to my favorite sister, Angela Wolak. She believed in this book project from the beginning and has been an amazing source of advice, support, and encouragement throughout the years of writing. She is the best.

The Challenges of Compromise

The year 2013 was not a particularly great one for the U.S. Congress. The year began on the heels of the 112th Congress, a record-setter as the least productive term of Congress in modern memory. In total, 284 laws were enacted, a significantly lower number than the last time control of Congress was split between the two parties and a number dwarfed by the nine hundred or so laws passed by the so-called Do-Nothing Congress of the 1940s.[1] By the end of 2013, Congress had set a new record in terms of the lowest number of bills enacted in a single year.[2] Congress would go on to set other records in 2013. In October, the federal government shut down for sixteen days as a result of Congress's inability to find common ground on a budget agreement, notable as the first government shutdown in nearly two decades and the third longest government shutdown up to that date. Another record was set in November, when Gallup registered the lowest level of congressional approval since they started asking the item in 1974.[3] Only 9% of Americans said that they approved of the job that Congress was doing, and 86% said that they disapproved. Public disapproval was registered in other surveys as well. Seventy-one percent of Americans felt that most members of Congress did not deserve to be re-elected, while less than half of Americans had said the same in a 1992 survey.[4] By the end of 2013, two-thirds of Americans were ready to call that current Congress the worst they had seen in their lifetimes.[5]

---

[1] In the 107th Congress, about one hundred more laws were enacted.

[2] It was the lowest number of bills in the first year of Congress since 1947, when these data were first consistently tracked. While the 113th Congress would not ultimately strip the 112th Congress of its place as the least productive Congress, it would end up claiming the title as the second-least productive Congress in terms of number of bills enacted.

[3] The Gallup poll was conducted November 7–10 with a sample of 1,039 adults.

[4] The 2013 poll was conducted by CNN/ ORC International from October 18–20, with a sample of 841 respondents interviewed by phone. The 1992 survey was conducted by Gallup from July 31 to August 2 with a sample of 1,001 respondents.

[5] The poll was conducted by CNN and ORC International, December 16–19, 2013, with a sample of 1,035 respondents interviewed by landlines and cellular telephones.

Compromise in an Age of Party Polarization. Jennifer Wolak, Oxford University Press (2020). © Oxford University Press.
DOI: 10.1093/oso/9780197510490.001.0001

In the years that have followed, not much improvement has been made. The 114th Congress ended up looking a lot like the 113th Congress. More bills were enacted than in each of the prior two Congresses, but only enough to make it the third least productive since the "Do-Nothing Congress" of the 1940s. Even with an uptick of bills passed in the 115th Congress under unified Republican control of government, it still landed among the top ten least productive Congresses since the 1940s. This Congress also delivered the beginning of the longest government shutdown in history. While congressional approval has rebounded a bit since that record low, public moods toward Congress remain pessimistic, hovering just below twenty percent approval in Gallup polling conducted at the end of 2018. Press accounts and news editorials have maintained a critical tone of Congress that was common to coverage of the 112th Congress. While Norman Ornstein had labeled the 112th Congress the "Worst. Congress. Ever." in a 2011 editorial, he was ready to transfer the title in 2016, arguing, "It may be no exaggeration to call the current, 114th Congress the worst ever—at least edging out the infamous 112th" (Ornstein 2011, 2016).[6]

As one unproductive year in Congress has stretched into two and three and more, many have worried that Congress is just not performing as it should. For many observers, Congress seems dysfunctional. Legislative productivity remains low, and it seems like little headway is being made in addressing the nation's problems. Legislative debates are defined by gridlock and stalemate, with partisan showdowns that lead to government shutdowns. Policy progress seems scarce, and political compromises appear uncommon. Partisan bickering prevails, and the political parties seem to rely on strategies of obstruction more than they engage in policy collaboration.

These patterns of low productivity and gridlock are at the heart of Americans' heightening dissatisfaction with Congress. In a Gallup survey, people were asked to explain why they were so disappointed in Congress.[7] A small number of respondents pointed to their disappointment with the rival party in Congress, and some complained about how Congress was approaching the issues most important to them. But rather than raise concerns about the policy priorities of lawmakers, citizens' most common complaint was about how Congress functions. Nearly sixty percent of the sample expressed frustration with gridlock and Congress's low productivity. Their major complaint was the failure of the political parties to work together to find compromises in Congress.

---

[6] The claim was challenged in 2013, when Terbush (2013) argued that title instead belonged to the 113th Congress in an essay entitled, "Confirmed: This Is the Worst Congress Ever."

[7] The poll was conducted June 1–4, 2013, by Gallup via telephone of a sample of 1,529 Americans. These data come from an open-ended question asked of the 1,271 people who said they disapproved of the job Congress was doing.

The seeming scarcity of policy compromise in Congress has also been cited by members of Congress as a source of dissatisfaction in their job. In a 2013 interview, Democratic Representative John Dingell voiced his disappointment in the changes he was seeing in the climate within Congress: "Today members are so busy getting re-elected, spend so little time there, there's so much pressure on them from outside to be partisan and to fight, not to do the things that we're supposed to, such as compromising and working together." In delivering his farewell address in 2018 after more than forty years in the U.S. Senate, Orrin Hatch also lamented the changes he saw in Congress. "The Senate, as an institution, is in crisis—or at least may be in crisis. . . . Regular order is a relic of the past. Compromise, once the guiding credo of this great institution, is now synonymous with surrender." Disappointment with Congress's failures to find shared ground are repeated by others leaving the institution as well. In announcing his plans to not seek another term in 2012, Republican Representative Steven LaTourette commented, "For a long time now, words like compromise have been considered to be dirty words. And there are people on the right and the left who think that if you compromise you're a coward, you're a facilitator, you're an appeaser" (Newhauser 2012).

Why does compromise seem so hard to achieve? The seeming scarcity of compromise in Washington might be the product of stubborn ideologues and divided parties within Congress, but it might also be a consequence of the demands of the electorate. Legislators who resist concessions and stand firm to their convictions might be doing just what voters want them to do. Classic models of policy representation dictate that legislators should vote in line with the ideological preferences of the district. To accommodate, to cede ground, to make concessions, to agree to compromise means making choices that might not line up with the preferences of the district back home. If this is true, however, then citizens must shoulder some of the responsibility for gridlock in Congress. If the American public sees no value to political compromise, then legislators who fight only for their convictions and refuse to try to find common ground are merely acting in line with the wishes of their constituents.

In this book, I challenge this wisdom. I argue that people value compromise as a way to resolve differences in times of political disagreement. Citizens want more from politics than just ideological representation—they also care about the processes by which disagreements are settled. They prefer politicians who are willing to compromise to those who vow to stick to their convictions. They believe government works better when Democrats and Republicans work together to find compromises. They are willing to accept policy compromises even on issues that they care about. They reward members of Congress who promise to make compromises and prefer that their own party nominates candidates who are willing to collaborate with the other side. When lawmakers support compromise legislation, they are not punished by their constituents. Instead, compromise bills are viewed as more legitimate, particularly among those who encounter policies that fall short of their preferred outcomes.

The Challenges of Compromise

Our laments about the absence of policy compromises in Congress are rooted in an acknowledgment that compromise is a necessary part of governing. The U.S. Constitution, itself the product of numerous compromises, establishes a system of government that nearly necessitates political compromise. If we had a two-party parliamentary system instead of our presidential system, the party who won the majority of the votes in the last election could implement their policies by casting party line votes. But instead, we have a system where power is distributed across the presidency, the House of Representatives, and the Senate, and each retains the ability to check or reverse the actions of another. Alongside separation of powers and checks and balances, the system offers multiple veto points where parties' policy progress can be derailed. Minority party factions can organize to delay and derail legislative progress, as can voices from interest groups. Committee leaders can stall legislation, and senators can filibuster.

Such a system is not without its virtues. It is a design that favors incremen-talism, and in that way ensures that policy outcomes are never too far away from the majority wishes of the public. Given our model of adversary democracy, where people do not share the same policy goals (Mansbridge 1980), there are reasons to deny the majority party unbridled power to pass ideologically ex-treme policy. But while these checks and balances can promote representation of moderate views, it is also a system that makes policy progress challenging, and one that can easily result in gridlock and stalemate. Because actors hold multiple tools to obstruct policy change, bills face better odds when they hold more than just the support of a simple majority. When Congress wants to pass significant legislative change, it usually requires broad support from both Democrats and Republicans (Krehbiel 1998; Mayhew 2005). To that end, compromise is often needed to achieve policymaking goals and pass important legislation.

On top of these structural challenges to forging compromises in Congress, we add a layer of party conflict. While policy change is easiest when one party controls Congress and the presidency, single-party control of government has been the exception rather than the rule over recent decades. From the 90th to the 116th Congresses, just over a quarter featured unified party control. While Democrats enjoyed long stretches of party control of Congress in decades past, party competition is on the rise and transfers of party control seem more fre-quent. Even when a political party gains unified control, it tends to be short-lived, typically one or two congressional terms at most. Given staggered terms of service and frequent House elections, the minority party has ready opportunities to rally to reclaim seats and greater influence in Congress. In an environment where the minority party remains competitive to retake control of Congress, legislators can choose to obstruct the majority party rather than consider compromises, under the hopes that they can regain control in the next session and work on their agenda as the majority party in power (Lee 2016).

The challenges of finding compromise have also grown as the political parties have become increasingly ideologically polarized within Congress. Within Congress, the number of liberal Republicans and conservative Democrats have fallen, and the average Republican in Congress is farther to the right of the average Democrat today than was true forty years ago (McCarty, Poole, and Rosenthal 2016). As both parties have staked out increasingly ideologically distinctive positions and the number of moderates in Congress has declined, political parties are clearly much farther apart than they once were. With these declines in the population of political moderates in Congress, there is less overlap in the policy goals of each party. With less in common, party compromise seems much harder to achieve.

Both the design of government and the deepening divide between the political parties represent significant challenges to the prospects for congressional compromise. Even so, these challenges are not insurmountable ones, so long as politicians are motivated to find points of agreement and tolerable concessions to the other side. However, reservations remain about whether members of Congress are indeed motivated to seek compromises. At the heart of these concerns are beliefs that the American people do not truly desire compromise from their members of Congress. Even if compromise is seen as something that is necessary in American politics, this does not mean that voters are willing to tolerate the concessions made by members of Congress who commit to policy compromises.

Compromises represent agreements where both sides make concessions in order to make gains that otherwise would not be possible. Because they require parties to make sacrifices to achieve outcomes that fall short of the party's ideal outcome, many worry that compromises are unpalatable outcomes to the electorate. As Dobel (1990, p. 1) argues, "no one likes to compromise." This sentiment is repeated in many press accounts, where journalists and columnists describe a public disdainful of compromise in articles titled, "Why Compromise Is a Bad Word In Politics" (Inskeep and Vendantam 2012), "People Want Congress to Compromise, Except that They Really Don't" (Cillizza and Sullivan 2013), and "People Say They Want Compromise But Not Really" (Kurtzleben 2015). In explaining his decision to retire from Congress, Senator Evan Bayh lamented Congress's reluctance to compromise, but laid some of this blame on the public as well, "Of course, the genesis of a good portion of the gridlock in Congress does not reside in Congress itself. Ultimate reform will require each of us, as voters and Americans, to take a long look in the mirror, because in many ways, our representatives in Washington reflect the people who have sent them there" (Bayh 2010). Republican Senator Jeff Flake echoed these sentiments in discussing the dysfunctions of Congress: "There just is no market for being one to compromise. And until voters will value that again, we're going to have the problems that we do today" (Nowicki 2018).

Studies of congressional decision-making also characterize the electorate as reluctant to tolerate compromise, where representatives who support compromises are thought to risk electoral retribution at the next election (Binder 2016; Gilmour 1995; Lee 2016). For Gilmour (1995, p. 4), members of Congress support compromises at their own risk, as "leaders who initiate and support compromise sometimes find themselves reviled as traitors rather than praised as pragmatic leaders." When legislators compromise, they dilute their ideological position in a way that disappoints the district. As Lee (2016, p. 51) proposes, "legislative compromises will often dishearten constituencies whose enthusiastic support a member or party needs. A glorious defeat is believed to work better for base mobilization than a successful deal where both parties get some share of the loaf."

Why would people dislike the prospect of compromise? One possible culprit is party polarization. Just as partisan differences in Congress have deepened and widened over recent years, the ideological divides within the electorate have grown as well. Party activists take more extreme policy stances than they did in the past (Fiorina and Abrams 2009). Strong partisans have become more ideologically consistent and divided along policy lines (Abramowitz 2011). Add in partisan redistricting, and representatives now face constituencies that are less ideologically moderate than they once were (Jacobson 2016). If members of Congress look to their districts and seem them as populated by partisan activists, then they may perceive few incentives to consider compromises. In a time of party polarization, it is thought that citizens do not want their elected officials to seek out compromises or look for bipartisan solutions (Harbridge and Malhotra 2011; Harbridge, Malhotra, and Harrison 2014).

If strong partisans and ideologues refuse compromise as a dilution of the policy goals they desire, then it undermines legislators' motives to pursue agreements during times when finding political agreement is difficult. Rather than collaborate across the aisle, members of Congress may instead choose to stand on principle and work to block and obstruct the agenda of the opposing party. In doing so, they differentiate themselves from the opposing side, offering voters a stark choice between ideological distinctive platforms (Gilmour 1995; Lee 2016). In a time when people are increasingly likely to hold negative opinions of the opposing party (Iyengar, Sood, and Lelkes 2012; Mason 2018), legislators have incentives to avoid making compromises with rival factions.

Others argue that resistance to compromise extends beyond just ideological opposition. When people think about Congress, their approval rests in particular in how politics is practiced (Durr, Gilmour, and Wolbrecht 1997; Hibbing and Theiss-Morse 1995, 2002). They aspire for a Congress that runs efficiently and smoothly, with a policy process that is both streamlined and expeditious. When they look to Congress, they usually see the opposite—with policy debates defined by drawn-out negotiations, disruptions, and delay as the sides try to find agreement. In surveys and in focus groups, people lament the inefficiencies that they see and seem intolerant of the deliberation and discussion that is a necessary precursor to achieving partisan compromises. From the perspective of voters, the politics of constructing compromise agreements appears more like partisan bickering. Hibbing and Theiss-Morse (2002) describe a public dubious of compromise, where people instead prefer that legislators act on their principles and enact the policies that Americans want.

When thinking about the kinds of traits we desire from our elected officials, we believe that Americans value politicians who stick to their principles and stand firm to their word (Cohen 2015). Nor is it unreasonable for citizens to demand this. During the course of campaigns, politicians make promises to the voters— of what they will achieve in office and what policies they will fight for (Gutmann and Thompson 2012). The demands of electioneering press candidates to take strong positions on issues during the course of the campaign—to secure the loyalty of the party base during the primary election season as well as to secure the support of campaign donors. These promises and pledges represent commitments that impede the progress of compromise once candidates become representatives in Congress. To compromise is to betray the promises made to voters while they were on the campaign trail. If members of Congress are to succeed in their jobs, they need to represent constituent preferences when they vote on legislation. When representatives vote against the interests of the folks back home or fail to fulfill the promises made on the campaign trail, they risk facing a tough battle at the next election.

Indeed, our normative expectation is that members of Congress should vote in ways that line up with the ideological preferences of their districts. Our classic models of policy representation emphasize ideological congruence, not pragmatic compromises. To make concessions and agree to compromise means making choices that might not line up with the preferences of constituents. When lawmakers resist concessions and stand firm to their convictions, they might be doing just what voters want them to do. Rather than see their legislators strike compromises, people may only want to see their policy interests represented and their partisan team prevail. If citizens deliver electoral rewards to legislators who stand firm to their convictions, then politicians will have little reason to make concessions to the other side simply for the sake of procedural progress.

It is therefore important to understand whether Americans truly want their members of Congress to make compromises or if they instead prefer that their representatives stick to their convictions. If Americans dislike compromise in politics, then citizens must accept some of the blame for the gridlock and stalemate of Congress. When legislators fight for their convictions and refuse to try to find common ground, they may merely be acting in line with the wishes of their constituents. In this book, I challenge the conventional wisdom that Americans dislike compromise in politics. I argue that in a time of polarized politics, we have underestimated people's willingness to support policy compromises. By assuming that people want only ideological representation from their member of Congress, we have overlooked how much people truly desire and demand compromise from legislators.

Compromises deliver policy outcomes, but they also represent a process of resolving democratic disputes in pluralistic society. As a political process, compromise is highly esteemed. From a young age, we are socialized to believe that compromise is a desirable way to settle our disagreements. In school, we learn about the U.S. Constitution as a document built on the compromises of rival interests and those with competing visions of national government. We learn about checks and balances as a founding principle of American government, a system designed to require elected officials find ways to negotiate their differences. Outside of political life, compromise is strongly valued in social settings. We are taught to settle our childhood squabbles through compromises. We are told to resolve workplace disagreements through forging compromises. We learn to accept the compromises that come in our personal relationships. We do these things not so much because we must, but because we believe that we should. We see compromise as a desirable way to resolve disagreements. As a norm of social and political life, our support for compromise has deep roots.

If we canvass surveys, we find broad public support for political compromise. Nearly all Americans support the principle of resolving political disagreement through compromise, and most Americans believe that compromise is what is best for the country. When asked what kinds of traits people admire from politicians, most say that prefer politicians who are willing to compromise to those who stand firm to their principles. The origins of these preferences is not ideological or partisan. People do not embrace compromise simply out of a desire to achieve moderate policy outcomes that are closer to their own preferences. Support for political compromise is instead rooted in our political socialization, and the lessons we have learned about the value of compromising. In school, in our workplaces, and in our personal lives, we often aspire to find workable compromises in those cases where no easy consensus is found. When asked to report how politicians should solve their disagreements, we expect that legislators should find compromises, just as we do in our own lives.

This is important for the prospects of compromise in politics. If only moderates desire compromises, then they will surely be scarce in an era when the size of the political center seems to be shrinking. But if people instead desire compromises in politics not so much because they personally like them but because they feel that they should support them, then it opens up routes to find agreements even during times of deep partisan difference. So long as compromise enjoys a principled base of support in the electorate apart from our partisanship, then our principled thinking about compromise has the potential to check our tendencies toward partisan reasoning in politics. Moreover, the socialized roots for political compromise will be deepest among those with greater educational experiences and engagement in civic life. Because these individuals are often the same people who are among the most ideologically constrained and politically engaged, this means that many of the most polarized voters are also the ones most exposed to socializing messages on the virtues of compromise.

If our principled thinking about compromise has the potential to check our partisan biases, then we need to be cautious about assuming that Americans are single-mindedly in pursuit of their partisan preferences in politics. Rather than demanding strict ideological congruence from their representatives in Congress, people think about political decision-making in nuanced ways and find themselves torn between competing policy goals and process preferences. I propose that people are not single-minded in their pursuit of preferred policy outcomes. Instead, their demands of politicians balance their partisan goals against principled thinking about how political disputes should be resolved. Even though their dispositions might often lead them to act in partisan ways, their socialized beliefs of how government should work to limit people's partisan tendencies.

When considering people's preferences in politics, we have traditionally focused on their policy preferences—the outcomes they want to see from Congress and their desire to move the country in different kinds of directions. Yet people care not just about what Congress does, but also how it works (Hibbing and Theiss-Morse 1995, 2002). These preferences influence how people evaluate the institution of Congress (Durr, Gilmour, and Wolbrecht 1995; Ramirez 2009). These preferences about how political disagreements should be resolved also have the potential to constrain the policy demands that people make of government. People value compromise as a way of resolving political differences, even if it delivers policy outcomes that might not perfectly conform with their preferences. If Americans are willing to accept compromises in politics, it opens up the prospects for representatives to consider compromises in Congress.

The Plan of the Book

In this book, I explore the origins of public support for compromise, as well as the boundaries of people's willingness to put this principle ahead of their partisan goals in politics. I then consider the consequences of the public's desires for compromise for Congress, in the demands people make of legislators as well as their reactions to compromise legislation in Congress. In Chapter 2, I start by developing what it means to compromise in politics and describe how political compromise is distinctive from other ways of resolving our political differences. I outline the virtues of compromise in a pluralistic society as well as its perils, and describe the reasons why Americans may be seen as wary about the prospects for compromise in politics. Even though people's ideological motivations may sour them to the prospects of compromise, I argue that people nonetheless think about compromise in both partisan and principled ways. Compromise is a democratic norm, one we support not because it benefits our personal stakes, but one we support because we believe that we should.

I next move on to investigate the origins of people's beliefs about the principle of compromise. In Chapter 3, I demonstrate that people's desires for political compromise have socialized origins. From a young age, we learn that compromise is a desirable way to resolve our differences. In adulthood, we support compromise for the same reasons that we support other democratic principles. Education promotes principled thinking, while those who have dogmatic personalities resist both compromise and other democratic norms. Even though some are predisposed to resist compromise by their dogmatic nature, education and civic engagement limit the expression of this and promote open-mindedness about compromise. Because our beliefs about compromise are learned independently of our partisan attitudes, our principled support of compromise has the potential to serve as a check on partisan thinking in politics.

Even if people like the idea of compromise in the abstract, they may well find it difficult to endorse in specific situations. I next consider the bounds of people's support for compromise, and the degree to which people's principled support for compromise informs their political preferences. In Chapter 4, I start by exploring whether people are willing to support political leaders who pledge to make compromises and tolerate compromise efforts within specific public policy domains. In reviewing evidence from multiple surveys, I demonstrate that people value compromise as a way to resolve differences in times of political disagreement. They prefer politicians who are willing to compromise to those who vow to stand firm to their convictions. When asked about their willingness to support compromises when it comes to specific policy issues, they widely endorse compromise outcomes across a diverse array of public policy domains. Citizens want more from politics than just ideological representation. Because citizens strongly support compromise in politics, it creates electoral incentives for elected officials to seek out compromises in politics.

Over the next three chapters, I continue to explore how people balance principled thinking against their policy goals in weighing their support for compromises in politics. Even as people value the principle of compromise, we know that they hold other competing desires—to see their party prevail, to see their preferred policy enacted, to see their representatives deliver desired policy results. When compromise comes at the cost of a partisan win or requires a sacrifice of policy goals, are people still willing to endorse compromises in politics? I explore how the pressures of partisan thinking, campaign competition, and policy conflict threaten people's willingness to support political compromise.

In Chapter 5, I start by considering whether partisan biases undercut public support for compromise. Using surveys and experimental data, I show that even strong partisans are enthusiastic about the principle of compromise in politics, where most are willing to call on their own party to nominate candidates who are willing to make compromises. Yet when faced with policy debates in Washington, their demands of politicians are more partisan, where people are far more likely to say that the other side should make concessions than to demand the same of their own party. People call for compromise among their own ranks as a result of their moderate policy preferences, while they think that opponents should make more concessions and do so as a matter of democratic principle. Yet even as politics is increasingly defined by battles between the political parties, many still expect that their own party should be willing to compromise, demands that seem rooted in principled thinking about the virtues of compromise.

In Chapter 6, I next consider whether people's preferences for political compromise persist in the face of the conflict and competition of contentious campaigns. When people encounter conflict and disagreement, it can encourage partisan thinking, as people take sides in the battle and pledge their loyalty to the party cause. When disagreement and partisan passions are high, we worry that citizens will be closed to the compromises and collaboration that are necessary to governing. I argue that campaign competition does not close the door to compromise. Rather, conflicts serve as a reminder that other people want different things than we do in politics. Citizens are prone to false consensus effects, assuming that most people share the same political desires that they do. Yet if we believe that all desire the same policy outcomes, then there is little need to consider compromise. By correcting these misperceptions and highlighting the heterogeneity of preferences in the public, competition cultivates greater support for compromises in politics.

In Chapter 7, I explore how the stakes of public policy disputes challenge people's willingness to tolerate compromises. Policy debates invite people to see politics in terms of battles to be waged and wars to be won. When faced with our partisan adversaries, we may dig in our heels and pursue partisan goals rather than open our minds to compromise. Yet even as people are guided by strategic considerations to win in policy battles, reminders about the legitimacy of the political process can encourage people to think about compromise in principled ways. While those on the winning side tend to resist compromise while those who face unfavorable outcomes embrace it, the pattern reverses when the political process violates norms of procedural justice. Even as partisan goals pull people away from considering compromise, reminders about democratic norms of fair procedures and political civility encourage greater public support for compromise. Across these chapters, I show that even as people's desires for political compromise are pitted against other partisan goals and policy aspirations, their views are still informed and guided by their principled views about compromise.

In the last section, I focus on the consequences of public preferences about compromise for how people evaluate elected officials in Congress. In Chapter 8, I explore whether people reward or punish members of Congress for their willingness to support compromises. Not only do people say that they like politicians who are willing to collaborate with the other side, they also reward lawmakers who are open to compromise. Using experiments, I demonstrate that people offer higher evaluations of legislators who are willing to strike compromises compared to those who pledge to stick to their convictions. I find little evidence that people punish in-party representatives for pledging to compromise, while out-party legislators are rewarded for their willingness to seek compromises. This suggests that legislators can successfully represent the wishes and desires of their constituents not simply through congruent votes, but also through their approach to legislating and their openness to compromise.

I then consider the consequences of legislative support for specific policy compromises within Congress. When confronted with policy changes, do people like them less when they are described the product of a legislative compromise? Do they punish elected officials for their support of compromise bills? In Chapter 9, I present the results of a set of experiments where participants were offered descriptions of recent policy debates, framed either as pieces of legislation or instead as the product of congressional compromise. I find little evidence that citizens punish their representatives for supporting policy compromises. Instead, policy compromises serve to boost the perceived legitimacy of the decision-making process, particularly among those who are ideologically opposed to the outcome. In the last chapter, I conclude by discussing the reasons why we have underestimated the public's willingness to compromise. I also discuss what these findings mean for the prospects of achieving policy compromises within Congress and how we should think about the policy demands of the electorate in a time of party polarization.

2

Public Support
for Political Compromise

Politics is defined by our conflicts—as well as how we choose to resolve them. Among the many ways in which we can address our differences, compromise has a particular symbolic importance. After all, politics is described as the art of the compromise. As Edmund Burke puts it, "all government, indeed every human benefit and enjoyment, every virtue, and every prudent act, is founded on compromise and barter. We balance inconveniences; we give and take; we remit some rights that we may enjoy others; and we choose rather to be happy citizens than subtle disputants."[1] Compromise is not only necessary to politics, but it is also thought to be virtuous. In the words of John Dingell, the country's longest serving member of Congress, "Compromise is an honorable word, as are cooperation, conciliation and coordination. Let us recognize that our Founding Fathers intended that those words would be the way the business of our country would be conducted."

Compromises represent agreements where both sides make concessions to achieve some mutually desirable outcome. When we compromise, we settle for something less that our ideal outcome out of a pragmatic sense that our agreement, even with its concessions, delivers greater dividends than failing to agree to anything. When we compromise, we set aside our goals of the elusive "best outcome" in favor of an achievable "better outcome." We consider compromises when we worry that we would be worse off with no agreement and when we believe it is better to make some progress toward those each side's goals than to make no progress at all. We compromise because we think we will gain more than we will lose, particularly once considering the losses from not brokering any agreement. If we choose to stand on principle, this unwavering stance can leave us fixed in place with no movement towards our goals.

---

[1] This from Edmund Burke's "Speech on Conciliation with America" from 1775.

Compromise in an Age of Party Polarization. Jennifer Wolak, Oxford University Press (2020). © Oxford University Press. DOI: 10.1093/oso/9780197510490.001.0001

Compromise is distinctive compared to other negotiations in politics, in part because it is more cooperative in nature and less defined by an adversarial or competitive character. Negotiation tends to focus on maximizing one's own fortunes and securing the best possible outcome. For a person heading into a car dealership to buy a new truck, the process of haggling down the salesperson to get the best possible price is much better defined as negotiation rather than compromise. Compared to other kinds of bargains that might be struck in politics, compromises symbolize a particular sense of reciprocity and mutual respect. The parties to a compromise are not necessarily out to win the best outcome for themselves at whatever the cost. Instead, a compromise starts in a place where both sides acknowledge that things they both want can be achieved if they work together. Compromises emphasize the need to reach some viable agreement over the goal of achieving the best possible outcome.

While compromises require cooperation between two sides, compromise is distinctive from other forms of collaboration and consensus-seeking in that it assumes the presence of deep differences. Compromise is not the result of finding our areas of shared ground alone—it reflects the dialogue of both what we are willing to concede, as well as what we hope to gain. In contrast to cases of cooperation where parties work together to achieve some mutually beneficial shared goal, compromises begin in places where points of disagreement may be just as numerous as the points of agreement. Our motivation to consider compromise may not even follow from any sort of shared aspirations or collective policy goals. Instead, the driving force for compromise may well be pragmatic in nature, such the necessity of compromises crafted to pass a budget or stave off a government shutdown.

Compromises are not about reaching consensus on all points of dispute or persuading one side to change its mind to concur with the views of the other. In this way, compromise has a pluralist spirit, recognizing that each side has its own interests and priorities. Compromises can emerge even in the face of deep disagreement, so long as the ideologically driven sides are able to identify some common objectives and consider some tangible policy concessions to their opponents. Parties need not resolve all of their differences in ideologies and interests to pen effective policy compromises.

Compromise is different from accommodation or appeasement in its bilateral nature. When we appease the other side, we make one-sided concessions as a way to try to quell the objections of our opponents or soften their stance. Compromise requires both sides to be willing to cede ground to the other side. This two-sided nature also helps distinguish compromise from simple bipartisanship as well. In a compromise, both sides make credible concessions to the other side. While compromises in Congress will typically be bipartisan efforts, politicians will sometimes label bills that had only token support of the opposing party as bipartisan collaborations (Baker 2015). Compromises require more than just the cross-party coalitions that can result when a few members of the minority choose to join the majority party. Compromises instead are the result of contingents of both parties coming together to broker agreements that satisfy demands from both sides.

Compromises often originate from pragmatic considerations, where we choose to pursue something less than the optimal outcome in pursuit of what is feasible. In many situations in both life and in politics, our optimal solution is simply not feasible. In these cases, we can defer our decision and hope that the constraints of the situation change, or we can work toward something that approaches our ideal but does not achieve it. In this way, compromise is akin to satisficing. In domains where we cannot obtain what is optimal, we endeavor for what is best given the constraints of the situation.

To the degree to which compromise reflects making the best of an unfavorable set of circumstances, we might expect people to hold a certain amount of antipathy or at least ambivalence about the prospect of compromise. This is reflected in how we have come to define compromise. *Compromise* is a word with multiple meanings. The first definition in the dictionary usually refers to its principled side, where a compromise represents an agreement where both sides make some sacrifices to achieve some mutually acceptable resolution. But compromise can also carry distinctly negative connotations. The secondary definitions in the dictionary emphasize the costliness of the concessions of compromise, evoking concerns about compromised standards and compromised positions. With compromise, we worry whether we has settled for something that is less than desirable, capitulated on key principles, or otherwise sacrificed more than we should have.

While we may recognize the necessity of compromise to make policy progress, it is not always easy to accept the concessions that compromises require. Compromises ask us not only to cede some ground to our opponents, but also make these concessions to achieve something less than our ideal policy outcome. For those with strong beliefs, compromise represents an abandonment of priors. To compromise suggests weakness, a lack of commitment to the cause. Making concessions to the other side can be seen as disloyal and as a betrayal of the vision of the party.

While parties may be reluctant to accept compromises as a way to settle their political disagreements, compromise can represent a virtuous way to resolve our disputes. Relative to other kinds of policy negotiations, compromise can manifest a deliberative character. We often idealize deliberation as a way of resolving our differences, celebrating the idea that people can come together to open-mindedly discuss competing viewpoints to reach common understandings about issues. In our deliberative settings, consensus is often seen as the ideal outcome (Barabas 2004; Habermas 1989). But while consensus may well be a viable goal for small group settings, it is an unlikely outcome for legislators to pursue in practice. The size of Congress coupled with the deep partisan and ideological differences within the institution mean that consensus resolution will be rare.

When consensus is unachievable, compromise can represent a normatively appealing alternative. Compromise resembles consensus-seeking in that both are facilitated when the two sides treat each other with respect and grant legitimacy to the concerns and perspectives of their opponents. Like deliberation, compromises often follow principles of reciprocity and mutual understanding, where the parties come together to find areas of agreement, identifying what is negotiable and what is off limits. But while consensus signals that the parties can move forward with shared purpose and shared understandings, the parties to a compromise can agree to the same path forward even if they do so for different reasons (Dryzek 2000). While compromises necessitate practical concessions, they do not require the sacrifice of the parties' ideological tenets. In this way, compromises recover some of the desirable attributes of deliberation in a way that does not require a weakening of prior ideological commitments. By respecting their opponents and understanding that they have different goals, parties can still pursue compromise agreements that improve the fortunes of both sides. Compromise retains the deliberative essence of recognizing and responding to the views of others, but in a way feasible within domains where partisan loyalties run deep. Parties need not abandon their principles in order to find effective policy compromises in practice.

By supporting compromises, parties acknowledge that their group interests might not always be the same as the interests of the nation collectively. Our policy objectives that we fight for are not necessarily universally shared. If we stand unwavering on our principles and always insist on the win, it suggests we see no legitimacy in the competing views of our opponents and that we refuse to promote what might be closer to the collective interest in favor of our own policy successes.

Compromises represent a way to acknowledge the will of the majority as well as the concerns of the minority party. In a majoritarian system, political majorities can act on their policy goals without having to engage with the views of the minority party. But even as Americans offer near universal support to the principle of majority rule, the practice of winner-takes-all meets with more ambivalent reactions (Anderson et al. 2005; Prothro and Grigg 1960). For many, a process that acknowledge the views of the many is more desirable than one that follows only the will of the majority (Weinstock 2013). Because of our shared norms about the importance of respect for dissenters and political minorities, many are drawn to the prospect of outcomes that incorporate the concerns of minority voices. To that end, compromise can resemble not just a principled way to resolve differences, but also a way we like to see disputes resolved in practice. Compromises represent one way in which decision makers can build on the ideas of the majority, while acknowledging the desires of the minority.

Compromises also have the potential to signal the legitimacy of political decisions. A process that affords voice to minority interests is a legitimate process, even if those interests are afforded no influence. However, in practice, people value more than just having voice in politics, where political voice without influence may do little to boost feelings of the legitimacy of policy outcomes. We know that processes that give participants not just voice, but also some influence contribute to people's feelings of trust and satisfaction with outcomes (Ulbig 2008). By incorporating some of the concerns of the minority, compromises have the potential to improve people's satisfaction with political institutions and policy outcomes.[2]

The Challenges of Accepting Compromises in Politics

Are Americans willing to accept compromises in politics? It is important to understand the preferences of the public as it informs the mandate of elected officials. If people do not want their members of Congress to be willing to compromise, then members who stick to their convictions are merely doing their jobs. There are reasons to worry that political compromise is unpalatable to electorates. While compromise is a part of our social lives as well as political life, the compromises we are asked to consider in politics differ in some important ways. The politicians who broker compromise agreements do so in settings that

---

[2] Even though compromise has its virtues in a democratic system, we cannot guarantee that any particular policy compromise will be virtuous. No doubt there are cases in history where strategies of intransigence or obstruction might have been preferable to compromises (Margalit 2010). Yet even when we look back on these sorts of dubious compromises, we cannot know with certainty whether the parties would have been better off without compromises. One of the challenges of striking compromises is the uncertainty—ambiguity about whether a better agreement was possible, or uncertainty about what might have happened without the compromise, or doubts about whether this was the right time to compromise. Given this uncertainty, judgments about the quality of specific compromises must remain subjective. There is rarely any good way to sort out in practice whether any particular legislative compromise represents the optimal outcome or the best negotiation possible. As such, I focus particularly on the mindset for compromise, and people's willingness to support the principle of compromise. To the extent to which I consider people's evaluations of specific compromises, I focus on cases where both sides and the press generally described the legislation as a compromise.

allow for personal interactions. They interact with other members of Congress who have been parties to prior compromises. These repeat interactions over multiple bills and multiple sessions of Congress facilitate the feelings of trust and reciprocity that contribute to successful compromises. These social ties are absent for observers in the American public, who instead evaluate the compromises of politics from a distance. As observers rather than participants, it is harder to assess whether the compromise truly represents a good outcome given the constraints of the situation. This could make it more difficult to accept compromises in politics relative those we are willing to accept personally in our social lives.

Our goals and aspirations in politics will often diverge from the motivations that drive compromise agreements in other domains. In the compromises made in the workplace or in our social lives, the stakes will often be personal and tangible. In politics, self-interest tends not to be a guiding force (Sears et al. 1980). Instead, we are guided in politics by social concerns and our values about the way the world should work. When the stakes are ideological and value-charged in this way, trade-offs become more difficult as it is harder to enumerate the costs and rewards of our policy concessions and gains.

Politics can be a difficult venue to find and accept compromise. In politics, we are often driven by our passions. The debates of political life engage some of our most deeply held beliefs, about our morals, our values, and our fundamental views about how the world should work. We suggest that neither religion nor politics should be invoked in polite conversation, given that both elicit strong feelings and raise disagreements that are not always easily settled. How we feel about politics is frequently affective, emotional, and tied to deeply rooted convictions. While some political debates are about how much we should spend on a cause or whether we should increase regulation, many debates are seen in terms of right and wrong or good and evil. Opinions about issues like abortion, the death penalty, same-sex marriage, and war evoke strong feelings and challenge our fundamental views about social and political life. When such issues are raised in politics, it is easy to imagine that they can provoke an uncompromising mindset. When people think about political debates in moralized terms, compromise can often see as an unacceptable outcome (Ryan 2016). To compromise could be seen as a betrayal of the principles we value most.

Even apart from those political debates that evoke moral principles, many issues can provoke passionate responses for those who have strong partisan allegiances. Just as members of Congress have become increasingly ideologically divided, some of the same patterns are seen in the electorate as well. While the polarization of the American public is not nearly as deep or encompassing as is seen among elites, the share of strong partisans and ideologues in the general public has increased in recent years (Abramowitz 2011; Bafumi and Shapiro

2009; Fiorina and Abrams 2008; Layman, Carsey, and Horowitz 2006). Citizens on the left and the right have more ideologically consistent views and increasingly choose to surround themselves with like-minded partisans.

Moreover, people seem to be increasingly guided by partisanship in their political choices (Druckman, Peterson, and Slothuus 2013; Levendusky 2009; Nicholson 2012). These partisan biases can be so deeply rooted such that they work outside of our conscious awareness (Lodge and Taber 2013). Just as people's fidelity to their political party is climbing, so is their antipathy to the other side. People are increasingly negative in their views about the opposing party and increasingly mistrustful of rival partisans (Hetherington and Rudolph 2015; Iyengar et al. 2019; Mason 2018). People act on these negative impressions. They are more likely to discriminate based on a person's partisanship than they are to discriminate based on that person's race (Iyengar and Westwood 2015). Even if we do not see the terms of the political debate in terms of right and wrong and good and evil, we may come to see our partisan opponents in such stark terms. For strong partisans and ideologues, those who are willing to compromise are those who are not true defenders of the party line. When our views are entrenched, it arguably contributes to an uncompromising mindset. As the political parties because increasingly distinctive in ideological terms, the political parties have less common ground between them. For those with ideologically polarized views, compromises represent substantial sacrifices.

Not all citizens are polarized in their political beliefs of course. Moderates and independents still make up a significant share of the electorate (Fiorina, Abrams, and Pope 2010). But even if many do not hold impassioned beliefs about political matters, the character of political life encourages adversarial politics. For most people, their main engagement in political life is through presidential campaigns. Campaign seasons are the times when people's interest in politics is greatest and their participation in politics is most likely (Patterson 2003; Verba, Schlozman, and Brady 1995). As people are pulled into civic life through campaigns, their engagement is typically partisan and adversarial in nature. Campaigns are about competition and conflict, not cooperation and compromise. The dynamics of contested campaigns pull us to our partisan corners. Debates, stump speeches, and horse-race news coverage paint politics as a battle to be waged and a war to be won. Our friends, family, and neighbors try to persuade us to give our time, our votes, and our allegiance to one candidate or another. The candidates try to recruit voters to their partisan teams, by making promises about how they will govern and what they will do once elected.

These signals do little to encourage people to consider compromise in politics. Instead, campaigns encourage people to fight for their side and champion their cause. Even if people are not strongly interested in politics or actively tuned into current events, campaigns can pull them into greater partisan engagement. The competitive mindset associated with campaigns should do little to encourage openness to compromise in politics. The conflicts and disagreements of politics draw people into politics, but in ways that promote people's partisan loyalties and solidarity to the cause. To the extent to which people are drawn into political life by the competitive side of politics, compromise may be seen an undesirable solution. Those on the winning side will resist conceding ground, as they wish to enjoy the spoils of their electoral win. Those on the losing side tend to be mistrustful and cynical in the wake of defeat, feelings that can also discourage them from working with the opposing side to find compromises (Anderson et al. 2005; Anderson and LoTempio 2002; Brunell 2008). Defending one's party against the opposing partisan team can be of greater importance than policy outcomes to those with the strongest party allegiances (Huddy, Mason, and Aarøe 2015).

When campaigns end, it is time for elected officials to take up the business of governing. This is the time when compromise is most important. But campaign seasons can constrain the possibilities for legislative compromises. Over the course of the campaign, politicians make promises to voters about what they will do if elected. Animated by the partisan battles of the campaign season, voters may have little interest in seeing their elected officials stray from these campaign promises to consider compromise (Gutmann and Thompson 2012; Hibbing and Theiss-Morse 2002). What people may want most from their elected officials then is a steely resolve and a willingness to fight for the interests of the district. For members of Congress who end one campaign already thinking about how they will tackle the next, these campaign pressures can inhibit the prospects for policy compromise.

Decisiveness and strong leadership are valued traits among elected officials (Cohen 2015; Kinder et al. 1980; Sigel 1966). When asked about the aspects of performance best define their vision of an ideal president, the most commonly offered response was that he provide strong leadership (Kinder et al. 1980). When asked to rank the relative importance of traits that a president might hold, most people said they value a president who provides strong leadership more than a president who cares about people, a leader who shares their values, or a president who is a caring and compassionate person (Cohen 2015). To the extent to which people demand elected officials who stick to their convictions, politicians have few incentives to consider compromise. When candidates run for office, we rarely expect them to promise to be great negotiators or champions for compromise. Instead, they tell voters that they will provide strong and decisive leadership and stand loyal to the party cause.

When thinking about policy-making in Congress, here too we have reasons to doubt the public's willingness to embrace compromise. When asked about how Congress should work, people want government to act expeditiously and efficiently. They perceive legislators as slow to act and reluctant to take on the problems that Americans care about. While deliberation, negotiation, and compromise are central to democracy, Americans are often frustrated when they observe the actual business of deliberation. Efforts to negotiate agreements are often seen as efforts to delay action on the issues that Americans care about most. Policy compromise is seen by many as selling out on one's principles (Hibbing and Theiss-Morse 2002). For many Americans, they would rather not see members of Congress deliberate, argue, negotiate, and seek compromises.

Why People Want Politicians to Compromise

These accounts about how the public thinks about compromise center on the importance of prior preferences, where people dislike compromise because it requires the sacrifice of political objectives they hold dear. To compromise is to concede to one's opponents, to sell out one's principles, to give up on policy objectives. Yet if we think back to the definition of compromise, it is about the character of the agreement reached as well as the process by which resolution is secured. It is not just about bipartisanship, where the two parties come together to find common ground. And it is more than just moderation and finding some middle-of-the-road solution. Rather, compromise is about mutual sacrifice for mutual gain—where both side make concessions to secure some outcomes that would otherwise not be obtained. When we choose to compromise, we make a decision to resolve a political disagreement in a particular way. To see policy compromises only in terms of their policy content is to ignore the important symbolic virtues of compromise as a principled way of settling political disputes.

Compromise is about the nature of the policy outcome as well as the process by which that outcome was produced. I propose that both aspects shape how people evaluate compromises in politics. When asked about how political disputes should be settled, people are guided not just by partisan considerations or policy goals, but also their principled thinking about the virtues of compromise. I argue that people value compromise as a way of resolving political disputes. They do so because they are principled thinkers when it comes to the fundamental norms and rules of democratic governance.

It may often seem that there are very few things in politics that most Americans strongly agree on. In our political lives, we debate what our priorities should be as well as how we should address societal problems. We disagree about which issues are most important, whether or not the president is doing a good job, or even how good or bad the economy is at the moment. But one place where Americans reveal general agreement is in their support of fundamental democratic principles. When asked about principles like majority rule and protection of free speech, citizens strongly support the democratic principles and procedural norms that lie at the heart of the American system of government. Among all the sorts of questions we ask in public opinion surveys, some of the greatest consensus is found in support for the defining principles of democracy. Ninety-five percent of Americans agree that "people should be allowed to express unpopular opinions." Fully 90% reject the idea that they can ignore the laws of government they did not vote for. Nearly 90% agree that majority rule should come with respect for the rights of the minority. Across the different kinds of questions shown in Table 2.1, there are high levels of agreement among Americans about the defining principles of democracy. Americans value the country's legal system and want to protect the freedoms contained within the Bill of Rights. They believe in majority rule and choosing elected officials by majority vote. Nearly all Americans agree with the fundamental rules of the game and embrace principles of free speech and equal protection (McClosky 1964; McClosky and Zaller 1984; Prothro and Grigg 1960; Sullivan, Piereson, and Marcus 1982).

Widespread support for these fundamental principles and values is seen as essential for the health of a democratic system. The persistence of democratic rule requires not just the right laws and institutions, but also public consensus on defining principles like procedural norms and fundamental values. Politics delivers plenty of disliked outcomes—lost elections, disagreeable policy changes, and unpopular leaders. When faced with these challenges, people could assign blame to the politicians or political parties—or to the procedures that made those outcomes possible. But if people respect election outcomes only if their preferred candidate wins or follow the mandate of only the laws that they agree with, then democracy cannot succeed.

Democratic governments can better weather the challenges of contentious politics when people grant legitimacy to the rules of the game. When faced with a disliked political outcome that was produced through fair and legitimate processes, people are more likely to accept the disliked hand that has been dealt (Gibson 1989; Gibson, Caldeira, and Spence 2005). We expect that when people respect the rules of the game, they blame the governing regime for their political dissatisfaction, rather than the system of government itself. This means that a democracy survives not just through its design, but in the collective belief in its principles. In choosing to see government actions that abide by the rules as legitimate, citizens contribute to the stability of democratic rule.

When scholars investigate people's support of democratic principles of equality or tolerance of disliked groups, they do so in part to better understand the degree to which citizens hold beliefs that reinforce the stability of democratic rule. In this way, the public's support for democratic principles helps define the character of good citizenship. Normative political theory lays out many expectations of the ideal citizen in a democracy. In addition to support for the principles

Table 2.1 **Support for Democratic Principles**

	Support for democratic value (%)	Lack of support for democratic value (%)
Decisions in the United States should follow the will of the majority, but the rights of the minority should always be protected.[a]	87	11
The party that gets the support of the majority ought not to have to share political power with the political minority.[b]	78	14
People should be allowed to express unpopular opinions.[b]	95	5
If you have to choose, which do you think is more important? Protecting people's ability to say what they want, or protecting people from hearing things that offend them?[d]	86	10
Any group that wants to should be allowed to hold a rally for a cause or issue even if it may be offensive to others in the community.[c]	67	30
It is not necessary to obey the laws of a government that I did not vote for.[b]	90	7
Which comes closer to your view? In politics, it's sometimes necessary to bend the rules in order to get things done, in politics it's important to respect the rules, even if it sometimes makes it harder to get things done.[e]	79	19
One of this country's greatest strengths is its reliable legal process—disagreements are settled in the court rather than in the street.[a]	81	18
Do you think that people who routinely avoid jury duty are failing to live up to the responsibilities of citizenship, or is this understandable given how busy people's lives are these days?[a]	72	25

[a] Telephone survey by National Constitution Center, July 10–24, 2002 ($N = 1,520$).

[b] U.S. Citizenship, Involvement, Democracy Survey, face to face, May 16–July 19, 2005 ($N = 1,001$).

[c] Telephone survey by the Freedom Forum/*American Journalism Review*, June 3–15, 2003 ($N = 1,000$).

[d] Telephone survey by the First Amendment Center, May 2016 ($N = 1,006$).

[e] Pew Research Center for the People & the Press, online, January 29–February 13, 2018 ($N = 4,656$).

of democracy, we expect citizens to be interested and engaged in politics. Good citizens are ones who are relatively informed about politics, or at least informed enough to act on the interests effectively (Delli Carpini and Keeter 1996; Nie, Junn, and Stehlik-Barry 1996). We value deliberation and open-minded discussion of differing points of view (Berelson 1952; Mutz 2006). Voting in elections and participation in civic life are defining features of what it means to fulfill the obligations of good citizenship as well (Putnam 2000).

Among these defining attributes of good citizenship, we might also include a willingness to consider compromises in politics. For Berelson (1952), the good citizen is guided by principled thinking. Berelson defines this as not only support for the rules of the game, but also the spirit of compromise. "Among such principles are the rules that violence must not be involved in the making of electoral decisions; that the majority decision must be accepted as final in any particular instance, until legitimately appealed to a court, a legislative body, or the citizenry; that the citizen must have due respect for constituted authority; that the citizen must share respect with other parts of the community and thus be ready for political compromise" (Berelson 1952, p. 320).

Compromises build on democratic ideals such as a respect for one's opponents and a recognition of the legitimacy of their views (Rostbøll 2017). Being open-minded about compromising with political rivals could be seen as a democratic good in the same fashion as support for civil liberties, respect for rule of law, or feelings of civic duty. When people obey laws and respect the rights of others, it promotes the stability of the democratic system. When people engage in politics, listen to their opponents, and consider compromise, we also expect a better functioning political system. Just as we value respect for the rules of the game, there are reasons to value norms of compromise and open-minded collaboration.

If compromise represents a valued principle in American politics, then the reasons why we believe in the principle of compromise should share the same origins as our support for other democratic principles. We have traditionally seen Americans' support for democratic principles as socialized (Nie, Junn, and Stehlik-Barry 1996; Owen and Dennis 1987). In school, we learn about the importance of democratic values that serve as the foundations to our system of government. We are taught about how documents like the Declaration of Independence and the Constitution establish the fundamental principles for the American system of government. Because these lessons are traditionally taught in a way that celebrates America's history, our earliest understandings of civics and politics are positive. These early uncritical lessons about our system of government serve as the foundations of our beliefs about democracy as we enter adulthood (Miller and Sears 1986).

Likewise, compromise is often described as a virtuous way to settle political disagreements within American politics. The pragmatic necessity of political compromise in the United States finds it origins in the design of the Constitution. Our sense of compromise as a virtuous way to resolve our disputes arguably finds some of its origins there as well. As a founding document, the Constitution itself is a celebration of compromises, representing the negotiated differences of northern and southern states, large states and small states, those who wanted an expansive government and those who wanted a smaller one. These compromises enabled the founding of the country and set the stage for other important compromises in the country's early years, including compromises about where to locate the capital and how to admit new states into the union. This history of political compromise in turn has been incorporated as part of American political culture, celebrating the compromises that were involved in the drafting of the Constitution, and how compromises allowed for the founding of the country.

Against this historical backdrop, compromise is often seen as a desirable way to solve our political differences. In schools, in social settings, and in our civic lives, we learn that we should be open to compromise and that compromise is a desirable way to settle disputes. Lessons about the virtues of compromise are often part of people's education in history and government. We learn in school about the compromises that the Framers made in crafting a Constitution and how politicians negotiate their differences in a system of checks and balances. Outside of formal civics lessons in school, we also informally learn the merits of compromise. In our day-to-day experiences, we engage in social learning about compromise as a way to bridge our disagreements. Preschoolers feuding over a toy are taught to forge compromises to end the battle, middle-schoolers learn the compromises that come within friendships, and high school students learn ways to resolve differences through compromise in student government or school clubs. In this way, we come to endorse compromise because we learn that we should.

If people support political compromises for principled reasons tied to deep-rooted socialized lessons about how government should work, then this should inform how people approach politics. Norms are a powerful guiding force in people's social and political behavior. Our self-interested political instincts are not always democratically virtuous. We might feel dread about a jury summons, lazy about waiting in line to vote, or bored by the prospect of reading the newspaper. Yet even in cases where we might not personally feel drawn into these political opportunities, we still often engage in democratic ways—following politics, showing up for jury duty, and waiting in line to cast to ballot—out of a sense of civic obligation that we should do so. Even if people do not necessarily care about becoming political experts, they will seek out information out of a sense of obligation that they should be politically informed (Delli Carpini and Keeter 1996). Even though voting is a costly act with limited personal rewards, many take on these costs because they feel a civic obligation to do so (Riker and Ordeshook 1968). I expect that even when people personally desire some policy outcome, they will nonetheless support the principle that politicians should compromise—because they believe it is the right thing to do in a democratic system of government.

Compromise as a Contested Value

If we consider compromise a democratic value, it is one that finds itself in tension with other political goals. Public support for compromise is distinctive among political beliefs in that it lies at the intersection of policy goals and procedural considerations. For the most part, we have studied people's policy goals as independent from their preferences about political process. We explore why people want liberal or conservative policy outcomes, and we separately investigate what kinds of procedures we should use to settle these ideological disagreements. The case of compromise, however, puts policy objectives and process goals into conflict. To support a compromise is to endorse a procedure that is widely seen as a fair and legitimate way of resolving differences. But to support a compromise also means sacrificing policy goals. When the two meet, which pressure prevails?

We know that a similar tension emerges in people's thinking about other democratic principles. Even as we know that people are very supportive of democratic values in the abstract, they are less consistent about how they apply these values to specific situations. Consider the case of tolerating the rights for free speech for a group that is offensive to others, as shown in Table 2.1. Here, most support the group's civil liberties, but 30% oppose letting the group hold the rally, presumably out of concern for the feelings of those who would be offended or hurt by the speech. Likewise, an overwhelming majority believes that people hold a civic obligation to participate in jury duty when called, but one out of four feels that people's busy lives could earn a reprieve for skipping out. When people are faced with a democratic value on one side, but a competing goal or objective such as order or security on the other hand, this tension between two appealing but competing objectives makes it harder to stand in steadfast support of the principle (Peffley, Knigge, and Hurwitz 2001).

In the case of compromise, citizens must weigh their principles about how policy disputes should be solved against their partisan and policy goals. Yet the principle of compromise differs in an important way from the other principles we often consider as the fundamental values of American democracy. The free-doms enumerated in Bill of Rights and principles of majority rule and minority rights are written into our country's founding documents. To support constitu-tional principles is to play by the rules of the game. However, the principle of resolving our differences through compromise does not share any sort of similar legal basis. Compromise might be pragmatic or even at times virtuous—but it is not formally mandated or required in politics.

At best, being willing to compromise is akin to good sportsmanship. We compromise because we think we should, rather than because we must. Resistance to compromise is not undemocratic per se, as compromise is more of a norm or obligation than an absolute requirement of democracy. To reject the extension of free speech or due process to members of a group you find distasteful or disruptive is a violation of democratic principle—legally, these groups are entitled to civil liberties and equal protection under the law. When people fail to act in tolerant ways, the health of democracy is threatened. In the case of compromise, it is less apparent that settling our differences via majority rule is any less democratic than resolving disputes through compromise. If someone decides that they cannot tolerate any compromise or concessions on an issue, it is their prerogative to do so. Majority rule should be implemented with respect for minority rights, but this can surely be achieved in a world without compromise.

Indeed, one can credibly stand as a supporter of democratic principles even if they reject compromise with their opponents. Even as we have those who support compromise on normative grounds, there are also those see politics as steadfast, principled battles in defense of one's convictions. For some, politics is about deliberation: learning about alternatives, discussing different perspectives, and hearing what others have to say. For others, politics is about competi-tion: waging partisan battles and fighting to secure policy victories. The practice of deliberative democracy has its advocates; as does participatory democracy (Mutz 2006). So while there are normative arguments for seeing politics as a domain where we should deliberate, collaborate, and compromise, there are also arguments in favor of politics as a domain where we stick to our convictions and fight for what we believe is best.

Support for political compromise represents a contested value. Because there are merits to both considering compromise and fighting for one's convictions, compromise has a two-sided nature. Even if people voice strong support for the idea that compromise is a desirable way to resolve political disagreements, this does not guarantee that they will be willing to endorse compromises in prac-tice. Even as people support the principle of compromise, they may well be far less likely to stand by this principle when reminded of other pragmatic policy goals. Through this book, I consider the bounds of people's support for compromise when the principle is placed in opposition to other competing values in politics. I argue that even if people's support of compromise is not absolute or unconditional, we have good reasons to believe that belief in the principle of compromise will still regularly inform people's support for compromise in specific situations and constrain the degree to which people are motivated solely by their partisan policy priors.

Our principled beliefs about democratic norms guide our choices and inform our judgments about how political challenges should be resolved (Gibson and Bingham 1983; Lawrence 1976; McClosky and Brill 1983; Sullivan, Piereson, and Marcus 1982). Democratic norms and values anchor our beliefs toward making the more democratic choice even in difficult domains. In the case of principles like majority rule and obedience to the law, we know that many are willing to find exceptions, opposing equal protection for those they find threatening and depriving disliked groups of their civil liberties (McClosky 1964; Prothro and Grigg 1960; Sullivan, Pieresen, and Marcus 1993). The fact that people's support for democratic values declines when such trade-offs are made explicit has been taken as evidence by some that people's support for democratic values is weakly held and easily eroded (McClosky 1964; Prothro and Grigg 1960). But another way to see this is that even when people are forced to make trade-offs between democratic values and other considerations they care about, their pragmatic considerations are checked by their principled support for democratic values. Even if the connection between principles and practice is imperfect, our support for democratic principles still guide our opinions in practice.

If people see a willingness to compromise in politics as a fundamental value of democracy, then their abstract thinking about democratic values has the potential to temper their tendencies toward motivated reasoning and partisan thinking about how political disagreements should be settled. Even if a strong partisan with rigidly held beliefs abhors the idea of making concessions to the other side through compromise, he or she might still be willing to tolerate compromises out of a socialized sense that people should be willing to work together in politics. Even if openness to compromise does not have the same legal origins as other principles of democracy, the pressures we feel about accommodating the preferences of our opponents arguably has the same socialized origins as the pressures we feel to respect the civil liberties of disliked groups or grant due process to those who threaten our sense of safety and security.

Implications of Understanding Compromise as a Contested Value

If compromise is a contested value, then this has important implications for how we think about the public's demand for political compromise. It implies that people care about more than just their policy goals. We have often assumed that people put their partisan and ideological preferences first politics, where people desire congruent policy outcomes and ideological representation about all else. Yet when we ask people about the kinds of roles they think representatives should serve, we find that their answers are not nearly so black and white. People are willing to allow legislators to put national interests ahead of those of the district (Doherty 2013; Grill 2007). When asked about how legislators should balance competing pressures in casting votes, people acknowledge that members of Congress will sometimes need to follow their own judgment even if it is incongruent with the specific will of the district (Barker and Carman 2012; Grill 2007). As such, we should not assume that people always desire policy representation above all else. Even if people value ideologically congruent votes, they may still be willing to sacrifice some policy aspirations for the sake of a successful policy compromise.

If people think about compromise in both principled and partisan ways, it gives meaning and importance to citizens' preferences about how politicians should settle disputes. We might be tempted to say that it matters little whether the people want politicians to compromise or not. After all, at the end of the day, elected officials are the ones involved in the business of debate, deliberation, and hammering out compromises—and they make these decisions, not the public. But if people have a symbolic attachment to the idea of compromise and believe in it as a way of resolving political disputes, then these beliefs could inform people's expectations of elected officials and in turn how they evaluate legislators and government institutions. People's principled desire for compromise in politics could encourage lawmakers to pursue compromises that serve the public interest.

Moreover, if support for compromise in the abstract can be demonstrated to be built on the same foundations that undergird public support for other democratic values, then it means that compromise draws a base of support outside of the content of current political debates. In the case of democratic values, we argue that generalized support for the rules of the game should be independent of substantive political preferences if they are to promote the health of a democratic system. When our side loses an election, our confidence in the legitimacy of the system should prevail even when faced with an undesirable outcome. If our views of how government should work are independent of whether democratic institutions deliver our preferred outcomes, it should promote the stability of government. Likewise, if people believe in compromise as a way to settle disputes, independent of the particular partisan stakes at hand, then it means that socialized support for democratic values can serve as a check on partisan thinking in politics. Even though we may want our side to win, we also want to settle our political differences the "right" way. So long as this principled support for compromise has roots that are distinctive in origin from our partisan leanings or policy beliefs, they have the potential to serve as a check on our partisan tendencies in a time of polarized politics. If true, then many will endorse political compromise as a process of resolving differences—even if it results in a policy outcome other than what they personally might desire.

If people think about compromise not just as an outcome in politics, but also as a process for resolving political differences, it highlights the importance of governing processes not just for how people evaluate government, but also for the policy goals they endorse. While studies of public opinion often focus on people's policy preferences and their evaluations of policy outcomes, people also have substantive preferences about how they want to see government work. People support like free speech and rule of law (Chong, McClosky, and Zaller 1983; McClosky 1964; Prothro and Grigg 1960; Sullivan, Piereson, and Marcus 1982). They value processes that they see as fair, representative, and unbiased (Tyler 2001). They like government processes that are efficient, effective, and responsive (Hibbing and Theiss-Morse 1995, 2002).

These preferences about how political decisions should be made are consequential. When political processes align with people's preferences about how government should work, it promotes trust in government and positivity about the political system (Hibbing and Theiss-Morse 1995, 2002). People care so much about the procedures that in evaluating their experiences with the courts and police, their views about how they were treated through the process matter more than the outcome they received (Hurwitz and Peffley 2005; Tyler 1990; Tyler and Huo 2002). If people see compromises not just in terms of what is won or what might be lost, but also as a process of resolving differences, this means that our process views inform the policy demands we make of elected officials. People may not be single-minded seekers of their policy objectives as has been long assumed in politics. Instead, people might willingly consider the sacrifice of policy goals in pursuit of a desirable decision-making process.

I proceed by first demonstrating that people think about political compromise in principled ways. Using surveys, I show that support for political compromise finds similar origins as support for other kinds of democratic norms and principles. Socializing forces like education and engagement in civic life are better predictors of people's willingness to endorse the principle of compromise than partisan goals or policy views. Over the chapters that follow, I then consider the durability of public support for compromise in the face of competing values—to see if people like compromise not only in the abstract, but also specific situations. I show that even as people enter politics to pursue their partisan policy goals, their preferences are still guided by principled thinking about political compromise.

3

Compromise as a Democratic Value

The origins of our political beliefs are found in childhood. By elementary school, most children already recognize the president and other symbols of government, and these early views of government are rarely critical ones. Government is seen as nurturing, and the president of the United States is perceived as a friend and helper (Easton and Dennis 1969; Greenstein 1965). As children move through elementary school to middle school, their early affective attachments become more cognitively rooted. In their exposure to contemporary politics and in their social studies lessons, children learn more about how government works and their views of politics become better informed, more nuanced, and often more critical (Sears and Brown 2013).

Yet even as children develop more sophisticated views about the workings of government, their lessons about the design and virtues of the American system of government tend to remain positive in tone. When describing the design of government, textbooks rarely invoke a critical voice. Middle-schoolers are more likely to learn about the virtues of checks and balances than they are to learn of the trade-offs between presidential and parliamentary designs. Many social studies curricula take a normatively positive tone in their emphasis on civic education, with lessons highlighting the importance of voting, the value of political freedoms, citizens' obligations to obey the law, and the virtues of democratic institutions (Evans 2004; Torney-Purta et al. 2001). As a result, children not only tend to support democratic principles from a young age, they do so increasingly as they move from grade school to high school (Avery, Sullivan, and Wood 1997; Owens and Dennis 1987; Torney-Purta et al. 2001; Zellman and Sears 1971). Our early affective attachments to government and these lessons about the virtues of democratic government are often though to contribute to Americans' strong support for democratic principles into adulthood. Through our political socialization, we learn to value the design of democratic government and the rights and responsibilities implied by democratic rule.

These socializing forces have the potential to cultivate support for the principle of compromise as well. Like other democratic principles, we are taught

Compromise in an Age of Party Polarization. Jennifer Wolak, Oxford University Press (2020). © Oxford University Press.
DOI: 10.1093/oso/9780197510490.001.0001

about the virtues of cooperation and compromise from a young age. Our parents may suggest that we find compromises when we are feuding with friends or siblings. Our teachers tell us about the importance of compromise to establishment of the U.S. Constitution. Our history textbooks document the compromises that contribute to the founding of the nation. Even children's books on the drafting of the U.S. Constitution speak of the virtues of compromise. In one book aimed at elementary students, the deliberations around the Constitutional Convention are described as difficult but successful, where, "the spirit of compromise saved the day" (Maestro and Maestro 2008, p. 24). The importance of compromise is often part of the social studies curriculum. Designers of national standards for the teaching of courses in civics, government, and social studies include compromise as one of the important values of civic education, alongside other virtues like political engagement and following current events (Center for Civic Education 1995; National Council for the Social Studies 1994).

In this chapter, I consider the principled origins of how the public thinks about compromise. I start by describing people's willingness to endorse compromise in surveys. Just as people report high levels of support for democratic principles like free speech and rule of law, I demonstrate that people also reveal very high levels of support for the principle of compromise. I then consider the origins of these beliefs and confirm that people's support for compromise shares similar origins as their support for other democratic principles. To further show that people's support for compromise has socialized origins, I explore how exposure to socializing forces in adulthood moderates the imprint of people's personality traits on support for compromise. I focus on dogmatism and the degree to which people are predisposed to rigidly hold their views with confidence and certainty. While some are open-minded by their nature, the dogmatic possess personality traits that make them inclined to stubbornly stick to their positions. But when exposed to socializing forces like education and engagement in civic organizations, their resistance to compromise is diluted. Even if it is not in our nature to make concessions to our opponents, political socialization encourages us to come to support the principle of compromise. I close the chapter by showing that our desires for compromise are more principled than pragmatic, in that the origins of people's support for compromise are fundamentally different from the reasons why they desire bipartisanship and moderate policy outcomes.

Stated Support for Compromise

Do our early lessons on the virtues of compromise lead us to value compromise as a democratic norm in adulthood? If people think about political compromise in principled ways, we should expect to see very high levels of support for the practice of compromise in politics, just as we see high levels of agreement about other democratic principles. To see if this is the case, I first draw evidence from multiple public opinion surveys. Because the way a question is worded can frame how respondents interpret the question, the choices made in question wordings have the potential to influence the degree to which people endorse the principle of compromise. Since not all will agree on what question wording best captures underlying support for the principle of compromise, I report levels of support for the principle of compromise from several items. In doing so, I can minimize concerns that support for compromise rests solely on the choice of question wording used, and examine people's support for the principle of compromise even when its costs and benefits are framed in different sorts of ways.[1]

Across multiple surveys, as shown in Table 3.1, it is clear that Americans strongly value the principle of compromise in politics. In a 2011 survey, 89% of Americans said that it is best for the parties to work together and find solutions, while only 8% thought party members should refuse to compromise with the other side. In a time of partisan disagreement, nearly all express support for the idea of compromise—at levels that mirror what we see for democratic values such as majority rule and free speech. In a 2019 survey, 86% agreed that compromise should be the goal for political leaders. Similarly high levels of support for compromise are revealed in a 2014 survey, where respondents were asked what is best for the country—Republicans and Democrats compromising some of their positions or seeing the parties stick to their positions, even if less is accomplished. Eighty-five percent said that it is better for this country if Republicans and Democrats make compromises to get things done, and only 12% said that they prefer that the parties stick to their beliefs. Even when pitted against the importance of standing on principle, 78% of Americans said that it was more important for elected officials to compromise and find solutions. When asked whether a willingness to compromise is a sign of weakness, 77% reject this position. Across different question wordings, overwhelming majorities say that compromise is what is best for the country. Even as people disagree about what policies are best and which issues should take priority, there is widespread agreement that compromise is a desirable way to settle these differences.

While these questions show very high support for the principle of compromise, their wording may favor the principle of compromise in that they ask people to pit compromises in politics against generally less desirable alternatives—such as government shutdown, not getting as much done, or refusing to make concessions. It is surely much easier to say that you support

---

[1] For example, Neblo and coauthors (2010) argue that when survey questions are framed in positive terms, the public is more supportive of deliberation in politics than is suggested by Hibbing and Theiss-Morse (2002).

Table 3.1 **Global Preferences for Compromise in Politics**

	Endorses compromise (%)	*Does not support compromise (%)*
In politics today, is it better for Republicans and Democrats to work together and negotiate their differences to reach agreements, or is it better for party members to stick to their positions and refuse to compromise with the other side?[a]	89	8
Please listen carefully as I read each statement and tell me if you would agree or disagree with that particular statement: Compromise and common ground should be the goal for political leaders.[b]	86	13
Which do you think is better for the country? Should the Democrats and Republicans compromise some of their positions in order to get things done, or stick to their positions even if it means not getting as much done?[c]	85	12
In general, is it more important for government officials to compromise to find solutions or stand on principle even if it means a government shutdown?[d]	78	20
In politics, willingness to compromise is generally a sign of a weak position. (Percentage disagree)[e]	77	22
Which statement best describes your preference: "Politics should be about finding a compromise between people with different views" or "Politics should be about sticking to your convictions, and fighting to implement them."[f]	67	27

[a]*Time* survey of a sample of 1001 national adults interviewed by phone October 9–10, 2011.

[b]Georgetown Institute of Politics and Public Service survey of 1,000 likely voters interviewed by telephone, March 31–April 4, 2019.

[c]CBS News/*New York Times* survey of 1,644 respondents conducted via telephone (landline and cell) from February 19–23, 2014.

[d]Conducted by Public Religion Research Institute, September 11–October 4, 2015 and based on 2,695 telephone and online interviews using NORC's AmeriSpeak panel.

[e]AEI, American Perspectives Survey of 1,004 adults interviewed online September 6–8, 2019 through NORC's AmeriSpeak panel.

[f]Citizenship, Involvement, Democracy Survey, a face-to-face survey conducted May 16–July 19, 2005 with a sample of 1,001 respondents.

the normatively desirable outcome of compromise when paired against less desirable alternatives. However, public support for the principle of compromise carries over to other question wordings. In the last row of the table, I consider a question that provides perhaps the most balanced set of alternatives. In it, respondents were asked about how they view the fundamental nature of politics. While 27% said that politics is about sticking to your convictions and fighting to implement them, over twice as many (67%) said that politics should be about finding compromises between those with different views. People are strongly supportive of compromise as a way to resolve political disputes. If people were guided primarily by their desire to see their partisan side win, we should expect to see high support for the principle of sticking to one's convictions. The high support for compromise suggests instead that people are motivated by factors beyond just their desire to be on the winning side of policy disputes.

To find that Americans are more likely to favor compromise than sticking to one's convictions suggests that pretty substantial amounts of support exists for compromise, at least in the abstract. People support not just the rules of the game, but also hold principled views about how politics should be practiced. This high level of support is in contrast to what we might have expected, given prevailing wisdom that Americans are not keen to see their elected representatives sign on to compromises (Gutmann and Thompson 2012; Hibbing and Theiss-Morse 2002).[2] However, I find that people are more likely to think about politics as a domain of compromise over fighting for their convictions. For those who see a willingness to consider compromise as a defining attribute of a good citizen (Berelson 1952), Americans' levels of principled thinking about compromise seems on par with other good citizenship behaviors like knowledge and political engagement. In a time when less than 60% of Americans can name the vice president and around 60% of the eligible electorate turns out to vote in presidential elections, it is notable to find that two-thirds of Americans see compromise as fundamental to politics.[3]

Moreover, high levels of support for the principle of compromise have persisted over time. In eight surveys since 2001, CBS News and the New York Times have asked respondents, "Which do you think is better for the country? Should the Democrats and Republicans compromise some of their positions in

---

[2] Indeed, in documenting people's expectations for how government should work, Hibbing and Theiss-Morse (2002) find a public disdainful of compromise, where 60% of Americans agree that compromise is akin to selling out one's principles. Compared to the question wording of this chapter, their item is distinctly one-sided. Absent any reminder of the contested nature of the democratic value, its emphasis on the negatives of compromise might help explain why the majority resists compromise in this case.

[3] In a telephone survey of 3,412 adults conducted by the Pew Forum on Religion & Public Life from May 19 to June 6, 2010, 59% correctly named the vice president.

Table 3.2 **Principled Support for Compromise over Time**

Compromise (%)	Stick to positions (%)	N	Date
76	15	1,050	June 2001
73	17	850	August 2001
75	16	1,034	January 2002
83	12	1,053	June 2004
85	12	960	August 2011
85	10	1,452	September 2011
85	11	1,154	January 2012
85	12	1,644	February 2014

Notes: Surveys conducted by CBS News/*New York Times.* Telephone samples, including cell phones from 2011 forward.

order to get things done, or stick to their positions even if it means not getting as much done?"[4] As seen in Table 3.2, people's general desire for compromise between the parties has remained consistently high over time. There is a modest increase after 2002 that coincides with a small change in the question wording, but across the years, sweeping majorities of the American public has strongly endorsed compromise as better for the country than steadfast loyalty to partisan positions. This consistent support for compromise suggest that these beliefs have stable, principled origins that reach beyond the particulars of what is going on in politics at the time of the survey.

Socialized Origins of Support for Compromise

People are highly supportive of the principle of compromise, reporting levels of support comparable to the public's backing of democratic principles. This suggests that people think about compromise not simply in terms of the demands it makes for each side to make concessions, but also in a principled way—related to the virtues of compromise in democratic politics. I next consider the explanations for why people voice support for the principle of compromise. If people's support for compromise is part of the same syndrome of

---

[4] The wording in 2001 and 2002 is slightly different, asking, "Which do you think George W. Bush and the Democrats in Congress should do—compromise their positions in order to get things done, or stick to their positions even if it means not getting as much done?"

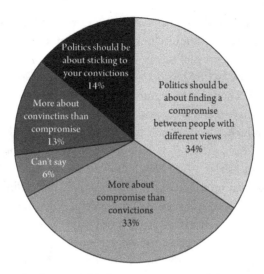

Figure 3.1 Support for the principle of compromise, 2005 CID survey.

support for democratic principles, then we should expect that both will share similar origins.

To test whether the same factors that explain support for democratic values also explain why people endorse compromise, I focus on responses to the last item in Table 3.1. In the 2005 Citizenship, Involvement, Democracy Survey, respondents were asked, "Which statement best describes your preference: 'Politics should be about finding a compromise between people with different views,' or 'Politics should be about sticking to your convictions, and fighting to implement them?'"[5] As worded, it measures support for compromise in the abstract, apart from any particular issue debate or partisan controversy. It also includes the credible alternative to resist compromise to fight for one's convictions, capturing the tension of compromise as a contested democratic value. As shown in Figure 3.1, most Americans believe that politics should be about making compromises, rather than sticking to one's convictions.

What kind of person prefers compromise to fighting for one's convictions? If beliefs about how we should settle our political differences can be understood in terms of democratic values, then support for compromise should be a function of the same sorts of factors that explain support for other kinds of democratic norms and principles. If we see the roots of support for democratic values as

[5] This was a face-to-face survey conducted in May through July 2005. Respondents answer on a five-point scale that ranges from clearly favoring the first description to distinctly favoring the second. The response options include *the first statement, more the first than the second, can't say, more the second than the first,* or *the second statement.*

socialized (Nie, Junn, and Stehlik-Barry 1996; Owen and Dennis 1987), then support for compromise should climb with years of educational attainment, just as those with more years of schooling are more likely to support democratic principles (Lawrence 1976; McClosky 1964; Prothro and Grigg 1960). If levels of education predict support for compromise, it will suggest that beliefs about compromise also have socialized roots.

Education's influence likely travels through several routes. The more time we spend in school, the greater the knowledge we have of democratic principles (Delli Carpini and Keeter 1996; Nie, Junn, and Stehlik-Barry 1996). The best educated are the best informed about the principles that define American democracy. Education is also associated with greater cognitive ability to engage in abstract reasoning, such that education will improve our capacity to understand and appreciate democratic norms and principles (Bobo and Licari 1989). Along these lines, I also expect that those who are more interested in politics will report greater support for democratic principles. Those who are attentive and engaged in politics should be more likely to encounter messages that reinforce civic norms and be more prone to learn to support democratic values (Chong, McClosky, and Zaller 1983).[6]

If we learn to support compromise through our political and social experiences, then the greatest threat to support for democratic principles is a closed mind. From the earliest studies of citizen beliefs, we have documented how some people by their nature seem to possess antidemocratic personality traits, characteristics that predispose them to be closed-minded and particularly wary of potential opponents. Such people, by their nature, seem to be more likely to be politically intolerant, less likely to support democratic values, and therefore likely to be more resistant to compromises (McClosky and Brill 1983; Marcus et al. 1995; Ryan 2013; Stouffer 1955; Sullivan, Pierson, and Marcus 1982).

The personality trait most relevant to a person's openness to political compromise is arguably dogmatism.[7] Dogmatism is an individual level trait associated with closed-mindedness and inflexible thinking (Rokeach 1960). To use Altemeyer's (1996, p. 201) phrase, the dogmatic feel an "unjustified certainty"

---

[6] If people instead think about compromise in partisan or strategic ways, we would instead expect political interest to be negatively associated with support for the principle of compromise, where those most keen on political pursuits have more to lose in endorsing the principle of compromise.

[7] Past work on personality and support for compromise suggests that personality's effects might be limited. According to extant literature, the Big 5 personality traits of openness, extraversion, conscientiousness, agreeableness, and emotional stability have modest effects at best on support for the principle of compromise. Hibbing, Theiss-Morse, and Whitaker (2009) find no effects for personality on support for compromise versus standing up for one's convictions, while Mondak (2012) finds weak positive effects for openness and curvilinear effects for conscientiousness, where the moderately conscientious support compromise more than those at high or low levels on the trait.

in their beliefs. People who are high in dogmatism are convinced of the absolute superiority and correctness of their views. As such, they are closed to alternatives, opposed to other ways of thinking about dilemmas, and dismissive of those who disagree with them. The dogmatic feel settled, resolved, and confident in their convictions and are unyielding and steadfast in their views.[8] A person low in dogmatism lacks this certainty and holds flexible beliefs that are open for reconsideration.[9]

I expect that those high in dogmatism will believe that politics is about sticking to your convictions and fighting to implement them, while those low in dogmatism will be more open to compromise. If some people by their nature tend to be closed-minded and utterly convinced of the virtues of their own point of view, then compromise represents a profound threat to these convictions. For those convinced that their beliefs are the correct beliefs, politics will be about fighting to implement their convictions, while compromise will be seen as threatening and unwise. As one's level of dogmatism increases, so should resistance to the idea of resolving disputes through compromise. Instead, the dogmatic will embrace a view of politics that emphasizes fervently fighting for what they think is best.

Finally, if support for compromise has similar roots as endorsement of other democratic norms, then openness to the principle of compromise should have little to do with a person's substantive political preferences. People's thinking about democratic norms is most principled when people apply these values in the same way regardless of the situation or group in question. Principled thinking about free speech means that one should be as willing to see a favored group hold a political rally as a group that is feared, disliked, or despised. Likewise, if people are thinking about compromise in a principled way, it should matter little whether they are Democrat or Republican, liberal or conservative. This is to some degree a tough test, as we would expect that feelings of compromise are likely more entangled with politicized thinking than abstract questions about the importance of free speech and following the law. Even so, I do not expect that support for the principle of settling disagreements through compromise is related to one's partisan or ideological leanings. I also do not expect that

[8] For the dogmatic, being convinced of the certainty of their views can serve as a sort of defense against the threats and insecurities raised by the outside world.

[9] Those high in dogmatism tend to be less supportive of democratic norms and higher in political intolerance. Dogmatism is the component at the center of the personality measure crafted by Sullivan et al. (1981) to explain support for general political norms. Dogmatism is also associated with levels of political tolerance and extending civil liberties to disliked groups (Davis 2007; Davis and Silver 2004; Gibson 1987).

principled support for compromise varies in any meaningful way across demographic groups like age, race, or gender.

To test my predictions, I include measures of education, political interest, and dogmatism. As controls, I include partisanship, ideology, strength of partisanship, age, race, and gender.[10] I explain the roots of support for the roots of compromise in Table 3.3. I model support for compromise alongside support for democratic principles, using a scale constructed from a set of seven items assessing people's support for civil liberties and rule of law. I use a seemingly unrelated regression approach, based on the simultaneous estimation of the models of support for compromise alongside support for democratic principles. This approach helps address the perils of correlated errors due to omitted variables across models, but more importantly, allows me to compare the effects of the predictors across models. In this way, I can test whether factors like education are significantly more important for explaining support for democratic values relative support for compromise. In the third column of Table 3.3, I report the results of tests that compare the size of coefficients across the equations, which informs to the degree to which the reasons people believe in compromise diverge from the support for formal democratic principles.

I find that the explanations for why people support compromise strongly resemble the explanations for why people endorse other democratic values. The dogmatic are less supportive of compromise and democratic values than those with less rigid beliefs, while support for democratic values increases as education and political interest increase. As illustrated in Figure 3.2, the magnitude of these effects is comparable across the two outcomes, and the chi-square tests for the equality of coefficients reveals no significant differences in the effects of these predictors.[11] Because the scale of democratic values manifests greater variance than the five-point compromise measure, some coefficients are statistically significant from zero in the democratic values model but not in the compromise model. The virtue of the seemingly unrelated regression approach is that I am able to test for whether these effects differ in magnitude across models, which is the key point of comparison. The only case where the effects significantly diverge between the two outcomes is in the case of strength of partisanship. I find that the coefficients are significantly different across models in a chi-square test, indicating that the strength of partisan predispositions are weighed differently in people's evaluations of the principle of compromise compared to their support of democratic principles. While the results in Figure 3.2 suggest that strong partisans may be slightly more likely to resist compromise than independents,

---

[10] Descriptions of how each is measured can be found in the appendix to this chapter.

[11] Predicted values at the minimum and maximum value of each predictor with other explanations set to their means, based on estimates in Table 3.3.

Table 3.3 **Explaining Support for the Compromise as a Principle**

	Belief that politics should be about compromises	Support for democratic principles	χ^2 (equality of coefficients)
Dogmatism	−0.046*	−0.069*	1.22
	(0.020)	(0.009)	
Education	0.068	0.068*	0.00
	(0.054)	(0.022)	
Interest in politics	0.065	0.052*	0.06
	(0.050)	(0.020)	
Strength of partisanship	−0.024	0.003	3.72*
	(0.014)	(0.006)	
Partisanship	0.001	0.002	0.04
	(0.008)	(0.003)	
Ideology	−0.039	0.013	0.54
	(0.071)	(0.030)	
Female	−0.001	0.000	1.19
	(0.001)	(0.000)	
Age	0.037	0.005	1.65
	(0.028)	(0.011)	
Nonwhite	−0.017	−0.013	0.01
	(0.034)	(0.014)	
Constant	0.747*	0.657*	
	(0.076)	(0.033)	
R^2	0.03	0.18	
N	846		

Note: 2005 Citizenship, Involvement, Democracy Survey. Seemingly unrelated regression estimates, standard errors in parentheses.

*p < 0.05.

strength of partisanship is not a significant predictor of either support for compromise or other democratic values.

Controls for demographic attributes and partisan and ideological beliefs are not significant in either model. While some have argued that party identification

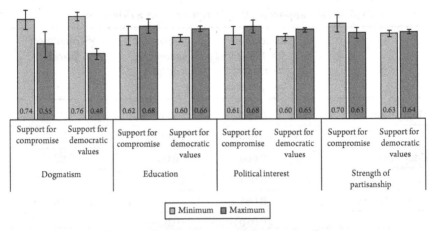

0.74	0.55	0.76	0.48	0.62	0.68	0.60	0.66

0.61	0.68	0.60	0.65	0.70	0.63	0.63	0.64

Support for compromise	Support for democratic values	Support for compromise	Support for democratic values	Support for compromise	Support for democratic values	Support for compromise	Support for democratic values
Dogmatism		Education		Political interest		Strength of partisanship	

☐ Minimum   ■ Maximum

Figure 3.2 Predicted support for compromise and democratic values.

is correlated with support for the principle of compromise (Wolf, Strachan, and Shea 2012), I find no evidence of this when it comes to people's principled support for compromise. Likewise, I find that ideology is unrelated to people's support for the principle of compromise. Liberals are no more likely to endorse compromise than conservatives.[12] Women are no keener to compromise than men, and the young are not any more likely than older people to embrace the principle.[13] Together, there is little evidence that people's partisan leanings or personal politics determine their openness to compromise. Overall, people's willingness to support compromise in politics shares similar roots to support for other democratic values. It increases with education, declines with dogmatism, and is unrelated to partisan and ideological dispositions.

Social Capital and Compromise

The best explanation for why some are closed to compromise in politics is that it is in their nature to be dogmatic and certain in their convictions. Those who hold their views with certainty dislike the prospects of cooperating with their

---

[12] This is contrast to prior work, where others have argued that liberals are more likely than conservatives to support democratic norms and apply them in tolerant ways (Davis and Silver 2004; Lindner and Nosek 2009; McClosky and Brill 1983; Sullivan, Piereson, and Marcus 1982).

[13] Some have argued that life experiences contribute to levels of tolerance and support for democratic norms, while others have argued that demographic differences do little to explain people's ideals of how government should work (Hibbing and Theiss-Morse 2002; Sullivan et al. 1981). Overall, I fail to find evidence that age, gender, race, or household income levels are associated with principled support for compromise.

rivals and believe that politics is about fighting for your convictions. Given that dogmatism is a stable personality trait connected to resistance to change, this suggests that some people will always fundamentally resist compromise and do so as a matter of principle. However, I expect that social learning through education and civic life will undercut the effects of dogmatism to promote support for norms of compromise and collaboration. Even if the default disposition of the dogmatic is to see politics as a battle to be waged, resistance to compromise is not absolute, but conditional on their social experiences. While some people by their nature may be open-minded about collaborating with opponents, those who are most dogmatic instead learn to be more open to compromise through their social and political experiences.

I consider first the effects of education on tempering resistance to compromise among those dogmatic in their beliefs. Even if we are not all cooperative by nature, we can learn to hear the other side and consider compromise. If people's support for compromise has socialized origins, formal education should curtail the effects of dogmatism. Even if our nature is to hold our beliefs with rigid certainty, education can communicate lessons about the need to respect the views of opponents and the importance of allowing the other side to speak their piece. As such, I expect that as one's level of schooling increases, dogmatism's effects on resistance to compromise will decline.

Social learning about democratic values can take place outside of the classroom as well. Democratic norms and values are not merely taught in schools, but they are also communicated and enforced by the political community (Nie, Junn, and Stehlik-Barry 1996). Compromise is arguably distinctive from other democratic values in the degree to which we are socialized to be open to this value not only through our political socialization in school, but also social learning in other domains. Compared to some of the more abstract democratic norms, we arguably have more hands-on experience with compromise. We think about compromises not only in politics, but also in our personal relationships, places of work, and our civic lives.

Political elites and political leaders have been demonstrated to be more supportive of democratic values and more likely to apply these abstract principles in specific situations, like extending civil liberties to disliked or threatening groups (Gibson and Bingham 1983; McClosky 1964; McClosky and Brill 1983; Stouffer 1955; Sullivan et al. 1993). To explain why elites are more tolerant and more supportive of democratic norms, scholars have used narratives of social learning: because elites inhabit a political environment that conveys and reinforces these kinds of values, political elites are more likely to encounter political messages that promote tolerance and support of the state (Sullivan et al. 1993). If political activists and elites learn to be more supportive of democratic values as a function of the messages they encounter, then it suggests that citizen support of democratic values will be similarly responsive to the character of the political environment.

To consider another route by which dogmatic people learn to be open to compromise, I focus on the social learning that can occur in places with high social capital. Regions with high social capital carry the potential to convey a variety of signals that reinforce the virtues of compromise as a democratic value. A place with high social capital is defined by high levels of interpersonal trust, norms of reciprocity, and active organizational life (Putnam 2000). In these kinds of communities, people often collaborate effectively on community dilemmas. Because they trust each other, they are willing to open the door to consider compromise. Because they are socially interconnected, they will be more willing to compromise now under the expectation that the other side will reciprocate at some future point. Because they are engaged in civic life, they possess the skills of deliberation and collaboration that help people find successful compromises.

Whether people are active participants in these kinds of activities or merely bystanders, places with high social capital and robust civic life should convey lessons about the desirability of compromise as a democratic value. Residing in a place that is civically minded with a rich community life could create a sense of shared interest in the common good. Places with high social capital could also manifest higher levels of compromise among political elites in government. Putnam (1993, 2000) argues that politicians are more effective in places with high social capital, perhaps because elected officials in such environments are predisposed to consider compromise with their opponents. In places with a lively civic culture of community participation and social trust, political leaders are more likely to say that they see the merits of compromise (Putnam 1993). In sum, in places where social capital is high, people are likely to encounter messages that reinforce democratic values from both political elites and the others in their community. For those who are the most dogmatic and resolute by nature, I expect that they will be more open to compromise when they reside in places with high levels of social capital.

In addition to considering the effects of one's environment in promoting support for compromise among those inflexible in their thinking, I also explore the effects of people's own engagement in civic life. Being an observer of the practice of democratic norms has the potential to spread support for these values, and personally practicing the skills of civic participation should only accentuate these effects. While democratic norms can be complex ideas to learn, we often see them best demonstrated in civic organizations. Whether it is a book club, a homeowners association, or a volunteer organization, participants traditionally follow social norms of deliberation and reciprocity—taking turns, letting other people speak their piece, and respecting that others might not agree with our opinions. Apart from observing democratic norms in practice, we can also engage in our own efforts to broker compromises, where we gain personal hands-on experiences with how compromises are made. Our ability to do so is facilitated by the civic skills we acquire through our organizational life (Verba, Schlozman, and Brady 1995). Participation in voluntary organizations is also social in nature. By interacting with others who share common interests, norms of trust and reciprocity are encouraged. Organizations emphasize the social side of politics. Even if we see politics as a domain of strong convictions and partisan battles, our organizational life puts us in an environment where we have personal relationships and friendships with people who do not always agree with our opinions. Our desire to maintain those social relationships might also nudge us toward compromise, as a way to find agreements where both sides achieve some objectives.

Social Capital, Dogmatism, and Support for the Principle of Compromise

For those high in dogmatism, politics is about fighting for your convictions, not compromising with the other side. Even so, I expect that socializing forces like education, social capital, and organizational involvement should undercut resistance to compromise among the dogmatic. In Table 3.4, I consider how these influences moderate the effects of dogmatism on principled support for political compromise. Because social capital is measured at the state level, I rely on a multilevel regression model to explore how the effects of dogmatism vary across states as well as individuals.[14] In models that do not include social capital, I rely on regression. I find, first, that education tempers the effects of dogmatism on opposition to compromise. While those with the strongest convictions tend to like compromise less than those who are open-minded, the differences between the two disappear as levels of education increase, as shown in Figure 3.3. [15] For those who have completed at least some college, dogmatism no longer has a significant marginal effect on support for compromise. The power of dogmatism in predicting opposition to compromise is strongest for those who have completed the least schooling. This is consistent with a narrative of social learning, where

---

[14] The model is specified with a random intercept associated with states and random coefficient term associated with the dogmatism measure. The covariance term between the two random effects was dropped as it was not statistically significant and did not improve the model fit.

[15] The plot shows predicted support for compromise across levels of educational attainment for those at the 10th percentile and 90th percentile of dogmatism. Predicted values are based on first model in Table 3.4; all other variables at their means.

Table 3.4 **Social Capital, Civic Skills, and Support for Compromise**

	Support for the principle of compromise		
Dogmatism	−0.125*	−0.136*	−0.132*
	(0.036)	(0.044)	(0.044)
Social capital	−0.061		
	(0.041)		
Dogmatism × Social capital	0.055*		
	(0.026)		
Organizational memberships		−0.033[a]	
		(0.018)	
Memberships × Dogmatism		0.019[a]	
		(0.011)	
Organizational volunteer participation			−0.041*
			(0.019)
Organizational volunteerism × Dogmatism			0.026*
			(0.013)
Education	−0.276*	−0.156	−0.182
	(0.131)	(0.139)	(0.133)
Education × Dogmatism	0.174*	0.124[a]	0.135[a]
	(0.062)	(0.073)	(0.070)
Interest in politics	0.082	0.078	0.075
	(0.051)	(0.051)	(0.051)
Strength of partisanship	−0.022	−0.024[a]	−0.023[a]
	(0.017)	(0.014)	(0.014)
Party identification	−0.004	−0.001	−0.001
	(0.007)	(0.007)	(0.007)
Ideology	−0.035	−0.045	−0.051
	(0.060)	(0.071)	(0.071)
Age	−0.001	−0.001	−0.001
	(0.001)	(0.001)	(0.001)
Female	0.031	0.038	0.036
	(0.029)	(0.028)	(0.028)
Nonwhite	−0.037	−0.026	−0.025
	(0.029)	(0.034)	(0.034)

Table 3.4 **Continued**

	Support for the principle of compromise		
Constant	0.941*	0.920*	0.917*
	(0.089)	(0.102)	(0.102)
Variance, intercept	0.000		
	(0.000)		
Variance, dogmatism	0.002		
	(0.001)		
R^2		0.041	0.041
N	842	842	842

Note: Multilevel regression estimates are in the first column. Regression estimates are in the second and third columns. Standard errors are in parentheses.

*p < 0.05.

ªp < 0.10.

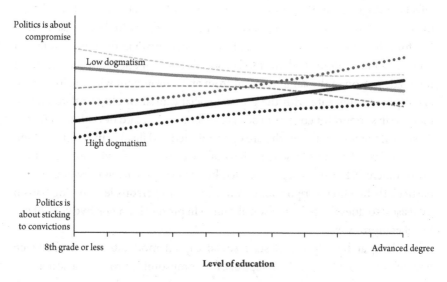

Figure 3.3 Dogmatism, education, and support for compromise as a principle.

people come to support democratic values like compromise as they are exposed to the socializing lessons of formal education.

The results also suggest that people think about compromise differently depending on the character of their state environment. While the dogmatic tend

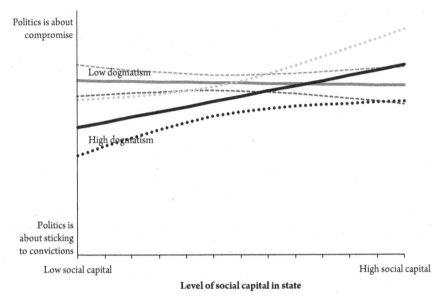

Figure 3.4 Dogmatism, social capital, and support for compromise as a principle.

to resist compromise, living in places with greater social capital diminishes the effects of dogmatism. For those who are not of a dogmatic orientation (below the median level of dogmatism), levels of social capital are of little consequence. But for those at or above the median level of dogmatism in the sample, support for compromise climbs with the level of social capital in one's state. For the most dogmatic person in the sample, a shift from an environment with the lowest social capital to the state with the greatest social capital would translate into an increase in support for compromise of 0.4 (about a standard deviation increase). As seen in Figure 3.4, those who are open-minded and flexible by nature see politics in terms of compromise regardless of the character of civic culture in their environment.[16] For those open-minded by nature, socializing pressures do not particularly heighten support for compromise. As a person's level of dogmatism increases, so does the power of social capital in promoting a positive view of political compromise.

Looking at how levels of state social capital moderate the tie between people's personality and their support for compromise provides a somewhat indirect test of how socializing pressures encourage people to consider compromise. However, I find the same moderating effect when considering more

---

[16] The figure plots predicted support for compromise across state environments for those at the 10th percentile and 90th percentile of dogmatism. Predicted values are based on first model in Table 3.4; all other variables at their means.

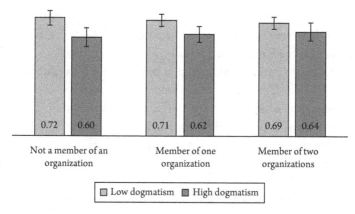

Figure 3.5 Dogmatism, organizational membership, and support for compromise as a principle.

direct measures of people's personal engagement in civic life. In the remaining columns of Table 3.4, I consider how people's involvement in organizational life moderates the effects of dogmatism on support for compromise as a principle.[17] I first find that as a person's number of memberships in voluntary organizations increases, the effects of dogmatism on support for compromise decline. In Figure 3.5, I present predicted support for compromise for those at the 10th percentile and 90th percentile of dogmatism. In the case of uninvolved citizens who are not members of any voluntary organizations, increasing dogmatism is tied to perceptions that politics is about fighting for one's convictions, as indicated by a significant marginal effect for dogmatism. For those who report membership in even one organization, the effects of dogmatism are reduced. The most dogmatic are still significantly more resistant to compromise than the least dogmatic, but the magnitude of the difference is reduced by more than a third. For those who are members of two organizations, there is no longer a statistically significant difference in support for compromise between the dogmatic and the open-minded.[18] Engagement in civic life mitigates the effects of dogmatism and promotes support for the principle of compromise.

As an additional check that these effects reflect the influence of civic life, I also consider whether active participation in organizational life has effects that are distinct from mere membership. If support for compromise is learned, the

[17] The personality trait of dogmatism is at best weakly associated with interpersonal trust ($r = -0.11$), membership in voluntary organizations ($r = -0.19$), and voluntary work in organizations ($r = -0.014$).

[18] Eighty-two percent of the sample is a member of two or fewer organizations and 94% of the sample volunteers for two or fewer organizations.

effects of organizational life should be strongest for those who not only join, but actively give their time to the group. In last column of Table 3.4, I test whether dogmatism's effects are moderated by the number of organizations in which the respondent is actively participating in voluntary work for the organization. I find that the effects of civic engagement are even greater when considering people's active participation in voluntary organizations. As seen in Figure 3.6, voluntary work for even a single community organization renders the difference in support for compromise insignificant between the dogmatic and the undogmatic. Involvement in organizational life tempers resistance to compromise among the dogmatic.

These results highlight some of the virtues of organizational life. Some have been pessimistic about the virtues of civic participation, raising worries that involvement in organizational life encourages intolerance or closed-mindedness. As Theiss-Morse and Hibbing (2005, p. 244) propose, "Voluntary groups perform wonderful services and have undeniable value to society, but their effect on democratic politics is tenuous and possibly negative." These results offer some optimism about the democratic value of organizational life, as active engagement in voluntary organizations is tied to greater willingness to support the democratic norm of compromise among those who otherwise would be expected to dogmatically fight for their principles. These results highlight the importance of political learning for people's support for compromise in politics. While some people are drawn to support compromise by their nature, for those who are the most likely to be stubborn in their convictions, support for compromise is learned.

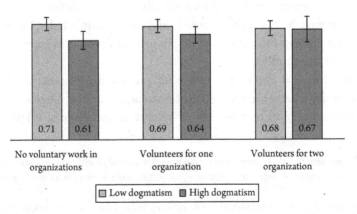

Figure 3.6 Dogmatism, organizational work, and support for compromise as a principle.

Preferences for Compromise, Bipartisanship, and Moderate Policy

Compromise lies at the intersection of what we want from government and how we want political disputes to be resolved. When people call for compromise, it is not simply because they desire the moderate policy outcomes implied by a compromise agreement. Instead, people endorse compromises because they find them a democratically desirable way to settle disputes and disagreements. I have argued that people's feelings about the principle of compromise are guided not by their policy aspirations, but instead by their abstract support for compromise as a democratic norm. So far, my results show that people are thinking about compromise in principled kinds of ways, where they endorse compromise for the same reasons they come to support other democratic values. As a further test, I next consider whether the origins of people's demands for compromise are truly distinctive from the reasons why they choose to call for moderate policy in Washington.

To do so, I rely on a survey that includes measures of not only people's willingness to support compromise, but also their expressed desires for both bipartisan politics and moderate policy outcomes. If compromise has distinctive socialized bases of support, then we should see that the factors that explain support for compromise diverge from the factors that explain support for bipartisan politics. Support for compromise should be more strongly related to exposure to socializing factors like education, while desires for middle-of-the-road policy outcomes should instead be tied to people's policy goals and partisan attachments.

In a 2014 survey conducted by the Pew Research Center, respondents were asked, "Which comes closer to your own views, even if neither is exactly right?" [19] The response alternatives were, "I like elected officials who make compromises with people they disagree with" and "I like elected officials who stick to their positions." Fifty-six percent selected the compromise option, and 39% said they prefer leaders who stick to their positions. I start by first considering the origins of people's support for compromise, as a way to confirm the relationships observed earlier in this chapter. If people think about compromise in principled ways, then we should see that calls for compromise increase among with greater education and exposure to socializing forces. I test this by first including a measure

---

[19] The questions were included in the first phase of the Political Polarization and Typology Survey conducted January 23 to February 9, 2014 with a sample of 3341 respondents interviewed by telephone.

of educational attainment.[20] As people's years of schooling increase, so do levels of exposure to the socializing messages that reinforce democratic principles and norms of compromise. As a second test of this socialization mechanism, I include a measure of campaign participation, as those who are most engaged in politics are the most likely to encounter messages that reinforce civic norms and democratic principles (Chong, McClosky, and Zaller 1983). It is measured as the sum of four items: being registered to vote, contributions to a campaign or election group, volunteering for a campaign in the past two years, and attending a campaign event in the last two years. If people are primarily partisan in how they think about compromise, then activists are likely to be among the most opposed to compromise. However, if people think about compromise in principled ways, then we should expect stronger support for compromise among the most politically engaged.

If people instead think about compromise in terms of their policy objectives, then resistance to compromise should be greatest among those with the strongest political passions, particularly strong partisans and those with ideologically polarized policy preferences. Political independents and those with moderate policy preferences should then be distinctly supportive of the prospect of compromise, as it should promote policy moderation and outcomes closer to their own ideal point. I include two measures to assess the intensity and extremity of people's political views. First, I consider the effects of strong partisan priors, by including a folded version of the seven-point party identification scale. High values indicate strong partisans, while low values indicate independents. To the degree to which strong partisans hold less centrist policy preferences, they should be less open to considering compromises. Second, I distinguish respondents who are policy moderates from those who hold consistently liberal or conservative views. To create a measure of policy moderation, I use respondents' stated policy preferences across a dozen policy issues.[21] A person who answers all of the policy questions in a conservative or liberal way is coded zero on this scale, while a person who gives equal numbers of liberal and conservative responses is coded 1. If people are guided by their policy goals when thinking about compromise, those who hold consistent ideologically liberal or

[20] Education is measured on an eight-point scale that ranges from *less than an eighth-grade education* to *postgraduate degree*.

[21] The scale includes two items about government activism and the regulation of business, three items about the value of government programs to help the needy, two items about racial discrimination and the need for government action on the issue, two items about the need for laws to protect the environment, two items about military strength versus diplomacy, and one item about the value of immigrants in American society. All items are dichotomous choice items and the liberalism score sums liberal responses from the set of items. The scale has a Cronbach's alpha of 0.84. The scale of policy moderation is the folded and reversed version of this liberalism scale.

conservative policy views should be less willing to consider concessions, while policy moderates should be more likely to favor compromise in politics.

Results are shown in Table 3.5. Consistent with the previous findings, both educational attainment and engagement in civic life are positively associated with support for political leaders who are willing to compromise. Holding other variables at their means, a person with the lowest level of educational attainment has a 43% likelihood of favoring leaders who are willing to compromise. This climbs to 75% for a person at the highest level of education. People's support for compromise has socialized roots. This same pattern is confirmed when considering support for compromise by levels of campaign engagement. A person who

Table 3.5 **Explaining People's Desire for Politicians Who Are Willing to Compromise**

	Prefers compromise	Preference for bipartisan outcomes	Policy moderation
Education	0.200*	0.025*	−0.029*
	(0.027)	(0.004)	(0.003)
Campaign participation	0.132*	−0.015	−0.054*
	(0.052)	(0.008)	(0.007)
Strength of partisanship	−0.029	−0.055*	−0.030*
	(0.047)	(0.008)	(0.006)
Policy moderation	−0.154	0.151*	
	(0.149)	(0.024)	
Female	−0.030	0.000	0.037*
	(0.089)	(0.015)	(0.012)
Age	−0.007*	0.000	−0.001*
	(0.003)	(0.000)	0.000
Constant	−0.176	0.651*	0.813*
	(0.217)	(0.036)	(0.023)
R^2		0.059	0.105
N	2968	2967	3106

Notes: 2014 Political Polarization and Typology Survey, Pew Research Center. Logit estimates are in the first column. Regression estimates are in the second and third columns. Standard errors in parentheses.

*$p < 0.05$.

has not participated in any campaign activities has a 55% likelihood of favoring politicians who compromise, all else equal, while a campaign activist has a 67% likelihood of preferring politicians who are willing to compromise.

If our willingness to compromise were a reflection of our policy preferences alone, we would expect that the most politically sophisticated respondents and the most engaged citizens would be the ones least likely to desire compromises in politics. Political sophisticates are among the most likely to engage in motivated reasoning, the most ideologically consistent in their views, and the least likely to engage in diverse discussion (Abramowitz 2011; Lodge and Taber 2013; Mutz 2006). There are good reasons to think that those with greater political sophistication are the most likely to stand in opposition to compromises in politics. However, I instead find that the traits of political sophisticates tend to be aligned with *greater* support for political leaders who are willing to compromise.

I find little evidence that people's support for compromise depends on their partisan and ideological leanings. Strong partisans are no more likely to oppose compromise than independents, and those with ideologically sorted policy beliefs are no more closed to compromise than policy moderates. Overall, people's willingness to compromise is not a reflection of a desire to achieve centrist policy outcomes. We desire compromise not simply because we lack strong preferences: we support compromise in part because we believe we should.

I next consider whether people think about compromise differently from the ways they think about bipartisan politics. I expect that socializing forces should be central to encouraging compromise, but less important to explaining people's demand for moderate policy outcomes. In the second column of Table 3.5, I consider how these same factors fare as explanations for people's desire for middle-of-the-road outcomes when it comes to policy decision-making. Using a thermometer scale, respondents were asked, "Thinking about how Barack Obama and Republican leaders should address the most important issues facing the country. Imagine a scale from zero to 100 where 100 means Republican leaders get everything they want and Obama gets nothing he wants, and zero means Obama gets everything and Republican leaders get nothing. Where on this scale from zero to 100 do you think they should end up?" I create a folded version of the measure, coded such that high scores indicate people's desire for outcomes that balance the partisan preferences of Democrats and Republicans, while low scores indicate preferences of clearly Democratic or Republican outcomes.

I find that those with higher education are more likely to favor compromise as well as bipartisan policy outcomes that balance the parties' demands, while those engaged in civic life are not any more supportive of middle-of-the-road partisan outcomes. While people's desire for policy compromise is unrelated to the strength of their partisan and ideological leanings, I find that policy moderation is associated with a stronger desire for balanced party outcomes, while strong partisanship undercuts this desire. The reasons why people like compromise are distinct from the explanations for people's desire for policy outcomes that balance Republican and Democratic preferences.

As a final test, I model the policy moderation measure as a function of the same set of predictors in the third column of the table. It is clear that the origins of people's support for political compromise are strikingly different than the reasons why people prefer moderate policy outcomes. Independents are significantly more likely than strong partisans to support a mix of liberal and conservative policy views. Education and campaign participation have the opposite effects as they did in the case of compromise. Increasing education is associated with more ideologically distinctive views, and campaign activists are less likely to be moderates than the uninvolved. The reasons why people like moderate policy outcomes are distinct from the reasons why they support compromises in politics. Demands for compromise are tied to greater education and engagement, while preferences for policy moderation are correlated with lower education and engagement as well as weaker partisan preferences.

Do People Demand Compromise from Elected Officials?

People think about compromise in different terms from how they think about moderate policy or bipartisan politics. Do they also ascribe unique political importance to compromise? Or is compromise merely a general social expectation, where we generally believe it is an effective approach to our disagreements across domains? To better understand our expectations of elected officials, I consider whether people hold politicians to a different standard when it comes to being willing to compromise in politics. To do so, I rely on a question wording experiment where some were asked about how elected officials should approach politics, while others were asked about their expectations for average citizens. If people are equally supportive of the principle of compromise across conditions, it will suggest that people broadly value compromise as a remedy to disputes. If people are more likely to believe legislators should be supportive of compromise than to expect the same for average citizens, then it suggests that compromise is uniquely important to people's expectations for how political disputes should be resolved.

The experiment was included in a module of the 2014 Cooperative Congressional Election Study, with a sample of 1,497 respondents. In it, I asked people about how people should approach contentious political issues. Half were

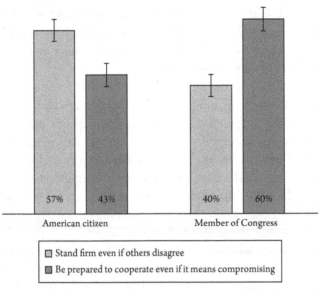

Figure 3.7 Compromise and people's expectations of politicians.

asked what a member of Congress should do when he or she feels strongly about an issue dividing the nation, while the other half were asked the same about an American citizen.[22] Respondents could choose between two options: "Stand firm for what he or she believes, even if others disagree," or "Be prepared to cooperate with other groups, even if it means compromising some important beliefs." Results are shown in Figure 3.7. I find that people are more likely to expect elected representatives to compromise than to expect the same of average Americans. Forty-three percent favored the compromise option when asked about their expectations for average Americans, while 60% favored the compromise option when they were asked about their expectations of members of Congress. The difference is statistically significant ($t = 6.75, p < 0.01$).

Conclusions

We often think about politics in terms of winners and losers—both in election seasons and in policymaking. Because of this, we have often assumed that Americans are also driven by a desire to win in politics. Indeed, people are happy to see their partisan team succeed on election day and glad when their preferred

---

[22] The specific wording asked, "When [a member of Congress/an American citizen] feels strongly about a major political issue and that issue is dividing the nation, what do you think he or she should do?"

policies are enacted in Washington. However, winning isn't everything in politics. People also have beliefs about how politics should be practiced. They believe that the sides should play by the rules, that rights should be respected, and that politicians should be open to making compromises. These beliefs are not something inherent to all citizens as much as they are something we learn through formal education and informal socialization.

People support compromise as a principled way to resolve political dilemmas. Even though we are often pessimistic about citizens' abilities to live up to the norms of good citizenship, on average, people see politics as a domain of compromise rather than a venue to steadfastly fight for our convictions. In exploring why people see politics in terms of compromise instead of fighting for one's convictions, their beliefs seem to have little to do with partisanship or ideology. Instead, support for compromise has similar roots as support for other democratic values. Education and personality are the best explanations for support for democratic values and have countervailing influences. While our predispositions to be strong-minded lead us to resist compromise, we become more supportive of democratic principles through education. Political socialization mitigates the effects of closed-mindedness and promotes greater openness to compromise. Even though some people by their nature resist compromise, social learning can shift people's perspectives away from a view of politics as battles to be waged and won. Even the dogmatic, who by their nature are unlikely to change their ways, become more open to compromise as their civic skills increase.

Many have argued that education and engagement with civic life cultivate a positive political culture (Mill 1910; Putnam 1993, 2000; Tocqueville 1969). Whether these factors similarly boost support for democratic values has been questioned (Miller and Sears 1986; Nie, Junn, and Stehlik-Barry 1996). I find evidence that suggests that people learn their support for compromise not only in school, but also in their civic lives. Both social capital at large and personal civic engagement promote greater openness to compromise as a principle, reducing people's tendencies to dogmatically pursue their preferred outcomes in politics. This suggests that we learn to support compromise in politics and that this social learning continues even after we leave school.

We know that the most engaged and participatory citizens are the ones who are most likely to be polarized in their political beliefs (Abramowitz 2011; Jewitt and Goren 2015). We might worry then that even if many citizens favored compromise, this support might be concentrated among the least engaged and least sophisticated subset of Americans. Instead, I find that strong partisans are just as supportive of compromise as independents and weak partisans. Support for compromise is not something unique to those with moderate preferences or weak partisan attachments. In fact, the origins of people's support for compromise are distinct from those forces that guide people to prefer moderate or middle-of-the-road policy outcomes. Ideologues and strong partisans are no more likely to oppose compromise than those at the middle of the ideological spectrum. Instead, support for compromise seems best predicted by principled thinking. Increasing education and political engagement are associated with greater willingness to support compromise as a political outcome. Because public support for compromise is rooted in views about how government should work, people's support for compromise can serve as a check against partisan thinking by political sophisticates.

Appendix
Measures

Support for democratic values is measured as the average of a set of items about support for personal freedoms, civil liberties, and the rule of law. The Cronbach's alpha for the items is 0.66.
Higher scores indicate greater disagreement with the following items.

"It is not necessary to obey a law you consider unjust."
"Sometimes it might be better to ignore the law and solve problems immediately rather than wait for a legal solution."
"The government should have some ability to bend the law in order to solve pressing social and political problems."
"It is not necessary to obey the laws of a government that I did not vote for."
"Free speech is just not worth it if it means that we have to put up with the danger to society of extremist political views."
"It is better to live in an orderly society than to allow people so much freedom that they can become disruptive."
"Society shouldn't have to put up with those who have political ideas that are extremely different from the majority."

Dogmatism is measured with a set of four items drawn from Rokeach's (1960) dogmatism scale. The Cronbach's item for the scale is 0.61.[23] The included items ask about agreement with the following statements,

---

[23] A fifth related item asks about agreement: "To compromise with our political opponents is dangerous because it usually leads to the betrayal of our own side." It is excluded here to avoid making an overly deterministic measure, although the results differ little if it is included in the dogmatism scale.

"Of all the different philosophies that exist in the world there is probably only one that is correct."

"In the long run the best way to live is to pick friends and associates whose tastes and beliefs are the same as one's own."

"There are two kinds of people in this world: those who are for the truth and those who are against it."

"A group which tolerates too many differences of opinion among its own members cannot exist for long."

Political interest is measured on a four-point scale of expressed interest in politics, on a scale defined as *very interested, somewhat interested, not very interested,* or *not interested at all.*

Education is measured on a seven-point scale ranging from less than an eighth-grade education to an advanced degree.

Partisanship is a seven-point scale ranging from *strong Democrat* (0) to *strong Republican* (6), based on a three-part branched question wording.

Ideology is measured on an eleven-point scale ranging from *liberal* (0) to *conservative* (1).

Strength of partisanship ranges from independent (0) to strong partisan (3), constructed as a folded version of the partisanship scale.

Social capital is measured at the state level, using Putnam's (2000) state scores.

Interpersonal trust is measured as the average of three items, each measured on an eleven-point scale, rescaled to range from 0–1, where higher scores indicated greater trust in other people.

"Generally speaking, would you say that most people can be trusted, or that you can't be too careful in dealing with people?"

"Do you think that most people would try to take advantage of you if they got the chance, or would they try to be fair?"

"Would you say that most of the time people try to be helpful or that they are mostly looking out for themselves?"

To measure participation in organizational life, survey respondents were given a list of sixteen different kinds of voluntary organizations, ranging from sports clubs to self-help groups to parents' organizations, and asked if they had been a member of such a group in the last twelve months. A seventeenth item asked about participation in any other similar voluntary organization. Responses were summed to a scale of organizational membership with a feasible range from zero to 17. In practice, the scale ranges from zero to 11 with a median of 1 and a mean of 1.24. Similar items were used to create a measure of participation in volunteer organizations. For the same list of groups, participants were asked if they had done any voluntary work for that organization in the same twelve month period. Responses were summed to a scale of organizational participation that ranges from zero to 11 with a mode of 0.00 and a mean of 0.44.

4

The Bounds of Public Support
for Compromise

When asked what they think of the principle of compromise, people voice strong support for it. They care about the ways that political decisions are made, and value compromise as a way of solving political differences. Yet even if people support the idea of compromise in principle, this does not guarantee that they will tolerate compromises in practice. Even if people believe that the parties should be willing to compromise, they may still be reluctant to say they will vote for politicians who promise to compromise. While people say that they think compromises are virtuous, they might not be willing to support compromises within policy domains that they care about.

What is appealing in principle can be harder to endorse in practice. We know that those who support democratic principles in the abstract do not necessarily act as tolerant when asked to grant rights to groups perceived as threatening or dangerous (McClosky 1964; Prothro and Grigg 1960; Sullivan, Piereson, and Marcus 1982). While the lessons of our political socialization may pull us toward a defense of democratic principles, our countervailing fears about disliked groups have the potential to push us in the opposite direction. The same may well hold true for compromise in politics. Even if we are socialized to believe that compromise is a desirable way to resolve disputes, we may resist the concessions that compromise agreements require in practice. When confronted with the prospects of ceding ground to opponents and settling for outcomes that might not be well aligned with other political goals, people's willingness to compromise may fade. After all, compromise is different from other democratic principles like freedom of speech in that it does not have a formal legal basis. Even if people value compromise in principle, it is not undemocratic to reject it out of loyalty to our cause. To reject a group's opportunity to protest or to constrain one's ability to speak freely represents a violation of the rules of democracy. To reject a compromise is fair game.

Compromise in an Age of Party Polarization. Jennifer Wolak, Oxford University Press (2020). © Oxford University Press.
DOI: 10.1093/oso/9780197510490.001.0001

When people are asked to not just consider the idea of compromise, but also apply the principle to specific domains where compromise might be pursued, are people still willing to endorse compromise in politics? In this chapter, I move beyond consideration of support for the abstract principle of political compromise to consider people's willingness to endorse compromises in specific domains. I first consider people's willingness to support political leaders who vow to compromise. When thinking about the kinds of traits we desire within elected officials, we know that people like politicians who offer strong leadership and a distinct policy vision (Cohen 2015). When asked to choose between a leader who will stand by his or her convictions and one willing to make the concessions demanded by compromise, are people still willing to call for compromise? Using surveys, I demonstrate people's willingness to support leaders who will compromise in politics. Even when pitted against other desirable traits that an elected official might possess, people are still keen to endorse politicians who will work with the opposing side to find compromises.

I also consider people's willingness to advocate for compromise within specific policy domains. Even if people think that compromises should be a part of politics, they may not be willing tolerate compromises in issue domains that they care about. To support compromise in the abstract is different than accepting partisan and ideological concessions within specific policy debates. In canvassing data from several surveys, I demonstrate that people like compromise not only in the abstract, but also as an approach to resolving specific policy disputes. Whether considering taxes, immigration, health care, guns, or the environment, a majority of Americans say they want to see politicians make compromises. Even when asked about their willingness to support compromises in specific domains, majorities still voice support for compromise remedies.

Preference for a President Who Is Willing to Compromise

What do people want from elected officials? People care about the policy positions that politicians take (Ansolabehere and Jones 2010; Canes-Wrone, Brady, and Cogan 2002), but they also have preferences about what kind of people they want they want to see represent them in Washington. When we ask people to explain what kinds of traits they desire among politicians, Americans say that they value leadership skills as well as honesty, a concern for average Americans, as well as having the right experience for the job.[1] Among many desired traits, leadership stands out as particularly valued. People say they want

[1] In a 2016 Quinnipiac University poll, 26% said that it was most important to them that the

politicians who are strong leaders and often put this trait ahead of all other attributes when asked what political traits they value most (Cohen 2015; Holian and Prysby 2015; Kinder et al. 1980; Sigel 1966). If people's ideal politician is a leader who stands up to challenges, does this threaten the prospects for compromise? Even if people endorse compromise as a way to resolve political disputes, they may not think highly of political leaders who are ready to make concessions and compromise. Instead, they may believe that the best politicians are those who take strong stands on the issues they care about. If people strongly prefer politicians who vow to fight for their convictions and stand loyal to the interests of the party, then it might matter little that people support the principle of compromise. Politicians who offer strong leadership will secure reelection even if they fail to deliver on policy compromises in office.

When faced with the choice between a leader who vows to fight for his or her convictions or one who is willing to compromise, which type of politician do Americans prefer? To explore this, I again compile questions from several surveys with different question wordings that each ask people about the kind of leader that they want to see in the White House. As seen in Table 4.1, most Americans prefer the leader who is open to compromise with his opponents. When asked which is more important in a presidential candidate, willingness to compromise or sticking to their core values, 50% said compromise and 42% said sticking to one's positions. In a 2015 ABC News/Washington Post survey, 58% of respondents said they want the next president to be "someone who mainly tries to compromise with the other political party."

When compromise is connected to goals of productivity and getting things accomplished, support for compromise is even higher. Sixty-four percent of respondents in a 2015 survey said the next president should be willing to compromise to get things done, and only 28% say he should stand firm on principle, even if it meant that less was accomplished. Likewise, in surveys in both 2012 and 2019, two-thirds of Americans say they want a president who compromises to get things done versus only one-third who favored a president who would stick to his principles no matter what. We traditionally have believed that politicians' core responsibility to their constituents is policy representation—to pursue policies that further the will of constituents and fight for the causes that people care about. Yet steadfast commitment to a cause is not seen as warmly in the eyes of the public as the pursuit of compromise. People say that they prefer politicians who are willing to cede ground to pursue productive compromises

---

President is someone with good leadership skills. Twenty percent valued a president who cares about average Americans and 16% named honesty. Fourteen percent said they wanted a president with the right kind of experience. Intelligence, level-headedness, and being a strong person were among the least valued traits. The poll was conducted September 8-13 with a sample of 960 registered voters.

Table 4.1 **Desired Traits of a President**

	Prefers a president who will	
	Be willing to compromise (%)	*Stand firm to convictions (%)*
Which of the following is more important to you in a presidential candidate? . . . Someone who will stick to their core values and positions, someone who will compromise with the other party.[a]	50	42
All else equal, would you like the next president to be someone who mainly tries to compromise with the other political party, or someone who mainly stands up for his or her side?[b]	58	37
Which comes closest to your own view? "The next president should be willing to compromise to get some things done, even if it means giving in on some things he or she campaigned on" or "The next president should stand firm on principle, even if it means he or she can't get some things done."[c]	64	28
If you had to choose, would you rather have a President who compromises to get things done, or sticks to their principles, no matter what?[d]	66	34
Would you prefer a U.S. president who compromises to get things done, or who sticks to his or her principles no matter what?[e]	66	33

[a]Survey by Pew Research Center for the People & the Press, conducted March 25–29, 2015, of 1,500 respondents interviewed by telephone (landline and cell).

[b]ABC News/Washington Post survey conducted March 26–29, 2015, based on 1,003 telephone interviews (landline and cell).

[c]USA Today survey conducted of 1,000 likely voters, by telephone (landline and cell) from December 2–6, 2015.

[d]The Economist/YouGov poll. Based on online interviews of 1,500 respondents conducted January 6–8, 2019.

[e]Evaluations of Government and Society Study, (ANES EGSS-4). Conducted February 18–23, 2012 via the internet using a national probability sample of 1,314 respondents drawn using random digit-dialing and address-based sampling through Knowledge Networks.

over those who vow to stand by the cause. The levels of overall support for leaders who compromise is somewhat lower than the very high support offered for the principle of compromise, suggesting that people may like the abstract principle more than they endorse it in practice. Even so, people regularly select the politician who is willing to compromise over the one who vows to stick to his or her convictions. In each wording, a majority of Americans favor leaders who are willing to work with the other side and consider compromises.

Is this desire for politicians who are willing to compromise eroding over time as levels of party polarization are increasing? The appeal of a politician who will fight for the party may be on the rise as the dividing lines between the political parties are deepening. In Table 4.2, I show how people's preferences for leadership styles have evolved over time. From 1987 to 2012, the Pew Research Center has asked people if they like "political leaders who are willing to make compromises in order to get the job done." Across the years of the survey, people report strong preferences for leaders who are willing to make compromises. Less than a quarter

Table 4.2 **Increasing Support for Leaders Who Compromise**

For each statement, please tell me if you completely agree with it, mostly agree with it, mostly disagree with it or completely disagree with it. "I like political leaders who are willing to make compromises in order to get the job done."

Completely agree (%)	Mostly agree (%)	Mostly disagree (%)	Completely disagree (%)	N	Date
16	56	16	4	4,244	May 1987
23	49	17	5	3,021	May 1988
23	48	17	6	3,004	May 1990
32	46	14	5	1,165	November 1997
32	45	15	4	985	October 1999
30	48	12	6	2,502	August 2002
28	49	13	6	1,264	August 2003
29	50	11	5	1,003	January 2007
37	42	12	5	1,506	April 2009
36	40	14	8	1,000	September 2011
39	41	11	5	1,504	April 2012

Surveys conducted by Pew Research Center and Princeton Survey Research Associates.
1987–1990: Personal interviews
1997–2007: Telephone interviews
2009–2012: Telephone interviews, including cell phone samples.

of Americans disagree with this statement, and agreement with it ranges from 70% to 80% across the years. Moreover, I find that people's desire for leaders willing to compromise has only increased over time. In 1987, only 16% completely agreed with this statement. By 2012, this had more than doubled, with 39% strongly agreeing that they like political leaders who compromise. Over time, people have only become more supportive of the idea that leaders should be willing to make compromises. As congressional productivity has lagged and gridlock seems on the rise, public demand for leaders willing to make compromises has climbed.

We also have little reason to believe that people's support for leaders who are willing to compromise has waned in the years since. While the Pew Research Center has not repeated this question since 2012, Gallup began asking a similar item about people's preferences for leadership style in 2010, regularly including it in surveys in the years since. Respondents are asked to place themselves on a five-point scale, where 1 represents a preference for leaders who compromise to get things done and 5 is a preference for leaders who stick to their beliefs even if little gets done. Across the surveys reported in Table 4.3, the most commonly

Table 4.3 **Preferences for Leaders Who Compromise, Over Time**

Next, we have a question about the best approach for political leaders to follow in Washington. Where would you rate yourself on a scale of 1 to 5, where 1 means it is more important for political leaders to compromise in order to get things done, and 5 means it is more important for political leaders to stick to their beliefs even if little gets done? You may use any number from 1 to 5.

More important to compromise (1/2) (%)	Compromise and sticking to beliefs as equally important (3) (%)	More important to stick to beliefs (4/5) (%)	N	Date
47	24	27	1,021	November 2010
47	23	28	1,018	January 2011
51	21	28	1,017	September 2011
53	20	25	1,510	September 2013
52	23	23	1,028	October 2013
50	26	23	1,017	September 2014
53	26	21	1,020	September 2016
54	28	18	1,022	September 2017
50	27	22	1,035	September 2018

Gallup polls, telephone surveys (landline and cell).

reported preference is for politicians who are willing to make compromises, with about half of the sample placing themselves at 1 or 2 on the scale. Around a quarter of people place themselves at the midpoint of the scale, indicating that they value compromise and sticking to beliefs as similarly important. The remaining quarter say they prefer leaders who stick to their beliefs. Considering the trends over time, the share of respondents who prefer leaders who compromise varies little between 2010 and 2018. The lowest level of support is in 2010 and 2011, when 47% state a preference for compromise, and highest in 2017, when 54% profess a preference for leaders who compromise. When considering public appetites for leaders who stick to their convictions, this seems to have eroded a bit over time. While 28% of respondents placed themselves at 4 or 5 on the scale in 2011, this falls to 18% in the 2017 survey. Overall, people's desires for leaders who are willing to compromise are quite stable over time, suggesting that these beliefs have principled rather than political origins.

How universal are people's desires for politicians who are willing to compromise? In the last chapter, I demonstrated that people's endorsement of the principle of compromise was unrelated to the strength of their partisan attachments and their desires for moderate policy. But when asked to consider what kinds of leaders are best, the imprint of partisan preferences may be greater—where those with the most moderate views call for leaders willing to compromise, and those with strong partisan and ideological beliefs call for politicians to fight for the party's agenda. If this is the case, then politicians who resist compromises might be merely heeding the call of the party loyalists—the activists who support the campaign and the ideologues who make up the party base.

I next consider whether the most politically engaged hold different preferences about what kinds of political leaders are best. I rely on a survey question included in the 2012 Evaluations of Government and Society Study, as reported in Table 4.1. Respondents were asked if they preferred a U.S. president who compromises to get things done, or one who sticks to his or her principles no matter what. I consider three indicators of political involvement: strength of partisanship, strength of ideological identification, and a history of voter participation. Logit results are reported in the appendix to this chapter (Table A4.1), and in Figure 4.1, I show the predicted levels of support for a president who makes compromises at high and low levels of belief strength and voter participation.[2]

I find that partisans and independents are equally likely to favor leaders who are willing to compromise. Sixty-three percent of independents say they prefer a president who is willing to make compromises, while 68% of strong partisans

---

[2] Strength of partisanship is a folded version of the seven-point partisanship scale. Strength of ideology is a folded version of a five-point ideology scale. Voter participation is the sum of answers to whether the respondent reported voting in the 2008 presidential race and 2010 midterms.

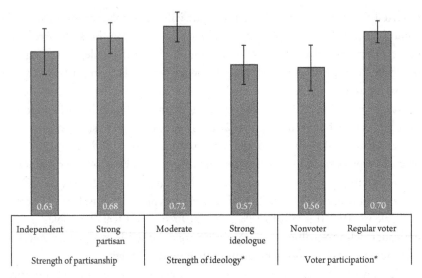

Figure 4.1 Party activists and demand for leaders who will compromise.

say the same. I find that ideologues and moderates diverge in their preferences for politicians who vow to stick to their convictions. While 72% percent of moderates offer a preference for politicians who are willing to compromise, only 57% of strong ideologues say the same. In the case of political engagement, I fail to find evidence that the politically active demand politicians who will stand by their convictions. Instead, voters are more likely to say they want politicians who are willing to make compromises than those who do not engage in politics. Seventy percent of regular voters said they favored politicians who are willing to compromise, compared to only 56% of nonvoters.

Overall, I find only partial evidence that the most politically invested citizens make different demands of political leaders. Strong partisans are no more likely to prefer a president who sticks to his convictions, and voters turn out to be more likely to desire leaders who compromise than nonvoters. It is only in the case of ideologues that I find evidence that the politically engaged want politicians to fight for their convictions and resist compromise. Even here, a majority of strong ideologues still voice a preference for candidate who is willing to compromise.[3] Most prefer politicians who are willing to compromise—and this includes many of those people with the strongest political passions.

[3] Moreover, these strong ideologues make up a relatively small share of the sample, as only about 20% of the respondents identify as strong ideologues.

Table 4.4 **Desired Traits in Political Leaders**

How would you rate political leaders who	Like a lot (%)	Like (%)	Dislike (%)	Dislike a lot (%)
Are willing to compromise	49	26	13	8
Stick to their positions, even if unpopular	44	23	15	13
Take a mix of liberal and conservative positions	28	32	25	9
Often side with members of the other party	16	28	31	17
Take conservative positions on nearly all issues	14	24	28	29
Take liberal positions on nearly all issues	11	21	27	35

Pew Research Center for the People & the Press. Telephone survey of 1,708 respondents conducted January 10–15, 2007.

Relative Desirability of Willingness to Compromise as a Trait

People say they prefer elected officials who are willing to compromise in politics over those who choose to stand on principle. But what if they are not asked to choose between two alternatives, but instead evaluate a willingness to compromise as one of several traits a political leader might possess? I next consider how people rate openness to compromise relative to other leader attributes. In a 2007 survey, the Pew Research Center for the People & the Press asked respondents about the traits they like to see in political leaders.[4] Response options fell on a four-point scale from *like a lot* to *dislike a lot*. Respondents were asked to evaluate several different approaches to lawmaking—including voting along ideological lines, favoring a mix of conservative and liberal positions, steadfast conviction to one's positions, and support for bipartisan efforts. Results are shown in Table 4.4.

[4] The specific wording asked, "As I read some characteristics associated with political leaders in Washington, please tell me how much you like or dislike each. We'll use a scale from 4 to 1 where '4' represents something you like a lot and '1' represents something you dislike a lot. On this scale, how would you rate political leaders who ..." The traits are listed in the table.

Among all of the named traits, willingness to compromise was the *most* desired trait of the group, with 75% reporting that they like candidates with this attribute. Once again, people have strongly favorable reactions to political leaders who are willing to consider compromise. The second most favorably rated trait was "stick to their positions, even if unpopular," which was liked by 65% of respondents. While people like leaders who will compromise, they also like the idea of strong leaders who stand up for their principles.[5] At first, this might suggest that the public might be merely giving lip service to the idea of compromise, agreeing with it in principle, but perhaps preferring decisive leaders in practice. This is where the evidence from Table 4.1 is particularly informative. When people are asked to choose between sticking to positions versus considering compromise, most Americans prefer a leader who will be willing to compromise. Yet it is also clear that the principle of compromise falls into tension with the other goals that citizens hold in politics. Even as citizens report a desire for leaders who are willing to make compromises, they also value principled position-taking. People express desires of politicians that may well be in competition with each other (Hibbing and Theiss-Morse 2002).

We might think that many like compromise simply because it increases the odds of securing moderate policy outcomes closer to their own centrist views. However, the remaining rows of the table suggest that this is not the case. People are more likely to say that they like a leader who is willing to compromise than they are to favor one who takes a mix of liberal and conservative positions. Both types are better liked than a party maverick who often sides with the opposing party, which less than half of respondents favor. Expectedly, the least liked candidates are ones who take consistently liberal or conservative positions, a strategy that tends to be valued by in-partisans and disliked by out-partisans.

To better gauge people's affinities for ideologically aligned candidates, it is useful to consider levels of support within subsets of congruent respondents, rather than look at the overall levels of support for consistently liberal or consistently conservative politicians. Among the subset of liberal respondents, 66% say that they like a candidate who takes consistently liberal views. Among self-identified conservative respondents, 69% say that they like leaders who are consistently conservative. Interestingly, both figures still fall short of people's levels of support for leaders who are willing to make compromises. People are more likely to say that they like politicians who are willing to compromise than they are to say they like leaders who hold ideological views consistent with their own.

[5] Preferences for politicians who compromise and those who stick to their positions are weakly related to each other ($r = 0.11$). Among those who like leaders who stick to their positions, 56% also like leaders who compromise. Among those who dislike leaders who stick to their positions, 47% like politicians who compromise a lot.

Table 4.5 Desired Traits in Candidates for Congress

	Year of survey	More likely to support (%)	No difference either way (%)	Less likely to support (%)	N
Candidate's approach to policy process					
A candidate would make compromises with people he or she disagrees with	2010	45	31	24	931
	2012	45	35	20	966
Candidate background					
An incumbent running for re-election	2010	16	55	29	915
	2012	15	65	21	944
A candidate who has never held elective office	2010	25	45	29	940
	2012	19	52	28	964
Candidate policy positions					
A candidate who supported the health care law	2010	40	23	37	957
A candidate who supported the government loans to banks during the 2008 financial crisis	2010	15	34	52	949
A candidate who would vote most of the time to support Obama	2012	29	44	28	967
A candidate who would vote most of the time to support Romney	2012	19	49	32	956
Among those with a partisan leaning					
A candidate who would mostly vote to support a president from the respondent's party	2012	49	43	8	822
A candidate who would mostly vote to support a president from the respondent's opposing party	2012	5	41	54	819

2010: Pew Research Center/National Journal Congressional Connection Poll. Telephone survey of 1002 respondents conducted May 20–May 23, 2010.

2012: United Technologies/National Journal Congressional Connection Poll. Telephone survey of 1001 respondents conducted July 19–July 22, 2012.

What if we consider the relative virtues of politicians willing to compromise relative other traits that a candidate might possess? In Table 4.5, I report on the kinds of traits people value in candidates for Congress, as reported in campaign season surveys conducted in 2010 and 2012. Respondents were asked whether various candidate attributes made them more likely to want to vote for the candidates, less likely to support that candidate, or made no difference.[6] While we might expect that the competitive and partisan nature of campaigns pulls people away from compromise, I find that one of the most valued traits a candidate can possess is a willingness to make compromises with the people he or she disagrees with. Forty-five percent of respondents said that this trait would make them more likely to support a candidate for Congress, while less than a quarter said it would be a strike against a candidate.

Being willing to compromise is more valued than being an outsider who has not served elected office, and it is also seen as more desirable than a candidate who is a familiar incumbent. It has greater or equal rewards as the positions a candidate has taken on prominent policy debates on health care and bank bailouts. Voting with the party's presidential candidate draw mixed enthusiasm at most among the full sample of respondents, but even among the subsets of congruent partisans, people's desires for congressional candidates loyal to the party only slightly outpace support for legislators to compromise. While people value policy positions and party loyalty when selecting congressional candidates, they also value candidates who are willing to make compromises with the people they disagree with.

Desire for Compromise on Specific Issues

People report that they prefer politicians who are willing to make compromise and rank this highly among other approaches that politicians might take. People care about more than just partisan policy congruence when thinking about what they want from their elected officials. If people like the principle of compromise and endorse compromise as an approach for political leaders, are they also willing to tolerate compromises on the policy issues that they care about? There are reasons to worry that the abstract idea of compromise becomes less palatable when it means we must accept concessions on policy issues that we care deeply about.

---

[6] Specifically, "Thinking about the elections for Congress this year, please tell me whether you would be more likely or less likely to vote for a candidate with each of the following characteristics, or whether it would make no difference in your vote either way."

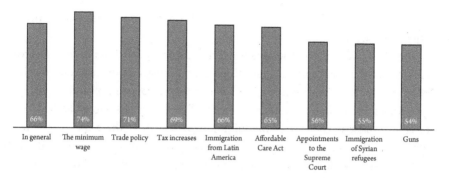

Figure 4.2 Desire for compromise by policy domain.

We know that Americans strongly support democratic principles—yet struggle when asked to apply them to specific cases. It is easier to embrace the idea of free speech than it is to allow hate groups to have books in libraries or to permit white supremacists to make speeches. It seems likely that people's willingness to support compromise erodes when people are asked to move beyond the general idea of compromise to consider it as a solution in specific policy domains. Even if compromise is seen a good way of solving disputes, it may not be viewed as the best way forward on matters of gun policy, abortion, or tax reform. While the average citizen is not always well-informed about politics, this does not mean that they are without policy preferences. When confronted by the issues that interest them most, people are more attentive and more animated to take action (Converse 1964). If people are strongly concerned about achieving the best outcome in these policy domains, they may reject the prospect of compromising with the other side.

To explore people's willingness to advocate for compromise in specific policy domains, I draw on a set of items that ask people about their willingness to endorse compromise on a slate of different policy issues. In a McClatchy/Marist poll conducted in the week before the 2016 presidential election, a sample of registered voters was asked, "Should government officials in Washington compromise to find solutions, or stand on principle even if it means gridlock?"[7] They were asked about their general preferences on this trade-off, as well as their favorability toward compromise on a slate of eight issues ranging from guns to the Affordable Care Act to immigration

---

[7] The survey was conducted November 1–3, 2016 with a sample of 1,587 participants interviewed by landline and cell phones. The items were asked only of registered voters, who composed 79% of the sample. I report the percentage who endorsed compromise among all of those giving a substantive response.

policy. In Figure 4.2, I report people's desire for compromise across these policy domains.

I find that two-thirds of the sample expresses a general preference for compromise versus standing on principle. When considering support for compromise within the specific issue domains, it is clear that compromise is a more appealing option in some policy areas than in others. People express the greatest desire for compromise in the case of the minimum wage, where three-quarters of the sample say they prefer that politicians pursue compromises. Respondents report wide support for compromise on matters of taxes and trade policy as well. Indeed, for about half of these issues, specific support for compromise meets or exceeds support for the principle as generally stated. This suggests that people are not necessarily more supportive of compromise in the abstract than they are in specific scenarios. About two-thirds of respondents say that they would prefer that lawmakers find to solutions through compromise on health care, rather than stand on principle. When considering Supreme Court appointments, immigration of Syrian refugees, and guns, support for compromise is lower—with just over half of respondents favoring compromise to seeing politicians stand on principle. However, even in the case of guns, the issue with the lowest level of support for compromise, most Americans (54%) prefer compromise to standing on principle. Across a diverse slate of policy issues, in every single case, a majority of Americans say they would rather see politicians compromise rather than stick to their policy principles. Even in the last week of a fiercely fought presidential campaign, people still express support for policy compromise across a wide range of contentious political issues.

These patterns are found in other surveys as well. In three different surveys over the years, the Pew Research Center has asked respondents about their preferences for party cooperation on a slate of policy issues. Rather than asking people about their desire for compromise in that domain, respondents are first asked which political party is closest to their own views on the issue and then asked in a second item whether that party should compromise on the issue to reach agreement or stick to its position even if no progress is made.[8] This represents a tougher test of people's willingness to tolerate policy compromises, as it requires people to report whether they want to see efforts

---

[8] The first question wording asked, "Please tell me which political party, the Republicans or the Democrats, comes closer to your view on each issue I name. First, which party's position comes closer to your views on [policy issue]?" The second item asked, "Do you think that the [party closest on issue] should compromise on this issue, so that the two parties could reach some agreement, or do you think the [party closest on issue] party should stick to its position on this issue even if it means no progress is made?" If no party was named in the first question, the second question was not asked.

Table 4.6 **Preference for Compromise, by Policy Issue**

	Year	Percent saying closest party should compromise (%)	N
Abortion policy	1997	32	846
	2007	26	1,268
The environment	1997	56	857
	2007	55	1,254
The federal budget	1997	66	938
Reforming the Medicare system	1997	58	893
Iraq	2007	47	1,354
Illegal immigration	2007	52	1,110
Federal taxes	2007	52	1,307
Most important problem	2007	66	1,001
	2010	67	842

All surveys by the Pew Research Center for the People & the Press.
1997: Telephone survey of 1211 respondents conducted February 20-23.
2007: Telephone survey of 1708 respondents conducted January 10-15.
2010: Telephone survey of 1383 respondents conducted February 3-9.

toward compromise among the party most likely to push for their desired policy outcome. In Table 4.6, I report levels of support for compromise across a diverse range of policy domains, including abortion policy, the environment, the federal budget, immigration, and federal taxes. By looking at support for compromise over a range of issues, it is possible to get a sense of the extent to which people are willing to see compromises on the issues they care about. For instance, compromising on technical matters of balancing a budget or negotiating industry regulations might be easier to accept than compromises on issues like abortion, guns, or immigration where passions run deeper.

For five of the seven specific issues named, people said they preferred that the party closest to them on the issue compromise rather than stick to its position. When it comes to matters of taxing and spending, immigration policy, the environment, and Medicare, people prefer that the parties consider compromise over seeing their allied party fight for their side in the debate. Sixty-six percent prefer compromise from their party when it comes to the federal budget, while just over half prefer that their party compromise on matters of the environment, immigration, and Medicare reform.

For two other issues, abortion policy and Iraq, most said that they prefer that the ideologically closest party stands firm, even if no progress is made. People's resistance to compromise on these issues likely reflects the substance of these particular policy debates. Abortion attitudes are deeply rooted, traditionally very stable, and connected to fundamental views about rights and morality. Compared to debates about how we fund Medicare or manage the budget, abortion attitudes grant less space for compromise. In the case of Iraq, the question was posed in January 2007, during a time of growing public criticism of the United States' involvement in Iraq.

Is this reluctance to compromise about the character of these issues, or is it a reflection of the intensity of people's preferences in these domains? If people are wary about ceding ground on the issues they care about most, it may be challenging to find compromises in policy domains that Americans see as most important. To see if people are generally closed to compromise on the issues that they care about most, I also consider people's support for compromise on the issues they see as most important. In both the 2007 and 2010 Pew surveys, respondents were asked, "What do you think is the most important problem facing the country today?" They were then asked which party they felt was better at addressing this problem and whether they would be willing to see that party make compromises with the other party on this issue. I find that people prefer compromise even on the issues they care about most. Two-thirds of respondents said that they wanted the party closest to them on this issue to work with the other side to find compromise. If anything, people seem more likely to want compromise on the issues that are most important to them.[9]

As further evidence of people's tolerance for compromise across a diverse range of issues, I consider how support for compromise varies over the range of policy domains that respondents named as most important. In Table 4.7, I show average support for compromise by issue domain, for all issues named by at least 2% of the sample as the most important facing the country. Across most of these issues, compromise is preferred to seeing one's party hold to their convictions. The main exception is the case of those who felt that morality, ethics, or family values were the greatest problem in America today. For these respondents, holding to convictions was preferred to seeing their party

---

[9] This suggests that resistance to compromise in the case of abortion policy and the war in Iraq are more about the substance of the issues than their relative importance to citizens.

Table 4.7 **Most Important Problem and Support for Compromise**

	Names issue as most important problem (%)	Favor compromise on that issue (%)
2007		
Iraq/war in Iraq	43	64
Health care	6	85
Dissatisfaction with government, politics	6	55
Immigration	5	59
Terrorism	5	62
The economy	5	87
Morality, ethics, family values	4	49
Unemployment, jobs	3	54
Education	2	76
Poverty	2	62
Partisanship/the political parties	2	47
2010		
Unemployment, jobs	26	74
The economy	25	70
National debt, budget, deficit	10	42
Health care	10	74
War in Iraq, war in Afghanistan	3	89
Dissatisfaction with government, politics	3	63
Morality, ethics, family values	2	25
Partisanship/the political parties	2	65

Pew Research Center for the People & the Press.
2007: Telephone survey of 1708 respondents conducted January 10–15, 2007.
2010: Telephone survey of 1383 respondents conducted February 3–9, 2010.

compromise. Interestingly, those who named Iraq as the most important issue for them tended to be enthusiastic about compromise as an outcome. While only 47% of the overall sample in 2007 survey favored compromise when it came to how parties handle the war in Iraq, among the subset who said Iraq was the most important problem, 64% said that they wanted the party closest to them to be willing to compromise on this issue. While people are not willing to compromise on issues like abortion, family values, and morality, for most other issues, people prefer that their own party is willing to compromise, rather than stick to their convictions.[10] Moral issues are the exception rather than the rule when thinking about people's intolerance for policy compromise.

Conclusion

People's willingness to express support for compromise extends beyond just agreement with the abstract principle. When asked what kinds of politicians they want to elect to represent them, most Americans say they prefer leaders who are willing to compromise. They like candidates for Congress who are willing to make concessions over those who vow to stand firm to their convictions. Demand for leaders who are willing to compromise seems only to have increased over time. Even strong partisans and the politically engaged say that they prefer to politicians who are willing to compromise over those who vow to stick to their convictions, although strong ideologues are less keen on leaders who compromise as compared to self-identified moderates.

Others have expressed skepticism about the sincerity of public calls for compromise, suggesting that even if people might say they like compromises in principle, they are not likely to support concessions in on the issues they care about (Gutmann and Thompson 2012). These surveys show that public support for compromise extends beyond just general endorsements of the principle of compromise. When asked about how a range of policy debates should be resolved, most Americans chose compromise as their preferred outcome. With the exception of moral issues like abortion, a majority of Americans are open to compromise on the issues that they care about most. From health care to the

---

[10] To what extent are people willing to compromise on all issues versus just some of the policy issues named? In the 1997 survey, 20% of respondents preferred that the closest party stick their convictions on every one of the policy debates named. In comparison, 28% said that they preferred that their party compromise across all of the named issues. On average, most people wanted to see their party compromise on most issues, with 66% saying that they wanted to see their party compromise at least half of the policy issues. The pattern is similar in the 2007 survey, where 17% resist compromise across the wider slate of issues. Fifteen percent said they wanted their party to compromise across all of the policies. Overall, 57% of respondents said they wanted to see compromise outcomes on half or more of the issue questions they answered. While the average respondent is not so keen to compromise that they wish to see it on every issue, most policy issues draw majority support for compromise as an outcome.

environment to immigration to gun policy, the prevailing mood of the electorate is a preference for compromise solutions.

Compromise is a contested value, in that it pits our policy goals against our principled views about how politics should be practiced. Even if people like the idea of compromise in principle, there are reasons to expect that other partisan goals can override people's willingness to apply these abstract ideas to specific situations (e.g., McClosky 1964; Prothro and Grigg 1960). It is surely easier to endorse the principle of compromise when we are not reminded of other important competing goals. Even so, most people still show high support for compromise even when paired against other valued principles, like strong leadership or standing by one's principles. Across many different ways of thinking about compromise in politics, whether it is in their expectations of elected officials or their desires for how specific policy debates should be addressed, a majority of Americans express a preference for compromise.

This chapter also highlights the tensions between compromise and other goals that people hold in politics. Even as people call on politicians to be willing to compromise, many also value elected officials who stand on principle. While a willingness to compromise is among the most highly desirable traits a politician might have, it is also clear that voters see virtues in other approaches to politics as well. Compromise is just one of many valued principles in politics. In considering people's willingness to call for compromises on public policy matters, we also see people's enthusiasm for compromise depends on what is at stake. Support for compromise varies depending on the issue domain considered, where compromise is a more appealing option in some policy areas than in others.

These findings highlight that people's willingness to support compromise is not absolute or unconditional. Instead, people's calls for compromise may depend on the circumstances and what competing considerations might apply to the decision at hand. As such, it is important to look not just at people's stated advocacy for compromise, but also examine the robustness of this support when put into direct conflict with the other political desires and aspirations that people hold. Over the next three chapters, I consider the tension between people's desires for compromise and other political goals. When policy goals are in direct conflict with principled thinking about compromise, is support for compromise eroded? I first consider the tension between partisan biases and principled thinking about compromise, to see if people hold their own party to the same standards as the opposing party when asked about which side should be willing to make concessions. I then consider whether campaign competition undercuts people's tolerance for cooperating with the other side, to see whether election victories supersede concerns about compromise. Finally, I consider the tension between democratic principles and policy victory in how people consider compromises in public policy debates.

To better understand the bounds of people's support for compromise in politics, I move from the descriptive evidence offered by surveys to consider people's support for compromise across a range of political contexts. To do so, I rely on experiments where I vary the stakes of policy debates as a way to better understand the conditions under which people are willing to put compromise ahead of other valued goals in politics. I also consider how people's support for compromise in surveys varies across both time and space, and how the desirability of compromise waxes and wanes across different political contexts.

Appendix

Table A4.1 **Who Prefers a President Willing to Compromise?**

	Desire for a president who will compromise
Strength of partisanship	0.074
	(0.095)
Strength of ideology	−0.216*
	(0.085)
Voter participation	0.298*
	(0.112)
Constant	0.394
	(0.218)
N	1,246

Logit estimates for 2012 Evaluations of Government and Society Study. Standard errors are in parentheses.
*$p < 0.05$.

5

Partisan Motives and Consideration of Compromise

Partisanship is a powerful force in politics, informing how people cast their ballots, evaluate the president, and assess policy dilemmas. Our partisan attachments find their roots early in life, as we form affective attachments to party labels even before we cognitively understand their content. Because our partisan identity is one of the earliest political connections that we acquire, it informs how we accumulate and organize new political information throughout our lifetimes. Partisanship serves as a guiding heuristic, facilitating judgments in domains where we lack the time or motivation to survey all available information. As a result, people have a remarkable tendency to see the world through a partisan lens. Our partisan attachments guide what kind of information we seek out, as well as how we evaluate the information we encounter. Particularly for those with strong partisan priors, new information rarely gets a neutral take. We prefer to seek out information that agrees with our partisan orientation and resist and counterargue positions that challenge our views (Taber and Lodge 2006). Given the accessibility of our partisan attachments, many of our partisan biases operate outside of our conscious awareness of this bias (Lodge and Taber 2013).

The importance of partisanship as a guiding force in how people approach politics seems to have only increased with the rising levels of political polarization in America. As party elites take increasingly ideologically distinctive positions, the power of partisanship in shaping attitudes appears to be strengthening (Druckman, Peterson, and Slothuus 2013; Levendusky 2009; Nicholson 2012). While average Americans are not necessarily more ideologically extreme in their preferences (Fiorina and Abrams 2009), their attitudes toward the parties are increasingly polarized. People view their own party in warm terms, while their antipathy toward the opposing party has climbed (Iyengar, Sood, and Lelkes 2012; Iyengar and Westwood 2015; Mason 2018). When asked about the attributes of co-partisans, they assign positive attributes those who share the same party affiliation, and negative traits to those in the opposing party (Hetherington, Long,

Compromise in an Age of Party Polarization. Jennifer Wolak, Oxford University Press (2020). © Oxford University Press.
DOI: 10.1093/oso/9780197510490.001.0001

and Rudolph 2016; Iyengar, Sood, and Lelkes 2012). These partisan biases can be even more consequential than racial biases and other group attitudes in predicting behavior (Iyengar and Westwood 2015; Muste 2014). People's partisan biases even inform their judgments within nonpoliticized domains, where partisanship is used as a cue to choosing dating partners, assessing physical attractiveness and choosing which applicant is most deserving of a scholarship (Huber and Malhotra 2017; Iyengar et al. 2019; Iyengar and Westwood 2015; Nicholson et al. 2016). For many, partisanship becomes a social identity, part of how they see themselves in political and social realms (Green, Palmquist, and Schickler 2002; Greene 1999, 2004; Huddy, Mason, and Aarøe 2015).

Because people use their partisanship not simply as a voting cue but also as a standard by which to identify political threats and rivals, it raises deep concerns about the prospects for political compromise. Even if people like compromise in principle, these instincts might be overwhelmed by partisan goals in practice. If partisans venerate their co-partisans and vilify those on the opposing side, it will be difficult to tolerate policy cooperation and compromise. Compromises ask partisans to cede ground and cooperate with their partisan adversaries. For moderates, compromises can be appealing, a way to secure policies that are closer to their own ideal outcomes. For strong partisans, compromises require greater sacrifices.

There are good reasons to worry about whether strong partisans are willing to tolerate political compromise. Partisans hold stronger identities than weak partisans and draw more value from seeing their own side win and prevail over opponents. Strong partisans reveal stronger attachments to party ideals and draw more instrumental value for having a policy outcome that is ideologically distinctive from the other side. Strong partisans are also more likely to overestimate the distance between themselves and the other side (Ahler and Sood 2018; Granberg 1993), making compromise feel even more costly as a strategy. Strong partisans may struggle to trust the other side to negotiate compromises in good faith, due to their tendencies to assign negative motives to those who take opposing views (Hetherington and Rudolph 2015; Hetherington, Long, and Rudolph 2016). As a result, those with strong prior views may only give lip service to the idea of compromise, while in practice rejecting concessions to the other side (Gutmann and Thompson 2012; Harbridge and Malhotra 2011; Wolf, Strachan, and Shea 2012).

In this chapter, I consider people's willingness to support compromise in cases where their partisan goals may be at odds with their principled support for compromise. I start by considering the degree to which partisan thinking undercuts people's stated support for compromise outcomes. Using survey evidence, I show that those with polarized party views are not any more likely to reject the idea of compromise than those who rate the political parties similarly.

I then move on to experimental evidence, to see whether people prefer different approaches to party collaboration depending on the partisanship of the politician in question. I find that people are as likely to say they prefer leaders willing to compromise whether from their own party or the opposing side. I then turn to longitudinal survey data, exploring the degree to which people make different demands of their own party versus the opposing party when it comes to policy collaboration. It is here that partisan differences are most pronounced. Even though most say that they believe that members of their own party should be willing to work with the opposing side in Washington, partisans are far more likely to report that the opposing side has an obligation to collaborate across party lines. Principled thinking about compromise informs people's demands of the parties in policymaking, but partisan priors also leave their mark.

Affective Polarization and Willingness to Compromise

The evidence presented so far suggests that people do not think about compromise in particularly partisan ways. In Chapter 3 of this volume, I find that strong partisans are not any more likely to reject the principle of resolving difference through compromise than independents. In Chapters 3 and 4, I show that when strong partisans are asked about what kinds of leaders they prefer, they are no more opposed to the prospect of compromise than independents. Even as our partisan biases shape our views of policy issues, our impressions of political leaders, and our feelings about members of the other party (Conover and Feldman 1989; Hetherington, Long, and Rudolph 2016; Iyengar and Westwood 2014; Nicholson 2012), our willingness to endorse compromise does not seem to rest on the strength of our partisan priors. So long as the public's desires for political compromise find their origins outside of partisan politics, then it implies that people will be open to compromise even in times of party polarization. The only case where prior preferences seem to matter is in the case of strength of ideology in Chapter 4, where the intensity of ideological self-identification predicts greater resistance to political leaders who are willing to compromise. While a majority of strong ideologues express a preference for a president who is open to compromise, they are less enthusiastic on this point than self-identified moderates. However, I fail to find that the ideological consistency of people's beliefs predict resistance to compromise in Chapter 3.

I conduct one more test to explore whether general support for compromise is related to the intensity of people's partisan passions. In this test, I focus on the effects of affective polarization, exploring whether tolerance of compromise outcomes drops among those who hold the most polarized feelings about the two parties. Rather than reflecting the strength of people's partisan attachments, opposition to compromise may instead come from those who hold the most intense feelings of partisan animosity. While activists on both the right and the left are increasingly sorting their beliefs in ideological ways, the expressed policy preferences of Americans remain relatively moderate rather than polarized (Fiorina and Abrams 2009). This could explain why independents do not seem to differ much from those with strong partisan preferences in their desires for compromise in Washington. In considering the fault lines of partisanship in American politics, the partisan divide is most keenly expressed in people's perceptions of the political parties (Lelkes 2016; Mason 2015). Even if policy views remain fairly moderate, people's affections for their own party have intensified and their animosity toward the opposing party has surged (Hetherington, Long, and Rudolph 2016; Iyengar, Sood, and Lelkes 2012). To the degree to which people dislike, mistrust, and wish to avoid spending time with their partisan rivals, it will be difficult to sign on to the cooperation, collaboration, and concessions that political compromise requires.

To see whether the partisan animosities associated with affective polarization lead to a resistance to compromise, I rely on responses to the 2016 American National Election Study. To measure affective polarization, I use a common measure of polarized party affect—the absolute value of the difference between people's ratings of the Democratic Party and the Republican Party on the feeling thermometer scale (Iyengar et al. 2019; Iyengar and Westwood 2014; Mason 2015). Greater values indicate more polarized affect toward the political parties. Low scores on the measure reflect those who rate the two parties similarly. I also include measures of strength of partisanship as well as strength of ideology, measured as folded versions of the seven-point identification scales.[1] I include three measures to control for the contributions of political socialization in explaining support for compromise. I include measures of education and political engagement as proxies of exposure to socializing messages about the virtues of compromise. I also include an indicator of trust in government, under the expectation that confidence in government is tied to support for compromise and party collaboration.[2] I control for gender, age, and race.

To assess support for compromise, I rely on two items—one about principled support for compromise and one about people's preferences for leaders

---

[1] Those who do not identify with an ideological category are coded as zero on the four-point indicator of ideological strength.

[2] Education is measured on a five-point scale ranging from less than a high school education to earning a graduate degree. Political engagement is measured as the sum of how many of six campaign participation acts that the respondent participated in. Trust is measured using a five-point indicator of how often the respondent trusts the federal government to do what is right.

who are willing to compromise.[3] In Table 5.1, I confirm that support for the principle of compromise is not related to levels of affective polarization.[4] We might worry that those high in affective polarization are unwilling to consider compromise due to their intense dislike for their partisan rivals. To the degree to which partisan rivals represent hated foes, it will be hard to consider making the concessions that political compromise demands. However, I find that even those whose affections for their own party are as intense as their hostilities toward the other side are open to the prospect of compromise. I also confirm that strong partisans are as willing to endorse the principle of compromise as independents and that ideologues do not differ from moderates in their support for the principle of compromise.

Considering people's preferences for leaders who make compromises versus those who stick to their principles, I again fail to find a significant effect associated with levels of affective polarization. Neither the intensity of partisan affect nor the strength of partisan identification predict resistance to supporting leaders who are willing to make compromises. The only difference that emerges is tied to strength of ideology, where those who self-identify as strong ideologues are more likely to say they like politicians who stick to their positions as compared to self-identified moderates.[5] Those who self-identify as political moderates have a 69% predicted probability of preferring a political leader who makes compromises over one who sticks to his or her convictions. This drops to 56% among those who identify as strong ideologues. Yet even though strong ideologues are more likely to value politicians who stick to their convictions, most strong ideologues still prefer a politician who is willing to compromise with the other side to one who stands firm. Strong ideologues also remain a small share of the electorate. Even though more than a third of respondents identify as strong partisans, less than 7% identify as extremely liberal or conservative.

Overall, I find only modest evidence that partisan and ideological priors direct people's support for compromise in politics. Rather than being rooted in partisan priors, support for compromise is best predicted by factors related to exposure to political socialization, such as educational attainment and political engagement. Those with more years of schooling are more likely to support

---

[3] The first asks respondents about their support for the principle of compromise, based on rejection of the statement, "What people call compromise in politics is really just selling out on one's principles." Response options fall on a five-point scale ranging from "disagree strongly" to "agree strongly." The second item asks respondents about their general preferences for political leaders who are willing to strike compromises, and whether they preferred "a government official who compromises to get things done, or who sticks to his or her principles no matter what?"

[4] The null results for affective polarization are robust to specifications that exclude the other potentially collinear measures of partisan and ideological strength.

[5] This confirms the same result noted in Chapter 4 of this volume.

Table 5.1 **Affective Polarization and Support for Compromise**

	Support for the principle of compromise	Prefers leaders who compromise
Polarized party affect	−0.004	0.176
	(0.023)	(0.191)
Strength of partisanship	−0.003	−0.066
	(0.006)	(0.051)
Strength of ideology	0.007	−0.185*
	(0.006)	(0.052)
Education	0.060*	0.316*
	(0.005)	(0.041)
Campaign participation	0.014*	0.139*
	(0.007)	(0.054)
Trust in government	0.168*	1.063*
	(0.026)	(0.219)
Female	−0.017	−0.144
	(0.011)	(0.091)
Nonwhite	−0.047*	−0.157
	(0.012)	(0.106)
Age	0.0001	0.004
	(0.0003)	(0.003)
Constant	0.275*	−0.590*
	(0.025)	(0.215)
R^2	0.10	
N	3,370	3,361

Notes: 2016 American National Election Study. Regression estimates are in first column. Logit estimates are in the second column. Standard errors are in parentheses.

*$p < 0.05$.

the principle of compromise and express support for leaders who are willing to make concessions, as are those who are actively engaged in politics. I also confirm that greater support for government is associated with a greater tolerance for compromise. Even in a time of deepening party divides, strong partisans are not any less likely to voice support for the prospect of compromise in politics.

Even though Americans are increasingly likely to see the political parties in divisive ways, these feelings of partisan animus do not discourage people from supporting compromises in politics.

Calls for Compromise Among Co-Partisans

People's support for the principle of compromise seems mostly disconnected from their partisan instincts in politics. Yet even as people say that they generally like the idea of a president who is willing to make compromises, are they still willing to say the same when asked to specifically consider the traits they want to see in their party's nominee for president? I next consider people's willingness to support compromise as an approach specifically adopted by co-partisan politicians. Even if partisan biases do not inform demands for compromise in the abstract, they might still inform specific opinions about whether partisan allies should be keen to compromise. People may desire leaders who fight for their principles among those who share the same party affiliation, while demanding compromise from those in the opposing party.

To test whether this is the case, I turn to experimental evidence. With experiments, I can see if levels of support for leaders who compromise is conditional on the party of the politician. If people are guided by partisan biases in thinking about how the parties should approach compromise, then we should expect to see important differences in what people expect from their own party versus the opposing side. Republicans should be particularly keen to see Democrats make concessions, and Democrats should call on Republicans to be open to compromise. In the fall of 2013, I conducted a question wording survey experiment with a sample of 1,050 participants recruited as a national sample of adults.[6] Participants completed the experiment as part of a larger questionnaire administered over the internet.[7] In the experiment, I asked participants about the kind of candidate that they would like to see in the 2016 presidential race— one who resists compromise or one who works together with other groups. Half read a statement asking what kind of candidate they would like to see from the

---

[6] The sample was recruited through Qualtrics using their online panel. From their pool of around two million volunteers (recruited from web ads and permission-based e-mail lists), Qualtrics sent my questionnaire to a sample of 2091 respondents that was representative of the U.S. population in terms of age, race, and gender based on Census data. The response rate was 50% of those who received invitations to participate.

[7] The sample is 65% female and 19% nonwhite. In terms of partisanship, 36% identifies as Democratic, 23% as Republican, and 41% as independent or other. Ages range from 18 to 86 with an average age of 48 years.

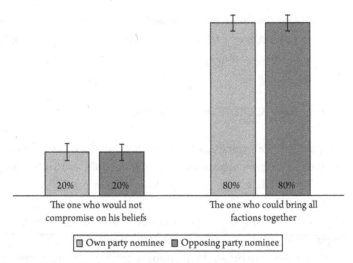

Figure 5.1 Preference for politicians who compromise, by party.

Democratic Party, while the other half were asked what kind of candidate they would like to see from the Republican Party.[8]

Using people's responses to a party identification question, I sort whether people were asked about a presidential nominee from their own party versus the opposing party.[9] Results are shown in Figure 5.1. I find that participants were equally likely to support a nominee who works with all the factions, whether that candidate is from their own party or not. I fail to find any differences across question wordings ($t = 0.05$, $p < 0.96$, $n = 862$). When asked about the kind of candidate they want to see nominated from their own party, 80% said they want to see a candidate who will work with all sides. When asked about the kind of candidate they would like to see nominated from the opposing party, again 80% expressed a preference for a candidate open to compromise. In a time of increasing party polarization and party competition, we have good reasons to believe that preferences about the traits of the next president might be informed by people's partisan biases. However, I fail to find evidence that people apply

[8] The specific wording read, "Turning to the 2016 presidential race, if the (Republican/ Democratic) Party nominated two equally qualified candidates for president in 2016, which would you prefer, the one who would not compromise on his beliefs, or the one who could bring all factions together?" This wording was selected as it is reasonably abstract, not tied to specific candidates or particular political events or battles. The choice of wording is also general enough to suggest compromise as a trait of the candidate, so as to avoid a definition of compromise tied specifically to narratives of policy moderation versus ideological extremity.

[9] For independents in the sample, answers to a seven-point ideology question were used to determine in-party versus out-party question wordings for liberals and conservatives who did not affiliate with a party.

different standard to the opposing party than they do their own. People were equally likely to dislike an uncompromising candidate when from their own party as when he or she was from the opposing party.[10]

The same pattern can be found in surveys. In November and December of 2015, subsets of likely Democratic and Republican primary and caucus voters were polled in separate surveys conducted by CBS News and the New York Times.[11] Respondents were asked about what they were looking for in their party's nominee for president in 2016. The Democratic sample was asked, "Would you rather have a Democratic nominee for President who is willing to compromise some of their positions with Republicans in Congress in order to get things done, or will stick to their positions even if it means not getting as much done?" The party names were reversed for the question asked of likely Republican primary voters.

As seen in Figure 5.2, an overwhelming majority (76%) of likely Democratic primary voters said they prefer a party nominee who is willing to compromise. Likewise, in the sample of Republicans, 60% of respondents favored a party nominee willing to compromise over a candidate who would stick to his positions. While Republicans as a group are somewhat less likely to say they want a party nominee who is willing to compromise, in both samples, a majority of likely primary voters said that they prefer that their political party nominate a candidate who is willing to compromise and get things done. Moreover, this sample represents the subset of the most engaged and most partisan people in the electorate—those who are likely to vote in their party's primary or caucus. While some have suggested that party activists create pressures that deter politicians from considering compromise (Gutmann and Thompson 2012), I fail to find support for this here. Even core supporters of the party say that they want their own party's nominee for president to be one who is willing to make compromises in politics.

[10] When considering the differences between partisans and independents, I find that strong partisans are more keen on the candidate who is uncompromising than independents are, but this holds true whether they were asked about a co-partisan or a nominee from the opposing party. The interaction between the treatment and strength of partisanship is not significant.

[11] CBS News/New York Times surveys. Democratic likely primary voters were interviewed by telephone or cell phone from November 6–10, 2015, n = 418. Republican likely primary voters were interviewed December 4–8, 2015, n = 369.

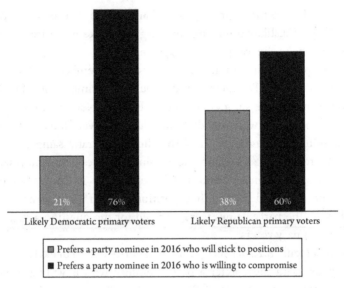

Figure 5.2 Primary voters' desire for a presidential nominee who is willing to compromise.

Strength of Partisanship and Calls for Compromise in Policymaking

My evidence so far suggests that people are not particularly partisan in their calls for compromise. Strong partisans are just as keen on the principle of compromise as independents, and most primary election voters say they prefer that their party nominate candidates who are willing to compromise. I next consider whether partisan biases emerge when people are asked about their willingness to see Democrats versus Republicans compromise within the realm of policymaking. When asked how the parties should govern, do people still express a willingness to see their own party make concessions to the opposing side?

To explore this, I take advantage of a set of surveys conducted by the Pew Research Center over the past decade. Over the years, the Pew Research Center has asked respondents what strategy they would like to see each of the political parties take over the coming year: Do they want Democrats (or Republicans) to work with the other side to find common ground, or would they rather see the party stick to their positions? For example, in 2006, respondents were asked, "Next year should the Democratic leaders in Washington try as best they can to work with George W. Bush to accomplish things, even if it means disappointing some groups of Democratic supporters, or should they stand up to George W. Bush on issues that are important to Democratic supporters, even if it means less gets done in Washington?" A second question is also asked about the reverse, and whether Republicans should work with Democrats or stand firm on the issues.[12] Versions of these questions were asked of a national sample in 2006 and repeated nine more times through 2018. The appendix to this chapter summarizes the details of each survey (Table A5.1).

In this question wording, respondents are not explicitly asked about their desire for compromise in Washington. Instead, they report on their general support for policymaking defined by cooperation versus fighting for the party's agenda. Even so, these surveys offer a way to examine people's mindsets for compromise and willingness to tolerate party concessions to the other side. Rather than inquiring about whether people prefer one leader type to another, the questions ask Americans what each party should do in practice: Should Republicans stand firm or cooperate with Democrats? If people are partisan in how they think about cooperation and compromise, then we should find among the strongest evidence of it with these questions.

Longitudinal data are of particular use here, as it is difficult to isolate partisan thinking within the context of a single cross-sectional survey. If people reject compromise in one survey, it might be a reflection of their partisan biases, or it might be a reaction to something specific in political circumstances, where support for compromise is bounded by characteristics of the current debates before Congress or the balance of power in Washington. By considering multiple surveys from different time periods, I can consider broad patterns of partisan thinking about policy cooperation in Washington. These surveys cover a time period that includes a good amount of variation in partisan control of government. Two surveys were conducted during George Bush's tenure as president, six were conducted during Barack Obama's presidency, and three were conducted after the 2016 election. This covers two switches in partisan control of the presidency and periods of divided government as well as unified government with both Democratic and Republican control of the Congress. This variation provides reassurances that these patterns are not bound to a single point in time, the party of the president, or the attributes of any single survey.

In Figure 5.3, I show people's preferences for each party to work with the other side, as a share of all respondents who answered the question. One of the first patterns to note is the overall high levels of public support for compromise. Across all survey years and both political parties, a majority of people say that they prefer that the parties to work with opponents to accomplish things, even if it means disappointing partisan supporters. When considering how policymaking should proceed, people want the political parties to reach across the aisle rather

---

[12] In 2006, 2007, and 2008, both questions were asked of all respondents, and the question order of the two was randomized. In surveys after 2008, respondents were randomly assigned to answer only one of the two questions.

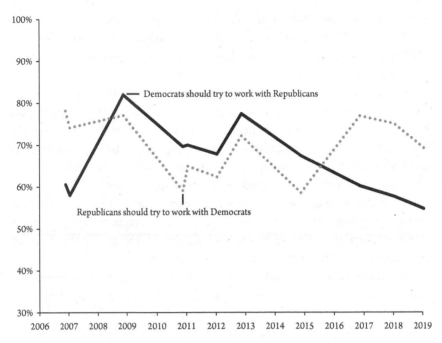

Figure 5.3 Preferences for each party to cooperate versus stand firm.

than stand up to opponents. The degree of support for party cooperation waxes and wanes across the years, and there is not much evidence of serious decay in public support for compromise over recent years. It is true that the lowest level of demand for compromise from Democrats is in January 2019, in the last survey in the series, where only 55% of respondents said they want to see cooperation over partisan resistance from Democrats. Yet this is only slightly lower than in January 2007, when 58% said they hoped Democrats would engage in compromise. In both cases, these surveys follow Democratic gains in midterm elections and relatively low levels of approval of the Republican president.[13] People are least inclined to support a cooperative stance from Republicans in the November 2010 and November 2014 surveys, where 59% call on Republicans to work with Democrats in Congress. Both surveys follow midterm elections that favored Republicans, where Republicans gain party control of the House of Representatives in 2010 and control of the Senate in 2014.

People appear to be more likely to expect that members of the president's party should be willing to collaborate than to say the same of the opposing party. In 2006 and 2007, people are more likely to say they want to see Republicans cooperate

[13] In the Pew surveys, about a third approved of the job President Bush was doing in 2007, and about 40% approved of President Trump.

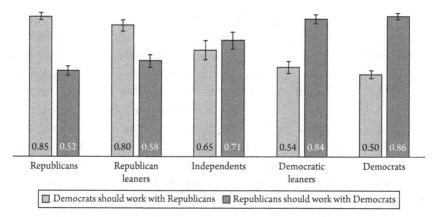

Figure 5.4 Partisanship and preferences for party collaboration.

than they are to say the same of Democrats, congruent with Republican control of the presidency. This flips after the election of Barack Obama, such that people are then more likely to expect cooperation from Democrats than Republicans. Likewise, after the election of Donald Trump, people are more likely to say that Republicans should compromise and less likely to say the same of Democrats.[14]

Do Democrats and Republicans make different demands of their own party than the other side? In Figure 5.4, I present calls for party cooperation by partisan subgroups in the sample, averaged across the surveys.[15] Among independents, collaboration is highly desired as an approach for both parties, where two-thirds of independents say they would like to see the Democratic Party and Republican Party work with each other. But among partisans, clear differences emerge. Democrats are far more likely to call on Republicans to compromise than to say the same of their own party, and the reverse holds true among Republicans. Half of Democrats say they want the Democratic Party to reach across the aisle, while 86% of Democrats call on Republicans to engage in party collaboration. Fifty-two percent of Republicans want to see their own party cooperate with Democrats, but 85% say they want Democrats to be willing to work with Republicans in Congress. Even as a majority of people call on their own party to collaborate on policy, they are much more likely to express a desire for party cooperation from the other side.

The pattern is generally symmetrical when considering the preferences of Democrats and Republicans, where both sides reveal similar biases about the

---

[14] This may reflect the wording of the items, given that the question wording for the president's party names the President while the out-party question wording does not.

[15] This includes responses from the surveys conducted from 2006 to 2018.

need for out-partisans to engage in collaboration. While others have suggested that Democrats are more keen to endorse compromise than Republicans (Grossmann and Hopkins 2016), this is not confirmed here. When we look at people's partisan desires across the years, Democrats and Republicans are equally likely to call on their own party to stand up to the other side. Partisans from both sides voice similar desires for cooperation from the rival party as well.

Even though support for the abstract principle of compromise rests on a nonpartisan foundation, people's reasoning about which political party should be willing to compromise bears the imprint of partisan reasoning. People hold different expectations of the opposing party than they hold for their own side. Partisans are divided on what they want from their party—about half say they want their party to be willing to reach across the aisle, and about half say they would rather their party stand up to the other side even if it means less would get done. But when asked about what the other side should do, nearly all partisans agree that the opposing party should be willing to collaborate. Only independents are equally likely to demand cooperation from Republicans as well as Democrats. Partisans instead tend to hold a double standard about which side should be willing to make sacrifices, where they are more likely to expect collaboration from rivals than to demand the same from partisan allies. While I have failed to find much evidence that partisan thinking guides people's support for the principle of compromise, people are prone to partisan reasoning when asked about whether their own party should cooperate with the other side in policymaking.

Why People Call for Compromise from Their Own Party versus the Opposing Party

I next explore the origins of these differences, and the degree to which calls for party collaboration follow from principled versus partisan considerations. I consider what motivates people to consider policy collaboration as the best option for their own party, and whether these explanations diverge from the considerations that drive people to call for cooperation from the opposing side. Using people's self-reported partisanship, I create dichotomous measures of the desire for one's own party to work with opponents and the desire for the opposing party to cooperate rather than stand firm. Self-identified independents are sorted into partisan camps based on a follow-up question that asks whether they lean toward the Democratic or Republican Party.[16]

---

[16] Those who say they do not lean toward a particular party are assigned into partisan camps based on self-reported vote choice in the most recent election. Remaining independent identifiers are excluded.

I rely the subset of surveys from the Pew Center that follow elections in 2006, 2008, 2010, 2012, 2014, and 2016 (as these surveys include measures of the covariates of interest). I test first the contributions of partisan priors. If people think about these questions in partisan ways, then ideologues and partisans should be more likely to expect the other side to be cooperative, while resisting the prospects of concessions from those who share their partisan goals. These demands should be muted among those with weaker partisan and ideological views. To test this, I include a dichotomous indicator of identifying as a strong partisan or not. I also include a measure of ideological strength, based on a folded five-point scale of ideological identification.

I also consider the degree to which people think about party cooperation in principled ways. If people think about cooperation and compromise not just in terms of what is won or what might be lost, but also as a process of resolving differences, then this may explain why they desire cooperation even from their own party. To explore the degree to which our views about government processes inform the policy demands we make of elected officials, I consider two factors: education and perceptions of the fairness of the election. I include education to capture the part of support for compromise that is socialized, where I expect that higher levels of education are associated with people's desires for cooperation both from their own party and the opposing side.[17] I also include people's perceptions of the fairness of the election. I treat this measure as a proxy for people's diffuse support for government.[18] I expect stronger support for party collaboration among those optimistic about the fairness of government processes and lower support for party collaboration among those who are dubious about the fairness of elections.[19]

Logit results are shown in Table 5.2, and predicted probabilities of recommending the parties cooperate are shown in Figure 5.5.[20] I find that partisans and ideologues are less likely to call on their own party to cooperate in Washington than partisan leaners and moderates. Among strong partisans, a majority say that they believe that their own party should be willing to cooperate with the other side. But the acceptance of this position is significantly higher among partisan leaners than strong partisans, where those with the strongest

---

[17] Education is measured using a seven-point scale of educational attainment ranging from less than high school to postgraduate training.

[18] I draw on a question about respondents' level of confidence that votes across the country that year were correctly counted, ranging from *not confident at all* to *very confident*.

[19] I also include fixed effects for survey year (with 2006 as the baseline category).

[20] The predicted values represent the baseline election year (2006) with all other variables at their means.

Table 5.2 **Why People Want Their Own Party and the Opposing Party to Cooperate**

	Desire for own party to cooperate	Desire for opposing party to cooperate
Partisan identifier	−0.287*	0.191
	(0.088)	(0.126)
Strength of ideology	−0.531*	0.110
	(0.124)	(0.182)
Confidence in election results	0.070*	0.245*
	(0.027)	(0.036)
Education	1.128*	0.411*
	(0.155)	(0.210)
2008	1.156*	0.532*
	(0.131)	(0.194)
2010	−0.343*	0.018
	(0.130)	(0.179)
2012	0.106	1.219*
	(0.136)	(0.264)
2014	−0.306*	0.048
	(0.117)	(0.165)
2016	−0.337*	0.288
	(0.128)	(0.187)
Constant	−0.558*	0.158
	(0.179)	(0.237)
N	3,917	3,971

Notes: Logit estimates. Standard errors are in parentheses. Data are from 2006, 2008, 2010, 2012, 2014, and 2016 Pew election surveys.
*$p < 0.05$.

partisan views have a 50% probability of recommending their own party cooperate, compared to 57% of partisan leaners. Strength of ideology is also associated with people's willingness to say that their own party should cooperate with the rival party. A moderate has a 58% probability of advocating that his or her own party should cooperate, compared to a 45% chance for a strong ideologue,

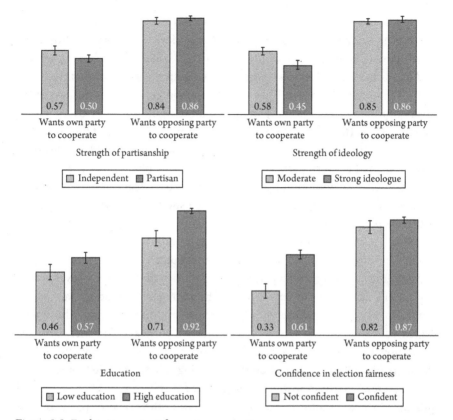

Figure 5.5 Explaining support for party cooperation.

all else equal. Clearly, the intensity of partisan priors shapes people's expectations for their own party, constraining people's support for compromise efforts from co-partisans.

Yet while partisans and ideologues are more likely to resist compromise as a path for their own party, they are no more or less likely to demand cooperation from the opposing party. Both moderates and ideologues agree that the other side should be willing to cooperate on policymaking, and those with strong partisan priors are no more likely to call on the other side to make concessions than those with weak priors. Partisan thinking governs only the expectations people hold about their own party's approach to policymaking.

To what degree are people's calls for party cooperation guided by principled thinking about collaboration and compromise? While people's partisan priors guide the demands people make of their own party, their calls for cooperation are not rooted in a strictly partisan logic. I find that those with higher levels of education are also more likely to expect their own side to cooperate. Among those with the lowest level of educational attainment, 46% say they would like to see their own party work with the other party, compared to 57% agreement among those with a post-graduate degree. The size of this effect is substantial, twice the size of the difference in beliefs of moderate partisans and strong partisans. A similar pattern is seen with the indicator of diffuse support of government. Among those who felt confident about the fairness of the election process, 61% said they want to see their political party cooperate on policymaking. This drops to 33% among those most skeptical of the fairness of the election. People's expectations of how their own party should pursue policy goals is guided by both partisan instincts and principled thinking. Americans demand party collaboration from their own partisan team in part because of their moderate views, but also because of their socialized views about how politics should be practiced.

When considering the reasons why people want to see the other side cooperate, principled thinking about partisan cooperation also informs people's expectations of the opposing party. Among those with the lowest level of education, 71% say that the other side should be willing to act cooperatively, which climbs to 92% among those with the highest level of education. Those with higher education are more likely to call on both parties to consider party collaboration. Likewise, the more confidence people place in the electoral system, the more likely they are to call on the opposing side to consider compromise. While people's partisan instincts shape their expectations of their own party, principled thinking informs people's desires of both their own party and the opposing party.

Conclusions

In surveys, people say that they like the idea of compromise in politics. But we worry that what people support in principle might not survive the partisan practice of politics. Against the backdrop of the growing literature on the pervasiveness of partisan reasoning, I find only partial evidence that people's views of compromise are guided by their partisan biases. From prior studies, we know that people can be profoundly partisan in their political thinking—in a way that closes them to outside arguments and colors their judgments within politics. But I find no evidence that feelings of affective polarization inform people's views about compromise. People who warmly evaluate their own party while strongly disliking the opposing side are no more resistant to compromise than those with more moderate evaluations of the political parties. Likewise, those who strongly identify with a political party are as willing to support compromise as political independents. When asked what kind of presidential candidate that they would like to see on the party's ticket, overwhelming majorities say that their own party should select a nominee who is willing to consider policy compromise. Even likely primary election voters say they would like to see their party nominate candidates who are open to compromise.

I find that partisan and ideological considerations leave their imprint on people's thinking about compromise in two ways. First, strong ideologues express less enthusiasm for politicians who are willing to make compromises than those who identify as ideological moderates. Second, people engage in partisan reasoning when asked about their expectations of how the political parties should resolve their differences. Even as most believe that the opposing party should be willing to collaborate and cooperate on policy, they are less likely to demand the same from their own political party. Partisan thinking also leads people to hold their own party to different standards than the opposing side. While people call for compromise among their own ranks as a result of their moderate policy preferences, they think that opponents should make more concessions as a matter of democratic principle.

People are of two minds when considering compromise in politics. They not only have policy goals, but also principled views about how disagreements should be resolved. When people's principled support for compromise is pitted against their partisan goals, both can leave their imprint on people's demands of elected officials. People are principled in that most Americans are willing to say that their own party should compromise, but partisan in that they are particularly likely to expect the opposing side to be willing to make concessions. People are principled in that socializing forces like education cultivate demand for cooperation from both political parties, but partisan in that their political leanings uniquely inform their expectations for their own party. For those with moderate views, the best outcomes will be obtained when both sides consider compromise. Strong partisans and ideologues, however, remain wary about seeing their own side cooperate even as they expect the other side to be willing to make concessions.

While people's tolerance for compromise is challenged by the partisan practice of politics, it is not fully eroded by partisan thinking. Many are willing to call on their own side to cooperate, even when that means making concessions to the other side. If people were strongly and uniformly partisan in their expectations of which parties should make concessions, then the electorate would surely need to shoulder some of the blame for the level of gridlock and stalemate in Washington. If voters demand that politicians on their side dig in their heels and resist ceding any ground to opponents, then representatives are just following the will of their constituents in resisting calls to compromise. But calls for partisan solidarity are far from unanimous. Even among strong partisans, a majority of people preferred that their own party work with the other side over a strategy of resisting concessions. These calls for party collaboration only increase among weak partisans and independents. This suggests that politicians can reap electoral dividends for compromising—as this is what most co-partisans in their constituency want, as well as what independents and out-party members of the district would prefer. People think about compromise in both partisan terms and in principled ways. While partisan biases inform people's expectations about how the political parties should collaborate on policymaking, they are not so potent so as to close the door to the prospect of policy compromise.

Appendix A

Table A5.1 **Details of Surveys**

Title of the survey	Dates in the field	Number of respondents	Type of sample	Margin of error (%)
November 2006 Post Election	November 9–12, 2006	1,479	National adults	±2.8
January News Interest Index	January 10–15, 2007	17,08	National adults	±2.9
November 2008 Reinterview	November 6–9, 2008	1,556	Voters	±3.0
November 2010 Post-Election	November 4–7, 2010	1,250	National adults	±3.3
January 2011 Political Survey	January 5–9, 2011	1,503	National adults	±2.9%
January 2012 Political Survey	January 11–16, 2012	1,502	National adults	±3.0
November 2012 Post-Election Survey	November 8–11, 2012	1,200	Voters	±3.4
November 2014 Post-Election Survey	November 6–9, 2014	1,353	National adults	±3.0
November 2016 Post-election Survey	November 10–14, 2016	1,254	Voters	±3.4
January 2018 Political Survey	January 10–15, 2018	1,503	National adults	±2.9
January 2019 Political Survey	January 9–14, 2019	1,505	National adults	±3.0

Note: All surveys were conducted by the Pew Research Center for the People & the Press.

6

Campaigns, Competition, and Support for Political Compromise

For most Americans, campaigns are at the center of political life. Contentious bills before Congress, presidential speeches, or the occasional scandal or court case might catch people's attention from time to time, but it is campaign seasons that are most likely to animate citizens to tune into politics. Conflict and competition capture our attention and encourage learning (Coleman and Manna 2000; Evans 2014; Lipsitz 2011, Mutz 2015; Wolak 2006). As campaigns rally people to engage in political life, they often do so in ways that promote people's partisan loyalties and solidarity to the cause (Lipsitz 2011; Mutz 2006). Campaigns spur us to take sides in politics: to select our favorite candidate, to choose between Democrats or Republicans, to decide who has most compelling campaign or strongest platform. People choose their favored candidate and compile reasons to dislike his or her opponent. Many choose to not merely root for the success of their political party, but to also engage in the campaign battle and take steps to secure electoral victory. They try to persuade others of the virtues of their favored candidate. They announce their support on signs posted in their yard and on stickers on their car bumpers. Some give their time and others give their money as an expression of support of their party or candidate.

Campaigns invite citizens to fight for their partisan team, to talk about politics with coworkers and try to persuade others of the virtues of the party and its candidates. People feel passionate about the things that their political party stands for, rooting for their side and rallying against the opposing party. Campaigns cultivate this as a way to mobilize party supporters and promote political participation. Candidates deliver criticism, critiques, negative ads, and angry attacks against their opponents as a way to encourage partisan fervor. Their rhetoric focuses on partisan talk, not discussions of compromise or cooperation with the other side. Partisan thinking is also reinforced in media coverage that depicts the campaign as a contest and a horse race. Together, these forces encourage people to see campaigns in terms of their battles and disagreements.

Compromise in an Age of Party Polarization. Jennifer Wolak, Oxford University Press (2020). © Oxford University Press.
DOI: 10.1093/oso/9780197510490.001.0001

Campaigns represent electoral contests marked by close competition, contentious debates, angry attack ads, and partisan arguments waged with our friends and coworkers. While a competitive partisan mindset is suited for campaigns, it is not necessarily conducive to the politics that follow campaign seasons. The partisan practice of politics encourages activism and engagement, but discourages open-minded thinking and tolerance for the other side (Mutz 2006). Yet this is what policymaking often demands—discussion, deliberation, and negotiation to find agreements that can be successfully passed into law. Primed to party loyalty by the adversarial nature of the campaign, there are reasons to believe that neither winners nor the losing side are ready for open-minded deliberation and compromise once campaigns end and the business of policymaking begins.

Campaign seasons are thought to constrain the possibilities for legislative compromises. Over the course of the campaign, politicians tell people where they stand on the issues and make promises to voters about what they will do if elected. Animated by the partisan battles of the campaign season, voters may have little interest in seeing their elected officials stray from these campaign promises to make compromises (Gutmann and Thompson 2012; Hibbing and Theiss-Morse 2002). Instead, constituents expect their representatives to head to Washington and fight for the issues that matter for the district. When representatives choose to accept compromises that dilute these promises, they run the risk of electoral retribution.

Does the competition of campaigns undermine Americans' willingness to consider policy compromises? While people strongly support the idea of compromise in principle, they are also guided by their partisanship when it comes to considering compromises in politics. Even as strong partisans voice support for leaders who are willing to compromise, they are more likely to call for the other side to cooperate than to demand the same of their own party. These patterns represent the tension between principle and practice in the minds of Americans. People care about policy outcomes, but they also care about the processes by which policy outcomes are achieved. Although they like the idea of resolving disputes through compromise, they also want to protect their own ideological interests in the debate. As a result, the compromises that people support in principle may not always be supported in practice.

In this chapter, I focus on how the conflict and competition of campaigns influence people's willingness to accept compromises in politics. Existing accounts suggest that when people encounter contested campaigns and partisan conflict, they will be drawn to their partisan corners and will be unwilling to consider compromise and cooperation (Gutmann and Thompson 2012; Wolf, Strachan, and Shea 2012). In the middle of a political battle, partisans will want to fight to protect what they believe in. Rather than collaborate, they will dig in their heels in the hopes of seeing their own side prevail. I challenge this conventional wisdom and argue that campaign competition instead has the potential to increase people's willingness to consider compromise.

In elections, partisans hope to see their own side triumph. But when it comes to the business of policymaking, I argue that people care about more than just a partisan win. Outcomes matter, but so does the process by which political disagreements are settled. In the face of deep divisions, compromises are appealing because they acknowledge the interests of competing sides. In the context of campaigns, conflict can encourage partisan thinking, but this competition also reminds people of the diversity of preferences within the American electorate. People resist compromise in part because they underestimate the degree to which Americans desire different outcomes in politics (Hibbing and Theiss-Morse 2002). By reminding people that not all Americans share their views, political conflicts can change people's perceptions of the necessity of compromises. If compromise is seen as a desirable way to balance the diversity of demands within the American electorate, then reminders of political disagreement should encourage people to consider compromise.

Using survey data, I demonstrate that competitive campaign contexts are associated with greater support for compromise, and these effects are concentrated among those least attentive to politics. When we learn that others have different partisan goals, compromise draws greater support. Using an experiment, I then explore how social cues affect support for compromise. I provide people with information about the preferences of other Americans to see how knowledge of the distribution of public demands alters public support for compromise. I confirm that people consider the desires of the electorate when they think about what policy outcomes are best. When people are reminded that others do not share the same political views, they are more willing to consider compromise.

How Disagreements Can Encourage People to Compromise

If the competition of campaigns frames politics as a battle to be waged, then people may feel they must fight for what they believe in. Americans may put loyalty to their party and their commitments to their policy goals ahead of their principled support for compromise. If this is true, it could explain why compromises seem increasingly uncommon in Congress. If voters cannot move past their ideological differences to make concessions to the other side, then members of Congress will choose to avoid compromise solutions as well. This is troublesome for the health of a democratic system if it is true. Compromise is meant to be a solution to the divisions and disagreements of politics, a way to resolve our differences that satisfies more people than just the majority coalition. However, if being confronted with these disagreements encourages people to adopt a partisan mindset, cooperation will be unlikely. The disagreements of politics that necessitate compromises could also be the greatest obstacle to finding that middle ground.

I argue, however, that the conflict does not close off the prospects for compromise. In fact, under the right conditions, competition and conflict have the potential to encourage greater openness to considering compromises in politics. Even as conflict and political disagreement engage partisan solidarity, they also shape our understandings of politics. Given that many Americans tune out the discussions of day-to-day current events, the conflicts of politics play an important role in capturing people's attention. As the conflicts and disagreements of politics encourage attentiveness to politics and pique political interest, they do so in ways that can reinforce the legitimacy of government. Campaigns are not just contests to determine who holds power next. They are also a form of democratic ritual (Rahn, Brehm, and Carlson 1999). Elections are the defining element of democracy for many people—the main way they find their voice in politics and the primary route for popular control. Elections carry with them at least some sense of solidarity and affirmation of civic virtue. We are brought together with our shared task of selecting our representatives. For many, an election is a reminder that our disagreements are part of living in a democratic system. Indeed, election experiences can contribute to public support of government (Ginsberg and Weissberg 1978). I propose that they also can encourage people to consider compromise in politics.

While elections may bring conflict, it is a structured within an institutional setting. Partisan sides battle to secure votes, but it is no free-for-all. Campaigns play out in a process defined by rules and norms and elections are governed by systems of rules. Not everyone likes the conflicts they encounter in politics, but their existence offers reminders that the political system is working as it should. Competition signals that people have voice in the process, that there is an opportunity to challenge current authorities, and that we have the chance to express our point of view—all of which are important to democratic rule. Campaigns air our political differences, but without the ability to disagree, we would not have a democracy. By seeing that others disagree and that many had a chance to participate, people seem more likely to accept unfavorable outcomes (Wolak 2014).[1]

In highlighting the diversity of political views in the electorate, the political disagreements of campaigns are informative to citizens. Disagreements might

---

[1] People on the losing side of an election are more likely to see the election process as unfair, but this is tempered in the presence of campaign competition (Wolak 2014).

inspire us to fight for our beliefs, but these conflicts also provide reminders that we do not all agree in politics. People overestimate the degree to which the American public shares the same priorities (Hibbing and Theiss-Morse 2002). It is a phenomenon known as a false consensus effect (Ross, Greene, and House 1977; Marks and Miller 1987). It is a form of attribution bias, where people perceive the attitudes and traits that they possess as common traits, while perceiving other contrary beliefs as rare or uncommon. For instance, people who hold feminist beliefs or worry about nuclear war also tend to think these beliefs are widely shared (Ross, Greene, and House 1977). We hold these biases in part because of a sense of ego defense, where we find it gratifying to think that others agree with us. But a key reason why we are prone to false consensus effects is based in information levels. When people lack information—which is a pretty common thing in politics—they use heuristics to fill in the gaps (Delli Carpini and Keeter 1996; Popkin 1994). When people are not sure about what others want, their own position serves as a heuristic about the desires of the public at large, and they assume that others agree with them on the issue. When asked to think about what other people want, they often project their own attitudes on the question (Conover and Feldman 1982, 1989).

These types of false consensus effects are particularly likely to be seen in the domain of politics (Mullen et al. 1985). In political life, many find themselves in homogenous contexts where the information they encounter is decidedly one-sided. Many discuss politics with only those who agree with themselves (Mutz 2006). They inhabit discussion networks that are pretty one-sided in their partisan composition (Huckfeldt and Mendez 2008). They live in election districts without strong two-party competition (Jacobson 2016; Jacobson and Carson 2016). In spending time with like-minded others, false consensus effects are reinforced (Wojcieszak and Price 2009).

For Hibbing and Theiss-Morse (2002), false consensus effects are one of the reasons why people come to dislike conflict and deliberation when they see it in Congress. People commonly believe that Americans agree on what the main priorities are and how they should be addressed. When members of Congress debate, argue, and filibuster, it reflects their efforts to delay acting to promote the public's interest. They suggest that one of ways to encourage people to tolerate disagreement and discord in Congress is to provide civic education about the necessity of deliberation and debate in Congress. I argue that political disagreement should also fill this role. If people dislike debate and deliberation because they overestimate public consensus on national priorities, then better information about how much the public disagrees should also promote tolerance of the contentious sides of politics.

I believe that encountering disagreement can encourage people to be more accepting of compromise in politics. Given that many people find themselves in homogenous political contexts, encountering political disagreement can be educative. If we tend to believe that most people agree with us and share our same perspectives, encountering political disagreement reveals that we misperceived the amount of public consensus on the issues. After all, the roots of compromise are social—acquired through our social and civic lives. If our willingness to endorse compromise has social origins, it would follow that our support for compromise is informed by what we know about the preferences of others. Learning that people have different priorities and hold different preferences is arguably relevant information to how we think our political differences should be settled.

I expect that living in places with greater political disagreement will be associated with greater support for politicians to compromise. This prediction is contrary to conventional wisdom about competition and conflict. Disagreement has been thought to make compromises difficult, accentuating the things that divide us and calling us to stand in partisan solidarity to secure the outcomes we treasure (Gutmann and Thompson 2012; Mutz 2012). I propose that conflict and disagreement can serve a very different role. Through our encounters with disagreement, we learn that people are sincerely divided on the issues, that not everyone likes the same candidate that we do, and that others have different priorities. In a world where we see differences rather than assuming national consensus, we see the reasons to forge bargains, consider concessions, and engage in compromise.[2]

Competition and Support for Compromise

To explore the relationship between competitive contexts and support for compromise, I rely on survey responses to the 2012 Evaluations of Government and Society Study.[3] In the survey, respondents were asked, "Would you prefer a U.S. President who compromises to get things done, or who sticks to his or her principles no matter what?" Most respondents say they prefer a president who is willing to compromise. Sixty-five percent want a president who will compromise to get things done, while 35% prefer a leader who sticks to his or her principles.[4] To measure the competitiveness and partisan diversity of a person's context,

[2] Campbell (2006) demonstrates that political heterogeneity is associated with higher levels of tolerance.

[3] The American National Election Studies' EGSS-4 survey was conducted via the internet using a national probability sample drawn using random digit-dialing and address-based sampling through Knowledge Networks. The survey was fielded from February 18 through February 23, 2012.

[4] This statistic and all successive analyses are based on survey-weighted data.

I use a state level measure[5] of the competitiveness of the presidential election in one's state during the last election.[6] I control for education and strength of partisanship, where I expect those with greater education and weaker partisanship will be more likely to favor politicians who support compromise.[7] I also control for partisanship, ideology, gender, and age.[8]

As the multilevel logit results in Table 6.1 show, living in a competitive political context is associated with greater support for a president who is willing to compromise. In contrast to predictions that campaign competition draws people to their partisan corners and closes them off to considering compromise, I find that people's support for compromise is highest in places with greater partisan divisions. In Figure 6.1, I plot the likelihood of endorsing compromise across different contexts. In a place with the lowest level partisan disagreement, people are only weakly supportive of compromise, where 54% say that they prefer a president who is willing to compromise (all other variables at their means).[9] Consider next a place that leans toward one party, but still has some partisan disagreement, such as a state where there is around a 60/40 split between Democrats and Republicans. In such a context, support for politicians who compromise is notably higher, where around two-thirds of respondents express a preference for a politician who favors making compromises.[10] In the places with the highest level of disagreement, 68% say they prefer a president who is willing to compromise over one who sticks to his or her principles.[11] Those who live in places of greater political heterogeneity report greater enthusiasm for the idea of compromise.

[5] The state is arguably the most salient geographical setting for most Americans. Local governments are often nonpartisan, while county lines or congressional district boundaries are often not salient dividing lines for citizens nor salient divisions in news coverage. Arguably, most citizens know whether they live in a battleground state or a noncompetitive state, and whether their state tends to be red or blue. The measure lacks some precision, as some respondents may live in partisan enclaves within competitive states, but to the degree to which this is prevalent, should bias against finding results for partisan diversity.

[6] Presidential competitiveness is measured as $4*p*(1-p)$ where p is the share of the two-party presidential vote won by the Democratic candidate in the state in the last presidential election. Scores on this measure range from zero to 1 in principle and from 0.25 to 0.999 in practice. Higher scores on this measure indicate greater partisan competition.

[7] Education is measured on a five-point scale, ranging from *less than high school* to *graduate degree*. Strength of partisanship is a four-point scale based on the folded seven-point partisanship measure.

[8] Partisanship and ideology are measured on seven-point scales where high values indicate identification with the Democratic Party and greater liberalism.

[9] In this sample, both Hawaii and Washington, DC, have this level of partisan agreement.

[10] This level of partisan disagreement is seen in states like Alaska, Maine, Louisiana, and Washington.

[11] This level of partisan division in seen in states like Ohio, Florida, North Carolina, and Missouri.

Table 6.1 Support for Leaders Who Compromise, as a Function of Competitiveness

	Preference for a president who compromises			
		Follows politics as moderator	News consumption as moderator	Frequency of political talk as moderator
Competitiveness	2.458*	20.062*	13.899*	7.205*
	(1.012)	(6.771)	(7.104)	(2.046)
Moderator (information exposure)		8.415*	21.355[a]	3.022*
		(3.182)	(12.892)	(1.046)
Competitiveness × moderator		−8.713*	−21.746[a]	−3.141*
		(3.304)	(13.406)	(1.079)
Education	0.254*	0.255*	0.243*	0.264*
	(0.067)	(0.068)	(0.065)	(0.070)
Strength of partisanship	0.028	0.014	0.021	0.034
	(0.094)	(0.101)	(0.103)	(0.098)
Partisanship	−0.040	−0.048	−0.024	−0.043
	(0.053)	(0.054)	(0.053)	(0.053)
Ideology	0.199*	0.190*	0.209*	0.198*
	(0.075)	(0.074)	(0.075)	(0.073)
Female	−0.102	−0.110	−0.114	−0.116
	(0.132)	(0.132)	(0.128)	(0.130)

Age	0.018*	0.018*	0.014*	0.018*
	(0.005)	(0.005)	(0.005)	(0.005)
Constant	-3.479*	-20.375*	-14.452*	-8.030*
	(1.203)	(6.518)	(6.854)	(1.999)
Random effects				
Variance, intercept	0.111	0.662	1.032*	0.195
	(0.088)	(0.427)	(0.465)	(0.122)
Variance, coefficient of moderator		0.079	4.528[a]	0.006
		(0.067)	(2.534)	(0.009)
Covariance, intercept and coefficient of moderator		-0.224	-2.077*	-0.035
		(0.162)	(1.019)	(0.027)
Deviance	1,448	1,434	1,422	1,438
N	1,201 (51)	1,201 (51)	1,199 (51)	1,201 (51)

Multilevel logit estimates. Standard errors are in parentheses.

*$p < 0.05$.

[a]$p < 0.10$.

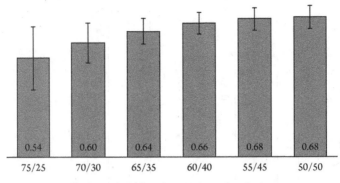

| 0.54 | 0.60 | 0.64 | 0.66 | 0.68 | 0.68 |
| 75/25 | 70/30 | 65/35 | 60/40 | 55/45 | 50/50 |

Closeness of presidential vote in state in last election

Figure 6.1 Diversity of political views in context and support for politicians who compromise.

People who live in competitive political contexts show greater support for compromise. I have argued that this relationship is the product of social information. Living in a place with diverse partisan views offers reminders that not everyone agrees in political life. The more that people encounter others who want different outcomes than they do, the less they will overestimate the amount of public consensus on the issues. In this way, diverse contexts should make compromise seem a more necessary and more desirable political outcome. If this story is true, then the effects of living in an environment marked by competition and disagreement should be most pronounced among those who are least politically informed and least inclined to follow politics. Those who regularly follow the news and talk about politics are most likely to recognize the dividing lines of politics and levels of partisan disagreement. News junkies learn of public disagreement from talk shows and news coverage. Folks who love to talk politics encounter disagreement in their informal conversations. They are more likely to know that Democrats and Republicans often want very different things. But for those least tuned into politics, diverse contexts are particularly informative about the prevalence of political disagreement. Our incidental exposure to yard signs or casual conversations or the like can provide knowledge about the heterogeneity of public preferences.

As a partial test of this mechanism, I next consider whether the effects of diverse contexts are heterogeneous across citizens. If the partisan disagreement in a competitive context teaches us that others want different things in politics and corrects false consensus perceptions, then the effects of partisan conflict in promoting support for compromise should be concentrated among those least tuned into politics. In the other columns of Table 6.1, I consider three moderating factors: how often one follows politics, reported levels of news consumption, and frequency of political talk.[12] In Figure 6.2, I plot predicted support for leaders who compromise across the range of partisan disagreement for those at the 10th percentile and 90th percentile of political attentiveness.

Considering first the differences across those with different propensities to follow politics, I find that diverse political contexts are particularly important to encouraging the least attentive to support compromise. In a place where one party dominates, those who rarely follow politics dislike politicians who compromise compared to those who keep up with current affairs. As levels of party competition increase so does support for compromise among those least attentive to politics. At moderate levels of political heterogeneity, the least attentive become just as likely to support politicians who compromise as those who regularly follow politics. In the most divided areas, the least attentive are in fact *more* likely to support politicians who compromise than those who regularly follow politics, although the difference is only near significant. When considering the marginal effects of residing in a politically diverse context, I find the largest effects for diversity among the least politically attentive. I also confirm significant and positive marginal effects for diversity for all but those at the highest level of attentiveness. For those who follow politics most of the time, the marginal effect for diverse contexts is not statistically distinguishable from zero. Heterogeneous political contexts are the most important to encouraging support for compromise among the least engaged.

A similar pattern emerges when considering an alternative measure of political attentiveness: self-reported consumption of news. For regular news consumers, the composition of their context is unrelated to their support for compromise in politics. But for those below the 75th percentile of news consumption, I find a positive and significant marginal effect associated with the heterogeneity of one's context. For those who consume the least news, support for compromise is low. As the amount of political disagreement in one's context increases, so does their support for leaders who are willing to make compromises. In places with greater partisan diversity, the difference between news junkies and news avoiders is no longer significant: both groups are equally as likely to say they prefer a president who is willing to compromise. Heterogeneous contexts are the most important to encouraging support for compromise among those least likely to follow the news.

[12] The degree to which one follows politics is measured on a four-point scale reflecting answers to the following question: "Some people seem to follow what's going on in government and public affairs most of the time, whether there's an election going on or not. Others aren't that interested. Would you say you follow what's going on in government and public affairs most of the time, some of the time, only now and then, or hardly at all?" News consumption measures self-reported levels of news use in a typical week for five sources: local TV news, national TV news, internet, newspapers, and radio. For each source, respondents are asked how many days they use the news source in a typical week for news other than sports. Responses are summed, then averaged to form a zero-to-1 scale, where 1 indicates use of all five sources every day. Political discussion is measured by responses to, "How many days in the past week did you talk about politics with family or friends?"

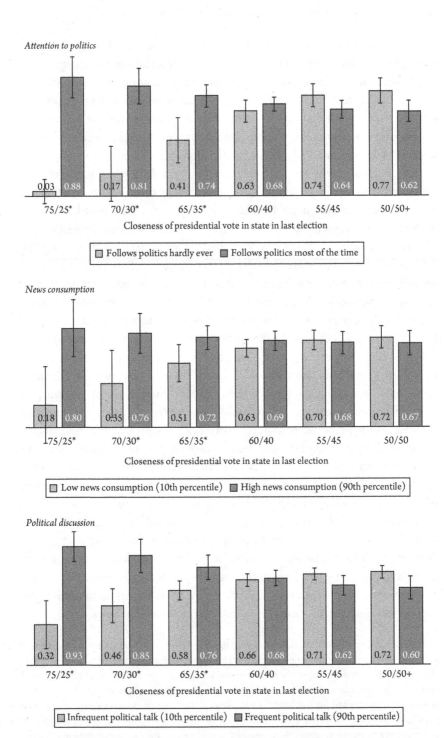

Figure 6.2 Factors that moderate the effects of competitiveness.

I also find that engagement in political talk moderates the effects of living in a diverse partisan context. For those who report that they do not talk about politics in an average week, most prefer politicians who stick firm to their convictions. As the level of political heterogeneity in their context increases, so does the likelihood of favoring a president who is willing to compromise. For those at the median level of political talk or below, partisan diversity is significantly related to greater support for leaders who compromise. For most people above the median level of political talk, there is no significant effect associated with living in a politically diverse context. But for those at the 90th percentile and above of frequency of talk, partisan diversity has a significant negative effect on support for compromise. For the political junkies who talk about politics every day or nearly every day, diverse contexts have the opposite effect than for those who rarely discuss politics, where increasing partisan diversity is associated with lower support for leaders who compromise.

Competitive contexts encourage people to be more supportive of compromises in politics.[13] Those who live in places with greater partisan disagreement are more likely to say they like politicians who compromise than those who live in places with greater partisan homogeneity.[14] Hibbing and Theiss-Morse (2002) argue that one key reason why people dislike debate and deliberation in Congress is because they think that such discussions are merely an effort to delay making the decisions that the American public wants. People tend to hold a sense of false consensus, overestimating the degree to which other people share their same preferences and underestimating the degree to which people want different things in politics. If people assume that there is wide agreement, then there is no need for deliberation and compromise. My results suggest that diverse political environments help correct false consensus effects.

Our traditional expectation is that those who are most invested in political life are the most likely to stand in the way of compromise. Because they care the most about political outcomes, they have the most to lose in ceding ground

[13] A concern might be raised that these results are a function not of learning that people disagree, but instead some level of conflict avoidance. While the survey does not include a measure of conflict avoidance, it does ask respondents, "Would you prefer to live in a place where most people have the same opinions you have about politics, or in a place where people have lots of different opinions about politics, or do you have no preference at all?" If I create a dichotomous measure of those who prefer to live in a place with like-minded others, these individuals are *less* likely to like leaders who compromise as the level of disagreement in their environment increases. This suggests that it is something other than conflict avoidance that encourages the least engaged to be most open to compromise as the diversity of one's setting increases.

[14] These results hold with controls for respondent partisanship, the share of the state voting Democratic in 2008, and the interaction of the two. These results represent something more than just the particular partisan composition of states with greater two-party competition.

to the other side. Yet these findings suggest that the least engaged and least attentive may be the most opposed to compromise in politics. Because they are tuned out of politics, they underestimate levels of political disagreement in the electorate. Perceiving homogeneity in the electorate, they may see little need for compromises to be made. As people learn more about the diversity of opinions—by seeking more news, engaging in more discussions, and living in an environment with greater diversity of views, resistance to compromise declines. This also helps explain why support for compromise is elevated among the most educated and politically involved, as shown in Chapter 3 of this volume. Not only are the political engaged more likely to feel the pressures of political socialization that cultivate support for compromise, they are also more likely to be aware of the political divisions of the electorate. When people are reminded of the differences within the electorate, they report greater support for politicians who are willing to make compromises.

Compromise and Social Information

Competition has been thought to be detrimental to the prospects for compromise, by encouraging the partisan practice of politics. I have argued that competition does more than just encourage us to rally in support of our party; it also reminds us that other people want different things in politics. Competitive campaigns provide cues about the prevalence of opposing viewpoints in the electorate—information that in turn influences people's views about what kinds of policy outcomes are best. To provide additional evidence of how knowledge of the preferences of others informs people's policy demands, I next turn to experiments. I move beyond the campaign context to explore how information from public opinion polls about the views of other Americans influences people's willingness to support policy compromises views.

According to theories of impersonal influence, people's policy demands are shaped by their perceptions about the beliefs held by other Americans (Mutz 1998). In contrast to the kinds of personal social influence that comes through our conversations with friends or coworkers, impersonal social influence is delivered from a distance—through what we learn about the beliefs of other Americans in media accounts and poll results. I expect that this kind of impersonal influence guides how people think about policy compromise. After all, compromise is not only a political value, but also a social one. We compromise not only because it serves our own needs, but also because we acknowledge its virtues as a way of addressing the interests of others. Information about the preferences of the collective help us better understand whether compromise is needed. While the compromises we make in our personal lives are often made face-to-face, the compromises we strike in politics are not made directly with other individuals. Instead, we navigate the prospect of compromise with generalized others—the collective of other citizens who do not share our same views. As such, people's feelings about the necessity and appropriateness of compromise will likely rest on how they perceive the political desires of others in the electorate.

To better understand how knowledge of other Americans' policy preferences encourages people to consider compromise, I rely on an experiment. In the study, I explore how people balance their desires for congruent policy outcomes against their knowledge that other people desire other political outcomes. To signal the will of the electorate, I manipulate the provision of polling data, where some are told that most people in the electorate share their views, some are told most disagree, and others are informed that the American public is evenly split on the issue. In the control condition, no information about public preferences is shared. I also vary whether participants read about a policy outcome well-aligned with their preferences or a policy change that challenges their predispositions. I have argued that people's support for compromise is guided by both principled thinking and their policy goals. As such, it is important to consider not just how people use information about the preferences of other Americans, but also how they weigh these considerations relative other goals like securing desirable policy outcomes.

In the experiment, I start by presenting participants with a brief description of a policy issue, focused on the case of national policy on physician-assisted suicide. I select this policy domain because it represents an issue domain of low salience but strong prior attitudes. As a policy domain where people are often guided by deeply held moral or religious beliefs, this choice represents a tough test of the theory—as we might expect that people might be reluctant to compromise on this issue. Important for the experiment, this issue is one that was not salient at the time of the experiment. Because it was not at the center of any recent policy discussions, I am able to manipulate the level of public support for the policy in a way that should be seen as credible to participants.[15]

To manipulate policy congruence, I vary the direction of the policy outcome. In one version of the vignette, the national government issues a ban on assisted suicide, while in the other version, Congress acts to legalize assisted suicide. Using a question from the pretest, I sort whether participants read about a policy change that conforms to their priors or challenges them. I manipulate the provision of information about social preferences by describing the results of a recent

---

[15] It is also a useful policy domain to select in that either policy change would represent a change from the status quo. This should increase the likelihood of symmetric effects across the versions of the policy change treatment, at least as compared to a vignette that upends some existing federal policy.

poll revealing levels of public support for the policy outcome. In the control condition, no information was provided about public preferences on the issue. In the first experimental condition, people were told that an overwhelming majority of Americans favored the policy outcome described in the vignette. In a second version, people were told that a majority of Americans opposed the policy that was passed. In a third version, respondents were told that the American public remained sharply divided on the issue, with as many supporting the policy as opposing it. Appendix A of this chapter provides the vignettes.

If people are mostly partisans who put their policy goals ahead of principled consideration of compromise in politics, then knowledge of others' views should be of limited consequence. Instead, the biggest variations in support for compromise outcomes should result from whether people read about a policy that conforms to one's preferences or challenges them. For those who read about policy changes well-aligned with their policy goals, compromise will be disliked for the policy concessions it demands. For those who read about policy outcomes that are contrary to their preferences, compromise will hold greater appeal—as a way to potentially make some policy gains past the new unfavorable status quo.

I propose that people's willingness to compromise also depends on the information that they hold about the preferences of others in the electorate. Given the results from the campaign competition analysis, I expect that the influence of social cues will be greatest when they challenge people's tendencies toward false consensus biases. When people are informed that most Americans share their preferences, I expect this information will be of limited consequence. People will be just as supportive of compromise in this case as in the control condition where no information about polling results was shared. If people generally assume that most share their policy preferences, then affirming this with polling data will be unlikely to move how they appraise the possibility of compromise. When informed that others agree with them, this information will reinforce rather than challenge false consensus effects among respondents.

I expect that information about the views of other Americans will be most consequential when it reveals that other Americans desire a different outcome than the respondent. As false consensus effects are disrupted, people will reconsider the need for compromise. Even if people are pleased with the policy outcome, they will be more willing to consider compromise after learning that most other people disagree with them on the policy. By this logic, people care not just about winning desirable policy outcomes, but also want to ensure that policy outcomes reflect the interests of the public at large. Even if people like to be on the winning side on policy debates, they also recognize that policy outcomes should follow from the demands of the electorate.

I also expect that when people learn that Americans are evenly divided in their support and opposition to a policy outcome favored by the respondent that support for compromise will increase relative the control condition. If people use information about the preferences of other Americans in ways that encourage the accommodation of those who disagree, then it should not matter much the degree to which people's false consensus biases are disrupted. To learn that the public is divided should also interrupt perceptions that most agree with the respondent. This manipulation also allows me to check whether people are using information in strategic rather than social kinds of ways. The social use of information implies that people accept compromise outcomes as a way to recognize the diverging preferences of generalized others. But we might worry that people instead use such information in strategic ways, to calculate the odds that their own side might be able to successfully prevail in securing their preferred policy. If people are strategic in their use of social information, then compromise should be less liked when people are told that the public is evenly divided. Rather than cede ground, people will stay loyal to their side, in the hopes of securing just enough support to gain the majority.

The experiment was conducted in fall 2013 with 1,050 participants recruited as a national sample of adults.[16] Participants completed the experiment as part of a larger questionnaire administered and completed over the internet.[17] After reading the vignette, respondents were asked what they think should happen: Congress should legalize physician-assisted suicide, it should ban it, or the sides should work out a compromise. Support for a compromise outcome is shown in Figure 6.3. Results from a logit model are shown in the Appendix B of this chapter (Table A6.1). In the control condition where no information about public preferences was provided, I find that those who read about policy changes that conform to their priors are reluctant to compromise, as only 27% select compromise as their preferred outcome. Most prefer to maintain the policy outcome described in the vignette, one that conforms to their policy aspirations in politics. For those who read about a challenging policy outcome, 44% are supportive of a compromise outcome, which is significantly higher support than seen among those who read about a congruent policy. For those who find themselves on the losing side of a policy debate, compromise holds far greater appeal.

---

[16] The sample was recruited through Qualtrics using their online panel. From their pool of around two million volunteers (recruited from web ads and permission-based e-mail lists), Qualtrics sent my questionnaire to a sample of 2,091 respondents, who were representative of the U.S. population in terms of age, race, and gender, based on Census data. The response rate was 50% of those who received invitations to participate.

[17] The sample is 65% female and 19% nonwhite. In terms of partisanship, 36% identifies as Democratic, 23% as Republican, and 41% as independent or other. Ages range from 18 to 86 with an average age of 48 years.

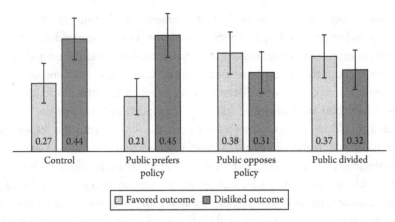

| 0.27 | 0.44 | | 0.21 | 0.45 | | 0.38 | 0.31 | | 0.37 | 0.32 |

Control   Public prefers   Public opposes   Public divided
                    policy   policy

☐ Favored outcome   ■ Disliked outcome

Figure 6.3 Information about public preferences and support for compromise
outcomes.

In the absence of information about public preferences, people are guided by
their policy goals when asked what political outcome is best.

When people are provided with information that most Americans share the
policy preferences of the respondent, the same pattern is found as in the control condition. There is no significant difference between how people answer
when they find that most share their views compared to the condition where no
polling results are mentioned. This is consistent with a false consensus narrative.
Lacking information about what other Americans want, respondents assume
that most people want the same things that they do. When told that most agree
with their view, their willingness to compromise is unchanged.

However, the pattern shifts when people are instead told that their view
is in the minority and that most Americans want a different outcome. Those
on the winning side are significantly more willing to consider compromise,
where now 38% selected it as their preferred outcome. Even when people
are informed that Congress has passed legislation that they desire, many are
willing to support compromise when they learn that most Americans prefer
a different outcome. Most still prefer to maintain the same policy outcome,
demonstrating the power of people's partisan policy goals. Even so, compared
to the case where people were told that most Americans share their goals, support for compromise nearly doubles when people learn that most Americans
dislike the outcome.

For those on the losing side, the pattern reverses. Having learned that the
policy they dislike is also opposed by most Americans, compromise seems a less
appealing outcome. Far fewer of those faced with disliked policy outcomes are
willing to consider compromise than is true in the control condition where no
information about public preferences are provided. Instead, they are more likely

to demand a policy outcome aligned with their interests and those of most other Americans.

What about the case where people are told that the public is evenly divided on the issue? If people are using information about the preferences of other Americans in solely strategic ways, we should see strong opposition to compromise among those who find themselves on the winning side of the issue. If the public is narrowly divided, then either side has a good chance of securing a policy success. As such, we might expect that policy winners will be particularly wary of calls for compromise and instead fight to defend their narrow win. Instead, I find a pattern that is statistically indistinguishable from the pattern seen among those told that the public opposes the policy change. People think about the policy the same way whether they are told that the public is evenly divided on the issue or that most people desire a different outcome. This is consistent with the argument that information about the preferences of others corrects false perceptions of social consensus. When we learn that others disagree with us, we are more open to considering compromise in politics. People's knowledge of the preferences of other Americans influences how they think political disagreements should be resolved.

Conclusions

We have reason to think that competition puts voters in a mindset hostile to compromise. When we consider Congress, competition is considered a rival to collaboration and compromise. In stretches of single-party control of Congress, minority party members have greater incentives to reach across the aisle and consider compromise. But when competition for control of Congress heightens, bipartisan collaboration holds less appeal. Rather than work with the other side, the minority party instead can focus on obstruction, highlighting the weaknesses of their opponents under the hopes that the next election will return them to majority power (Lee 2016). This competition for party control increases the pressure on policy moderates in Congress to hold the party line, prioritizing the electoral fortunes of the party over other objectives (Koger and Lebo 2017). To the degree to which compromise in Congress seems increasingly difficult to achieve, heightened partisan competition is likely a contributing factor.

When thinking about the effects of competition in the electorate, we worry that here too it may discourage people from considering compromise. If we were to think about which settings would be most likely to pull out people's partisan tendencies and encourage the prioritization of policy goals over principle, it would be in the case of conflict and competition. When politics is framed as a battle to be waged, there is little room for principled thinking. Instead, the situation demands that we stand in solidarity with our party to battle for the win—to triumph in the election, to succeed in passing that desired policy. Yet even as people are guided by their policy goals in considering what political outcomes are best, people's partisan passions are not so powerful that they see compromise only in terms of its potential to deliver desirable policy outcomes.

If people were wholly partisan, a closely matched fight should inspire greater resistance to compromise. Competition should encourage us to act in partisan ways. Instead, I find that conflict and disagreement have the potential to encourage people to consider compromise as a political solution. Those who live in places with greater party competition are more likely to say they want political leaders who are willing to strike compromises. Gutmann and Thompson (2012) suggest that reducing the level of disagreement and conflict in campaigns would help promote compromises in Congress, by reducing the pressures of partisan thinking among the electorate. My results suggest that this might not be necessary. Instead, electoral competition is tied to greater enthusiasm for politicians who are willing to compromise. Even though party competition within Congress might heighten strategic opposition to compromise among elites (Koger and Lebo 2017; Lee 2016), this reflects institutional factors rather than the demands of the electorate.

For citizens, competition does not cultivate strategic thinking. Instead, it serves to provide information about the diversity of public preferences. Part of the reason why people resist compromise is arguably because they believe that compromise is unnecessary. Given false consensus effects, people overestimate the degree to which public consensus exists on the issues. Believing that Americans mostly agree on the issues, they instead want politicians to act on this mandate, rather than sorting some compromise remedy. Encountering political disagreement serves to correct such misperceptions. I find that those who live in places with greater partisan disagreement are more likely to prefer politicians who are willing to compromise. These effects are particularly strong for those who are less tuned into politics. For those who rarely talk about politics and seldom follow the news, environments with greater partisan heterogeneity are particularly strongly related to support for leaders who are willing to compromise.

When asked about what policy outcomes are best, people consider both their policy goals as well as the policy demands of the rest of the electorate. When they find that their views are shared by an overwhelming majority of other Americans, they see little need for compromise and instead call for the policy outcomes that best match their own interests. But when people learn that the policy outcome they desire is opposed by most other Americans, they are more willing to advocate that a compromise be made instead of preserving that desired policy outcome. Even as people hold policy goals, they also desire outcomes that align with the demands of the American public at large. These so-cial considerations encourage support for policy compromise.

Political heterogeneity has virtues in a democratic system. Living in diverse contexts and talking with those who disagree with us can cultivate stronger feelings of political tolerance (Campbell 2006; Mutz 2006). I show that exposure to political disagreement can also encourage people to consider compromises in politics. Campaign competition and partisan conflict in politics do not rule out the possibility of policy compromise in the minds of voters. Even in a time of party polarization, party conflict does not close the door to compromise. Political competition has the potential to pull us toward our partisan camps, but it also reminds us of our differences. This knowledge can counteract our partisan resistance to compromise in politics. This might explain why people's support for compromise persists even as ideological divides within the electorate have deepened. As the differences between the parties are clearer, people may better recognize the diversity of public preferences and the need for finding compro-mise solutions.

Appendix A

Experimental Vignettes

Legalization of Assisted Suicide

Control

Bill Poised to Legalize Physician-Assisted Suicide

Congress votes soon on a bill that will permit physician-assisted suicide as an option for the terminally ill.

Under the bill, assisted suicide will be legalized, ending any penalties for doctors who prescribe medication to terminally ill patients who wish to end their own lives.

Public Support

Bill Poised to Legalize Physician-Assisted Suicide: Americans Voice Strong Support for the Legislation

Congress votes soon on a bill that will permit physician-assisted suicide as an option for the terminally ill.

Under the bill, assisted suicide will be legalized, ending any penalties for doctors who prescribe medication to terminally ill patients who wish to end their own lives.

According to a recent Gallup poll, an overwhelming majority of Americans support the bill, with 78% of Americans saying that physician-assisted suicide should be allowed.

Public Opposition

Bill Poised to Legalize Physician-Assisted Suicide: Americans Voice Strong Opposition to the Legislation

Congress votes soon on a bill that will permit physician-assisted suicide as an option for the terminally ill.

Under the bill, assisted suicide will be legalized, ending any penalties for doctors who prescribe medication to terminally ill patients who wish to end their own lives.

According to a recent Gallup poll, an overwhelming majority of Americans oppose the bill, with 78% of Americans saying that physician-assisted suicide should be banned.

Public Divided

Bill Poised to Legalize Physician-Assisted Suicide: Americans Divided in Their Feelings about the Legislation

Congress votes soon on a bill that will permit physician-assisted suicide as an option for the terminally ill.

Under the bill, assisted suicide will be legalized, ending any penalties for doctors who prescribe medication to terminally ill patients who wish to end their own lives.

According to a recent Gallup poll, Americans remain sharply divided on this issue, with 48% saying that physician-assisted suicide should be allowed and 47% saying it should be banned.

Assisted Suicide Ban

Control

Bill Poised to Ban Physician-Assisted Suicide

Congress votes soon on a bill that will prohibit physician-assisted suicide as an option for the terminally ill.

Under the bill, assisted suicide will be criminalized, with steep fines and penalties for doctors who prescribe medication to terminally ill patients who wish to end their own lives.

Public Support

Bill Poised to Ban Physician-Assisted Suicide: Americans Voice Strong Support for the Legislation

Congress votes soon on a bill that will prohibit physician-assisted suicide as an option for the terminally ill.

Under the bill, assisted suicide will be criminalized, with steep fines and penalties for doctors who prescribe medication to terminally ill patients who wish to end their own lives.

According to a recent Gallup poll, an overwhelming majority of Americans support the bill, with 78% of Americans saying that physician-assisted suicide should be banned.

Public Opposition

Bill Poised to Ban Physician-Assisted Suicide: Americans Voice Strong Opposition to the Legislation

Congress votes soon on a bill that will prohibit physician-assisted suicide as an option for the terminally ill.

Under the bill, assisted suicide will be criminalized, with steep fines and penalties for doctors who prescribe medication to terminally ill patients who wish to end their own lives.

According to a recent Gallup poll, an overwhelming majority of Americans oppose the bill, with 78% of Americans saying that physician-assisted suicide should be allowed.

Public Divided

Bill Poised to Ban Physician-Assisted Suicide: Americans Divided in Their Feelings about the Legislation

Congress votes soon on a bill that will prohibit physician-assisted suicide as an option for the terminally ill.

Under the bill, assisted suicide will be criminalized, with steep fines and penalties for doctors who prescribe medication to terminally ill patients who wish to end their own lives.

According to a recent Gallup poll, Americans remain sharply divided on this issue, with 48% saying that physician-assisted suicide should be allowed and 47% saying it should be banned.

Appendix B

Logit Model

Table A6.1 **Desire for a Compromise Outcome, Given Information on Public Preferences**

	Prefers compromise outcome
Disliked outcome	0.772*
	(0.265)
Public support for outcome	−0.288
	(0.294)
Public support for outcome × Disliked outcome	0.342
	(0.383)
Public opposition to outcome	0.539*
	(0.270)
Public opposition to outcome × Disliked outcome	−1.114*
	(0.374)
Public divided	0.482[a]
	(0.274)
Public divided × Disliked outcome	−1.010*
	(0.370)
Constant	−1.014*
	(0.203)
N	1,047

Logit estimates. Standard errors are in parentheses.
$*p < 0.05.$
[a]$p < 0.10.$

7

Policymaking, Procedural Justice, and Support for Compromise

When asked about how political disagreements should be settled, people weigh their policy goals against process considerations. Compromises ask us to balance what we would personally like as an outcome against what we believe is the best way to resolve a policy dispute. People are not wholly partisan in their thinking, as they care about more than just securing policy outcomes congruent with their own interests. Nor are people purely principled in how they consider compromise. Despite strongly endorsing the idea of compromise as a way to resolve political disputes, their support for compromise is informed by their policy goals in practice. Across past chapters, I have shown that while partisan thinking serves as a force that can deter principled thinking about compromise, social considerations serve as a countervailing force, where people are more likely to agree to compromise when it yields policy outcomes that better follow the demands of the electorate.

In this chapter, I continue to explore the forces that guide people to be more open or closed to the prospect of policy compromise. I focus on the ways in which the processes of political decision-making structure people's willingness to consider compromise outcomes in politics. I start by considering the degree to which political conflicts make it challenging to accept compromises outside of campaign seasons. Conflict inhabits the heart of politics. When faced with policy dilemmas, we debate the things that divide us and often give little heed to the things we share in common. When we talk about lawmaking, we talk about disputes, disagreements, conflicts, and controversies. Whether it is the clash of competing priorities, policy disagreements among lawmakers, or battles between political parties, our encounters with politics emphasize conflict. Even after campaigns end, political life invites us to take sides—on which policy is best, what issues should be prioritized, and how problems should be resolved.

The conflicts that define policymaking not only inspire the need for compromise but also represent the obstacles that make compromises hard to find.

Compromise in an Age of Party Polarization. Jennifer Wolak, Oxford University Press (2020). © Oxford University Press. DOI: 10.1093/oso/9780197510490.001.0001

Partisan conflicts can encourage an uncompromising mindset by cultivating feelings of cynicism, dissatisfaction, and mistrust (Durr, Gilmour, and Wolbrecht 1997; Funk 2001; Hibbing and Theiss-Morse 2002; Mutz 2015). In the face of policy conflict, differences in power across factions invite people to see policy disagreements in strategic terms. If partisans believe they have the votes to pass their agenda, then compromise will hold little appeal. For those in the minority faction, compromise can be a pragmatic though unappealing option, one that requires concessions to disliked opponents. Even if people like the idea of compromise in principle, the conflicts of political life may make it challenging to pursue them in practice. I consider the degree to which people think about compromise in strategic terms, to see if policy conflicts cultivate partisan thinking among those on the winning side and curtail feelings of trust among those on the losing side.

I next explore how support for compromise might be encouraged among those disinclined to pursue it. To consider how the character of policy dilemmas conditions how people think about compromise, I focus on the effects of the processes of political decision-making. I propose that people's views about how politics should be practiced have the potential to check their partisan thinking about policy compromise. I expect that framing policy dilemmas in ways that make the process of political decision-making salient will moderate the imprint of partisan priors on support for compromise. I consider both procedural justice and political civility as forces that shape how people reason about policy compromise. Using experiments, I show that cues about the character of democratic procedures can encourage people to think about policy disagreements in principled ways. Even as people are guided by strategic considerations in considering compromise, they also care about the fairness and civility of the procedures that generate that policy outcome. If we learn that a desired policy outcome was achieved through a potentially unfair process, we are more likely to call for compromise, even if it means sacrificing some of our partisan goals. Likewise, people resist compromises with those who violate democratic principles of fairness and civility, even if a compromise would have brought them closer to their preferred policy outcome.

Winning, Losing, and Compromise

As campaign seasons draw to a close, the fates of the parties are determined on election day. As members of Congress and the president get to work on their respective agendas, are citizens keen to see politicians make compromises with their rivals? Even if campaign competition does not undermine people's willingness to consider compromise, there are reasons to believe that neither winners nor the losing side are ready for open-minded deliberation and collaboration with their rivals. For those on the winning side, it is time to secure the policy outcomes that the party fought for during the weeks leading up to election day. With the partisan battles of the campaign fresh in mind, those in the majority may be reluctant to consider any concessions to the party they just defeated at the polls. Instead, the election victors will want to stand loyal to the principles they fought for in the campaign and enjoy the electoral spoils that come with winning elections. In a majoritarian system, partisans have good reasons to pursue the party's agenda rather than make concessions to their opponents.

For those on the losing side, compromise might be the most practical option. Finding themselves in the political minority, compromise offers a path for policy influence even in the wake of electoral defeat. Even so, many have raised doubts about the willingness of those on the losing side to move beyond the deep divisions of the campaign season. Having lost their campaign battles, people may be reluctant to work side by side with their opponents. After an election loss, people place less trust in government than those on the winning side (Anderson and LoTempio 2002; Banducci and Karp 2003; Brunell 2008) and feel less satisfied with democracy (Craig et al. 2006; Singh, Lago, and Blais 2011). Those on the losing side lack efficacy, doubting their own ability for political influence as well as whether their voice will be heard in politics (Clarke and Acock 1989). These feelings all make it harder to consider compromise. To strike compromises with your rivals, you need to trust that your opponents will work in good faith and hold to their word. Lacking trust and efficacy, those on the losing side may be reluctant to enter into collaboration with their partisan opponents.

If policy conflicts encourage an uncompromising mindset among both election winners and losers, then compromise will be hard to reach. Even if people are willing to support compromise as a way of settling disputes, their principled support for compromise may not inform their policy demands in practice. I start by considering how information about the balance of party power shapes people's willingness to call on politicians to consider compromise. I focus on the desirability of compromise when policy debates are framed in terms of what might be won and what might be lost. In previous chapters, I have focused mostly on people's willingness to support compromise in general situations—as an approach of politicians and as a way of conducting politics. In this chapter, I focus on the tension between what people want to happen and what people believe should happen when it comes to specific public policy disputes. In the abstract, the principle of compromise may hold strong normative appeal. But when faced with a specific piece of legislation and the tangible stakes of legislative policy debates, people's partisan instincts may prevail.

To consider the effects of strategic thinking on support for compromise, I rely on an experimental design similar to that considered in the last chapter, but rather than focusing on the balance of public demands, I manipulate the balance of partisan power within a legislature. By manipulating each party's odds of seeing their side prevail, I can consider the degree to which people think about compromise in strategic terms. In the study, respondents first read a short description of a state legislature debating how to manage natural resources on state lands. Republicans were described as interested in pursuing natural gas exploration for its economic benefits, while Democrats were described as opposing the proposal out of environmental concerns. The text of the vignettes can be found in the appendix of this chapter.[1]

I then varied the information that people received about each party's odds of winning a policy debate. In the control condition, participants were given no details about which party holds the greater odds of prevailing. In a second condition, people were informed that their own party holds an advantage and will likely succeed in passing their version of the bill. If those on the winning side are strategic about the kinds of decision-making processes that lawmakers choose to use, we should expect them to reject compromise in favor of majority rule. Confident that their party will prevail, they will resist concessions to the other side. In a third condition, respondents are told that the opposing party holds that advantage and that their own party is unlikely to prevail. If people are primarily driven by strategic thinking, compromise will be a desirable option. If the opposing side will likely succeed at implementing their proposal, compromise is the best alternative to try to secure a more appealing policy outcome. Yet it is also possible that support for compromise drops in this condition. Rather than pragmatically seeking compromise, negative feelings about the outcome might lead those in the minority might resist concessions, where people are wary about sacrificing policy goals and collaborating with their rivals in the legislature.

I also consider how the mere presence of political conflict affects people's willingness to contemplate cooperation. In a fourth experimental condition, the parties are described as evenly matched, where either side could potentially prevail in passing their version of the policy through the legislature. This frame echoes the kinds of press coverage common to legislative debates, where journalists describe policy battles as contests to be won or lost, emphasizing details of which party leads and which tactics each might use to their advantage (Atkinson 2017;

---

[1] I determined whether the partisan vignette represented one's in-party or out-party using responses to a seven-point scale of partisanship in the Cooperative Congressional Election Study. Independents who do not lean toward either party were further sorted into partisan camps using questions about party registration and the respondent's preferred candidate in the 2012 presidential election.

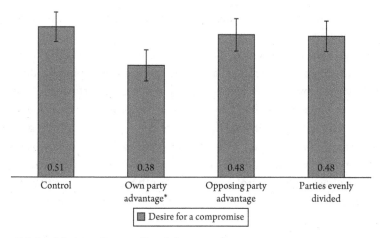

Figure 7.1 Legislative policy conflict and support for compromise.

Cappella and Jamieson 1997; Lawrence 2000; Patterson 1994). If conflict alone invites people to think about politics in terms of their partisan rivalries, then a close partisan battle should also discourage consideration of compromise. In strategic terms, an evenly divided legislature should provide strong incentives to stand firm. If either party could prevail, then savvy partisans should dig in their heels and vow fidelity to the party's cause, to try to secure the narrow advantage necessary for a win. If people's resistance to compromise is rooted in a desire to win and secure desired policy outcomes, then compromise should be a particularly unpopular option when the partisan teams are evenly matched.

I explore this using an experiment placed on a module of the 2014 Cooperative Congressional Election Study, with a sample of 1,488 respondents. First, participants read a version of the experimental vignette about the legislative policy debate. After this, they were asked about what outcome they most preferred—the policy offered by their own party, the position of the opposing side, or a compromise outcome.[2] Figure 7.1 summarizes support for the compromise option across the experimental conditions.[3] I find first that compromise is the modal preference across all conditions. Even when presented with specific policy debates, people still seem quite open to solving policy disputes through compromise. In the control condition, where information about the balance of

[2] Specifically, it asked if legislators should expand natural gas exploration on state-owned lands, restrict natural gas exploration, or work out a compromise solution.

[3] The sample is balanced across the four conditions in terms of partisanship, strength of partisanship, ideology, environmental attitudes, gender, age, and race. I find similar results when survey weights are applied.

votes between the two parties is absent, 51% selected a compromise as their preferred outcome.[4]

Turning to the differences across the experimental conditions, I find partial evidence in support of the idea that people to think about policy outcomes in strategic ways. I confirm that when people find that their party holds greater political power, they are less likely to say that a compromise is their ideal policy outcome. Among those who read the vignette that reported that their own party was likely to prevail in the policy dispute, only 38% endorse compromise as their preferred policy outcome. This is significantly lower support for a compromise than is observed in the control condition.[5] For those who expect that they will win the policy dispute and secure a desired policy outcome, compromise is a less attractive option.

I fail to find support for the idea that those allied with the out-party are any more disdainful of the prospect of policy compromise. When faced with a likely policy defeat for their own party, 48% of respondents say compromise is their ideal outcome—which is not significantly different from the level of support for compromise in the control condition where no information about the balance of party power was provided. Those who those learn that their party is unlikely to prevail in the policy debate are significantly more likely to call for compromise than those on the winning side, but this difference is driven by the resistance of the majority faction rather than the desires of the minority party. We have reason to worry that those in the minority faction will be wary of their opponents and mistrustful of political processes in ways that make compromises challenging (Anderson et al. 2005; Brunell 2008; Craig et al. 2006). However, I find little evidence of resistance to compromise among those who favor the party that is out of power. Even though lawmakers in the minority party might be wary of compromise in favor of trying to obstruct the party in power (Lee 2016), those in the electorate who find themselves in the minority faction are no less willing to call for policy compromises.

While we might expect that people might dig in their heels to fight for their side to win after learning that the two parties are evenly matched, I fail to find support for this. Those who learn that either side could prevail are just as likely to support compromise as those who receive no information about the strategic odds of winning the debate. Even in the face of a closely matched partisan battle, people are not guided by a desire for fidelity to their partisan teams.

---

[4] Notably, this question wording should not create strong pressures to give some sort of socially desirable (but insincere) endorsement of compromise. People are doing more than just accepting some disliked compromise; they are specifically selecting it as their desired policy outcome.

[5] Support for compromise is significantly lower in this condition relative the control vignette as well as both of the other experimental conditions.

Nor does close competition seem to derail people's willingness to work with their opponents. Scholars have proposed that the conflicts of politics can corrode people's trust in government (Cappella and Jamieson 1997; Hibbing and Theiss-Morse 2002; Mutz and Reeves 2005; Mutz 2015). Even so, emphasizing the divides between the parties does not appear to dilute enthusiasm for compromise among participants in this study. Political conflict alone is not enough to spark strategic resistance to policy compromise within legislatures.

When confronted with specific policy debates on issues they care about, people remain quite supportive of the idea of policy compromise. Yet describing policy disputes as partisan battles with winners and losers has the potential to lead people to put their policy goals ahead of principled consideration of compromise. People who anticipate that they will be on the winning side of the policy dispute are less willing to endorse compromise as their preferred policy outcome. Those on the losing side feel differently, and are more keen to see the legislature pursue a compromise. Policy winners and losers are not equally open to compromise.

Encouraging Compromise in the Face of Conflict

How can compromise be encouraged in a domain defined by conflict and disagreement? Even though we often dislike conflict in politics, it is arguably unavoidable. Indeed, it is central to a democratic system. We value a system where we are free to fight for what we believe in—to participate in the debates and discussions that determine political outcomes. Even if we do not win the battle, we look forward to the next round, with the hopes that our fortunes will be reversed. Rather than try to prevent disagreements, we instead set up political institutions as a way to manage conflict and organize political debate. In democratic systems, we create rules for how we debate the issues and institute systems to resolve our differences in fair ways. When elected officials follow these rules and respect procedural fairness, it reinforces the legitimacy of the political system.

For citizens to weather the blows that conflict inflicts, we rely on our trust in the legitimacy of the political system. If we do not believe that we have the opportunity for voice or that we will have future opportunities to obtain the outcomes we seek, then we will have trouble accepting policy results that displease us. But if we see the system as legitimate and believe that government procedures are fair, then we can better tolerate political conflict and its costs. When we trust political institutions, it helps grant legitimacy to unpopular decisions (Gibson 1989; Gibson, Caldeira, and Spence 2005). When people do not receive their desired outcome, their inclination to challenge the results is inhibited by feelings of legitimacy about the processes and institutions that produced the outcome. When people are confronted with a disliked partisan outcome, these principled considerations check our partisan tendencies to otherwise reject this disliked outcome as illegitimate.

I consider how reminders about procedural legitimacy temper people's partisan demands in their willingness to consider policy compromises. The forces that encourage people to consider compromise are arguably the same systems used to manage a political world defined by conflict: mutual agreement on the rules of the game. A key reason why people support compromise in politics is because they believe that they should. Through political socialization, citizens come to see compromise as a desirable solution to political and social conflicts. Even though they might have other partisan goals, compromise is a principled choice. To the extent to which this is true, procedural considerations should serve as a force that reminds people to think about compromise in principled ways.

We know that people are concerned not only with securing desirable political outcomes, but also with how those debates are resolved (Hibbing and Theiss-Morse 2002). When people encounter news stories about a bill before Congress or a presidential initiative, they learn not only about the policy outcome but also the process that generated it—and the partisan disagreements and policy disputes that preceded that outcome. These details about the processes of political decision-making shape how people think about politics (Hibbing and Theiss-Morse 1995, 2002). Even as voters become more partisan in their thinking and increasingly guided by motivated reasoning, they still care a good deal about the character of political procedures. People care so much about the procedures that in evaluating their experiences with the courts and police, their views about how they were treated through the process matter more than the outcome they received (Hurwitz and Peffley 2005; Tyler 2000).

When faced with partisan debates and policy conflict, people's first instincts might be partisan—to favor outcomes that best align with their interests. But when people encounter cues to think about the legitimacy of the political process that produced the policy outcome, I believe they will be reminded about their principled support for compromise. Discussion of how political conflicts *are* resolved should make salient our concerns about how political disputes *should* be settled.

To explore how the character of political processes shapes people's support for compromise, I turn to experiments. I vary the character of procedures used to implement policy changes, presenting people with a procedure that either follows democratic principles of fairness or with an unfair process that violates principles of procedural justice. People care strongly about being treated fairly in the political system. Fair procedures provide reassurance that institutions are following the rules in ways that will produce fair outcomes (Tyler 1990). When elected officials fail to respect the rules of the game, people lose trust in those institutions and see them as less legitimate (Gangl 2003; Gibson 1991). I expect that descriptions of procedural fairness will influence how people apply principled thinking versus partisan reasoning to policy dilemmas and compromise. I test this by manipulating not only the fairness of the procedures, but also the direction of the policy outcome, varying whether people read about a policy outcome that conforms to their prior preferences or instead opposes them.

When policy debates are framed in ways that emphasize the fairness of political procedures, I expect to see a pattern of results similar to what was shown in the previous experiment on conflict, where those on the losing side of a policy debate are more enthusiastic about compromise than those on the winning side. For those on the losing side to cede ground to our opponents and consider concessions and compromise, we need to have some trust that our opponents will play fair and follow the rules. If our opponents respect the rules of the game, it encourages us to see the system as legitimate and invites us to consider compromise as a principled way to resolve our differences. When we believe that the system is fair and legitimate, it should be easier to support compromise, particularly for those on the losing side.

I expect this pattern to be reversed in the presence of process cues about procedural injustice and unfair procedures, where those on the losing side are less willing to consider compromise. If people perceive that they have not been treated fairly within the political system, they will be disinclined to work cooperatively within it. Having found that the winning side has used unfair tactics to secure their policy goals, it becomes hard to trust their opponents to play fairly when it comes to finding a suitable compromise. Rather than considering concessions to their rivals, they will instead resist compromise. If we see that our opponents do not respect the rules, it should be harder to tolerate concessions and more difficult to consider compromise. Just as we find it difficult to trust government when procedural justice is violated, it should be hard to pursue compromise with untrustworthy opponents who break the rules.

For those on the winning side of the policy debate who secured their policy victory through violations of norms of procedural justice, I expect they will more willing to support policy compromise. Because people weigh both policy considerations and procedural concerns in their support for compromise, I expect that these procedural justice violations will lead people to prioritize process considerations over their policy preferences. Even though it might mean sacrificing a desirable policy outcome, those on the winning side will cede ground and consider compromise, a potentially compensatory gesture that acknowledges the party's procedural violations.

To explore how people balance partisan thinking and principled reasoning when it comes to considering compromise, I consider how procedural violations alter support for compromise outcomes when unfair procedures were used compared to a neutral control condition where process details are not mentioned. The experiment centers on a vignette in the form of a newspaper article. This article describes a policy debate in New Jersey, where Democrats and Republicans in the state legislature are debating whether forests on state-owned land should be accessible to commercial lumberjacks. One version describes a decision by the state to open state forests to logging, while the other version describes a bill that prohibits further logging on state lands. Experimental participants were randomly assigned to read one version, and environmental attitudes assessed in a pretest questionnaire were used to determine whether people were reading about a desirable or challenging policy outcome.[6]

I also manipulated the fairness of the procedures used by the winning side in the state legislature. In the control condition, no information about the processes was provided, while in the second version, the winning side was described as breaking the rules to push through the legislation, violating open meetings rules, and calling special sessions with insufficient prior notice. A subtitle was also added to the newspaper article mentioning these allegations of broken rules. As a manipulation of procedural justice, it is relatively subtle. Legislators were not described as taking bribes or usurping power from other branches of government. Instead, legislators on the winning side were said to have broken rules about when and how legislative meetings are called. I selected this relatively subtle manipulation as it resembles the ways procedural violations typically occur in contemporary politics in the United States. This creates a tough test of the theory: if people respond differently even in the face of this kind of minor procedural violation, then fair procedures must be quite important to how people think about compromise. The text of the vignettes can be found in Appendix A of this chapter.

I conducted the experiment in the summer of 2013 using a sample of 425 participants recruited through the Amazon Mechanical Turk.[7] After reading the

---

[6] If I instead determine whether people encounter favorable or unfavorable policy outcomes based on their partisanship and which partisan side won, I find similar results.

[7] I include a free response question asking people to explain why they feel that way as a check to ensure that respondents read the article. I exclude eleven respondents who did not answer this question.

On the Mechanical Turk, interested participants can complete small tasks for small sums of money. Samples drawn from the Turk are more diverse than other convenience samples like student subject pools, but still are not representative samples of the American public. This sample is 32% female and 29% nonwhite. In this sample, 11% have a high school education, 46% have completed some college, and 43% have a bachelor's degree or more. The sample is left-leaning, where 42% identify as Democrats, 14% identify as Republicans, and the remainder identify with other parties or as independents. The sample also skews young, where 68% of the sample is under age 30, 17% are between 30 and 39 years of age, and 15% are ages 40 and over.

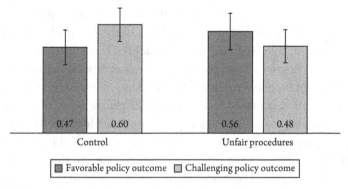

Figure 7.2 Environmental policy, procedural justice, and support for compromise outcomes.

news article, experimental participants were asked, "What do you think should happen in this state?" and given options that the state should block logging on state-owned land, the state should allow logging on state-owned lands, or that the sides should try to work out a compromise. From this question, I create a dichotomous measure of support for compromise as a political outcome. Levels of support for compromise are shown in Figure 7.2. In Appendix B of this chapter, I report logit results from a model of support for compromise as a function of the fairness of the procedure, the favorability of the policy outcome, and the interaction of the two (Table A7.1).

I find that the effects of policy success on willingness to compromise are conditioned on the fairness of the process. Considering first the case where no details of the decision-making process were mentioned, I find that those who secure favorable outcomes tend to be less likely to prefer a compromise than those who read about disliked policy outcomes. This pattern mirrors that in Figure 7.1, where those on the winning side are less keen on pursuing a policy compromise than those on the losing side. Among those on the winning side of the policy debate, 47% choose a compromise as their preferred outcome, while 60% of those on the losing side favor compromise.[8]

However, the pattern is reversed when experimental participants were told that the policy process was unfair, as indicated by the significant interaction effect in the logit model reported in the Appendix B. While those who encounter disliked policy outcomes are usually keen to compromise, this is less true in cases where politicians violate principles of procedural justice. When rules are broken in policymaking, 56% of those on the winning side select compromise as the best outcome, while only 48% of those on the losing side of the

---

[8] This difference is near significant ($p < 0.065$).

debate prefer a compromise solution.[9] Betrayed by the unfair practices of their opponents, those on the losing side seem less likely to trust their rivals to engage in good faith collaboration. Absent feelings of trust, the collaboration and concessions required by compromise lose their appeal. However desirable a policy win might be, people care about more than just securing a victory. When a policy success is obtained by breaking the rules, people are more likely to advocate for compromise—perhaps as a way to compensate for these ill-gotten gains.

People's support for compromise depends on the character of political procedures used. While winners eschew compromise and those on the losing side favor it, the pattern is reversed when policy victories are achieved by bending or breaking the rules. If support for compromise was driven primarily by policy attitudes, we would expect to see that people like compromises only so much as they bring policy outcomes closer to one's preferences. If this were all there was to the story, then it should matter little how that outcome was obtained. People should be similarly resistant to compromise whether the procedures were by the book or when rules were bent. Instead, I find here that support for compromise is informed by both policy and process considerations. All else equal, policy winners are disinclined to compromise. But when those desired outcomes are secured by unfair means, people are more willing to consider compromise. Those on the losing side normally are happy to consider compromise, as a way to secure a more favorable policy outcome. But they are less likely to do so when the other side has been revealed to be violating procedural norms. Whether it is mistrust of their opponents or an unwillingness to consider compromise when other democratic values are not respected, unfair practices close policy opponents to considering compromise.

Incivility and Support for Compromise

When politicians break the rules and violate principles of fairness, it changes the way we think about compromise in politics. To further explore the degree to which information about government processes influences people's tolerance for policy compromise, I consider the consequences of political incivility. Incivility represents a form of political conflict that violates our norms of how politics should be practiced. Politicians who shout, talk over each other, and hurl insults back and forth violate our expectations about how elected officials should

---

[9] Under unfair procedures, the difference between winners and losers in their support for compromise is not statistically significant. The drop in support for compromise among those on the losing side between the control and unfair procedures treatment is nearly significantly different ($p < 0.07$).

deliberate. Civility is a valued norm in politics (Funk 2001; Mutz 2015).[10] People readily admit that they dislike political discourse marked by incivility and conflict, and angry and impolite political discourse has been shown to be damaging to public trust (Funk 2001; Hibbing and Theiss-Morse 2002; Mutz 2015; Mutz and Reeves 2005).

Political incivility resembles unfair procedures in that both violate our norms about how politics should be practiced. Yet incivility is distinctive from procedural violations in that it does not violate principles of fairness or the rules of the game. While politicians endanger the legitimacy of government by ignoring the laws and violating norms of fair play, the same does not hold for incivility. This is important to acknowledge, as it speaks to the mechanisms that are at work in these experiments. If people resist compromise with the opposing side when they break the rules, it may be due to a lack of trust and a reluctance to cooperate with opponents who will not negotiate in good faith. If politicians' use of incivility alters how people think about compromise, then it suggests that people's support for compromise is not only tied to our trust in the other side, but also global feelings about political procedures and how political disagreements are best resolved. If people's inclination to compromise is rooted in a sense of civic and social obligation, then incivility should hurt prospects for compromise.[11] When our opponents do not follow the norms of being civil to the other side, we should be disinclined to share similar social courtesies with them. On the other hand, when we are explicitly reminded that the other side acted with civility and respect, it should serve to remind us of the positive side of civic norms and promote a greater willingness to consider compromise.

To explore the effects of civility on support for compromise, I employ an experiment. I present participants with a newspaper article about an environmental policy debate, varying the policy outcome and politicians' reliance on civility in pursuing the outcome. The focus of the article is a legislative debate about extending mining operations in Wisconsin. Republicans are described as pushing for expansion of mining for its economic benefits, while Democrats are depicted as wanting to limit mining out of environmental concerns. Some read a vignette where their own party prevails in passing its legislation, where others

[10] Incivility is not just a political norm; it is also a social one. We dislike those who act rudely or antagonistically within our own lives and are similarly disappointed to see this kind of behavior from elected officials. In this way, incivility is similar to compromise in having shared roots at both social and political norms. Just as we feel the social pressure to act civilly to those we disagree with, we also feel socialized pressures that we should be open to compromises.

[11] If people care only about the trustworthiness of their opponents in considering compromise, it should matter little whether the other side acts in civil or polite ways.

read that the opposing side succeeded.[12] In the control condition, people read only about the mining bill. The incivility and civility manipulations include an additional subtitle and paragraph describing the civility level of the legislative debate. In the civility frame, the legislative discussion is described as polite, civil, orderly, and respectful. While leaders on the winning side disagreed with their opponents, they took care to treat the other side with respect. In the case of incivility, state legislators from the winning party were described as interrupting and heckling the other side. Rather than treating the other side with respect, party leaders were instead facing sanctions for name-calling and coarse language.[13]

I conducted this experiment in the fall of 2013 with a convenience sample of 585 participants recruited through the Amazon Mechanical Turk.[14] After reading the experimental vignette, participants were asked what would be the best outcome for the people in the state—blocking iron mining, allowing iron mining, or that the sides should try to work out a compromise. From this question, I create a dichotomous measure of support for a compromise outcome. Levels of support for compromise are shown in Figure 7.3. Logit results are reported in Appendix B (see Table A7.2).[15] In the control condition where no information was offered about the civility of the politicians, I find the familiar result where those on the winning side are significantly less likely to support compromise than those on the losing side. Among those on the winning side, 53% say compromise would be the best outcome, compared to 67% of those on the losing side. Those who obtained desired policy outcomes are significantly less

[12] I determine whether people are on the winning side or losing side based on their partisanship as reported in the posttest questionnaire. Pure independents are excluded from these results. If independents are folded into the analysis as "nonlosing" partisans, the results are substantively similar. Descriptively, pure independents reveal similar levels of support for compromise as partisan winners in the control and civility conditions and similar resistance to compromise as partisan losers in the incivility condition.

[13] The text of the vignettes can be found in Appendix A.

[14] The sample is 38% female and 20% nonwhite. In terms of education, 9% have a high school education or less, 43% have completed some college, 38% have a college degree, and 10% have an advanced degree. Like other samples drawn from the Amazon Mechanical Turk, the sample skews young. Fifty-two percent are aged 17 to 29, 28% are aged 30 to 39, and 10% are in their 40s, and 11% are aged 50 or over. The sample is left-leaning, as 63% identify as Democratic, 16% identify as independent, and 21% identify as Republicans. I have no prior expectation that Democrats and Republicans are differently responsive to incivility. I also explored whether there was any evidence of heterogeneous treatment effects. While there are some intercept differences in support for compromise among Democrats, there is little evidence that Democrats and Republicans respond in different ways to the use of civil or uncivil processes.

[15] Randomization appears to have been successful. I tested whether age, gender, race, strength of partisanship, partisanship, and prior issue preferences could be explained as a function of the

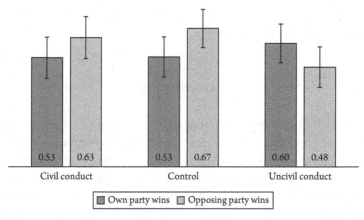

Figure 7.3 Party incivility and support for compromise.

likely to prefer a compromise outcome than those who are faced with a disliked policy outcome.

When people are given information that emphasizes the civil nature of the policy process, I find a similar divide between policy winners and losers, but unlike in the case of the control, the difference between the two is not statistically significant. Given additional description of the civility of the process, winners are similarly resistant to compromise, while those on the losing side are somewhat less likely to demand compromise—perhaps out of a sense of being more willing to accept a disliked outcome generated by a civil and respectful process.

In contrast, in the case of incivility, the pattern is reversed. Those who identify with the party on the winning side tend to be more likely to support compromise than those on the losing side. When one's own party wins the debate but acts in uncivil ways toward its partisan opponents, 60% believe compromise is the best outcome. For those on the losing side who encountered the impolite and uncivil behavior of their opponents, only 48% support compromise as the best outcome.[16] This pattern mirrors that found in the procedural justice experiment. People's willingness to consider compromise depends on the degree to which politicians respect procedural norms. Moreover, these results suggest that people care not only about whether their opponents follow the rules, but also whether they follow civic norms of civility. When the winning side is rude,

experimental manipulations or their interaction using analysis of variance. I found no evidence of significant differences across the cells of the experimental design.

[16] In the logit estimates reported in Appendix B, I find a significant interaction effect between an own-party win and the incivility frame, as well as a near-significant marginal effect of a policy win in the case of the incivility condition ($p < 0.1$).

impolite, and uncivil, those in the opposing faction are less likely to think that compromise is the best outcome.

Conclusions

When faced with debates over public policy, are people willing to consider compromise? I find that even when faced with the specific trade-offs of legislative policy debates, many are willing to endorse compromise solutions. While survey questions reveal strong support for the principle of compromise in the abstract, we might worry that this reflects social desirability biases, where people say they support compromise merely because they believe that they should. By exploring people's willingness to recommend compromise within public policy debates, these experiments affirm people's enthusiasm for compromise in specific situations. Across the studies, the modal response of the ideal outcome was typically compromise.

People's willingness to compromise is informed by both partisan concerns and principled thinking. When faced with policy dilemmas, people who secure desired outcomes are less likely to consider concessions and compromise than those who find themselves on the losing side. Policy conflicts engage strategic thinking among those in the majority faction. While we might worry about the willingness of those on the losing side to consider compromise due to their animosities toward their opponents, I find little evidence that those in the minority are closed to compromise. Nor do I find much evidence that the closeness of a political conflict discourages people from being willing to compromise with their opponents.

These results highlight the ways in which the conflicts of politics can make it more challenging to find compromises. Even though people support compromise in principle, they resist it in cases where it is clear that the party's goals can be achieved without making any sacrifices. When reassured that their party has enough votes to pass their agenda, people prefer majority rule to the concessions required by compromise. When people are unsure about their own party's chances for policy success, compromise is seen as a more appealing option. In the context of contemporary politics, parties often remain uncertain about their odds of policy success. Over recent decades, unified party government is the exception rather than the norm. Even when power is concentrated in the hands of one party, the design of government leaves the minority faction with plenty of opportunities to derail and delay policy change. In these situations, compromises are of greater pragmatic virtue—and also more likely to enjoy the support of citizens.

When asked about how political disputes should be settled, people do not simply pick the procedure that is mostly likely to generate a winning outcome. Instead, they make choices informed by democratic values and their socialized views about how democracy should work. Because our beliefs about compromise are learned independently of our partisan attitudes, our principled support of compromise has the potential to serve as a check on partisan thinking in politics. The expression of principled thinking about compromise is heightened in the face of reminders about other civic norms and democratic values. When we learn that we have won through unfair means, we are more ready to consider compromise. When we find that we have lost due to the procedural violations of our opponents, we pull back from consideration of compromise.

A similar pattern holds when norms of civility are violated. Absent information about the civility or incivility of the process, people on the winning side are less willing to compromise than those on the losing side. When explicitly reminded of the civility and decorum of the process, this difference between policy winners and losers declines, and both are similarly open to compromise. When people are told that the winning side acted in uncivil ways, those on the winning side become more likely to support compromise as a policy outcome. Those on the losing side instead turn away from compromise with their opponents in the face of this incivility. Even in a time of party polarization and greater partisan motivated reasoning, people do not simply want the outcomes that most closely match their interests. They also want politicians to respect procedural norms and rules, and will call for different kinds of outcomes if these norms are not respected.

Politics is about conflict and disagreement. Our differences invite us to consider compromise, but the conflict of our views also makes those compromises difficult. When our disputes take place within a political system we see as fair and civil, it is easier for those on the losing side to consider compromise. But when our opponents ignore the rules and violate norms of civility, compromise becomes more difficult. It helps to have the right kind of processes, where we disagree but in a setting where the parties agree to follow the rules and respect the other side. These experiments show that people care a good deal about the processes by which government policies are produced. People care not only about procedural fairness, but also norms of civility. Others have shown how violations to procedural norms and rules hurt trust and erode public legitimacy (Gangl 2003; Gibson 1991). I demonstrate that procedural violations also influence how we want to see political disagreements settled. Our willingness to consider compromise outcomes depends on the character of the policy process used.

When the public rewards their party for following the rules and observing norms of civility, it has the potential to reinforce legitimate actions from political elites. The more people care that proper procedures and norms are observed, the stronger incentives leaders have to follow the rules of the game. While people rely on the legitimacy of institutions to mitigate their own disappoints with losing, they also reinforce legitimacy in demanding that elites do their part to make sure that the rules are followed. In this way, citizens provide a feedback loop of reinforcement to potentially promote the legitimacy of democratic government.

Appendix A

Experimental Vignettes

Vignettes for Experiment 1: Conflict and Compromise

Version 1: Control

Democrats and Republicans are debating a bill that would alter how natural resources are managed on state lands. Republicans in the state legislature want expand natural gas exploration on state lands as a way to bring jobs to the region. Environmental concerns are paramount for Democrats, who argue that natural gas drilling should be restricted in favor of protecting the state's scenic landscapes.

Versions 2 and 3: Party Advantage

Given a state legislature controlled by Democrats, few expect that Republicans will be able to find the votes necessary to expand natural gas exploration on state lands.

Given a state legislature controlled by Republicans, few expect that Democrats will be able to find the votes necessary to restrict natural gas exploration on state lands.

Version 4: Parties Evenly Matched

Given a state legislature evenly split between Democrats and Republicans, either party could prevail in deciding how to best regulate natural gas exploration on state lands.

Vignettes for Experiment 2 on Procedural Justice and Compromise

Expansion of Logging

New Jersey Opens State Forests to Logging.

Trenton, NJ (AP)—This week, [Democrats/Republicans] in New Jersey's state legislature have passed a contentious measure that will fundamentally change how the state's protected forests are managed. Under the bill, commercial lumberjacks will be [allowed to chop and sell trees/banned from harvesting any trees] from New Jersey's prized state-owned forests.

According to the sponsors of the bill, expanding the parcels of land open to logging will unlock a lucrative new harvest for the state's forestry industry, which has struggled in recent years. "This change will increase the flow of logs to mills, create new jobs, and help our rural communities that rely on logging to sustain their economies. We have the ability to do something very simple to put about 2,000 people back to work," said Republican Andy Osterman, the bill's chief sponsor.

Opponents of the bill say that the expansion of the logging industry will scar the state's scenic forests and damage the streams and wetlands that run through state-owned forests. "We need to protect the rare plants of these forests as well as the animal habitats they provide. By shielding our forests, we will keep our streams and reservoirs pristine and protect the park land that provides us sanctuary for escaping our busy city lives," said Democrat Marty Phillips, who has been an outspoken opponent of the bill.

Restriction of Logging

New Jersey Blocks All Logging on State-Owned Lands

Trenton, NJ (AP)—This week, [Democrats/Republicans] in New Jersey's state legislature have passed a contentious measure that will fundamentally change how the state's protected forests are managed. Under the bill, commercial lumberjacks will be [allowed to chop and sell trees/banned from harvesting any trees] from New Jersey's prized state-owned forests.

According to the sponsors of the bill, these limits on the lands open to logging will protect state's scenic forests and help restore the streams and wetlands that run through state-owned forests. "We need to protect the rare plants of these forests as well as the animal habitats they provide. By shielding our forests, we will keep our streams and reservoirs pristine and protect the park land that provides us sanctuary for escaping our busy city lives," said Democrat Andy Osterman, the bill's chief sponsor.

Opponents of the bill say that closing these parcels of land to logging will only compound problems for the state's forestry industry, which has struggled in recent years. "This change will decrease the flow of logs to mills, cost us jobs, and hurt our rural communities that rely on logging to sustain their economies. This change in policy is going to put about 2,000 people out to work," said Republican Marty Phillips, who has been an outspoken opponent of the bill.

Unfair Procedures Case Adds This Subtitle and This Paragraph

- [Democrats/Republicans] claim [Republicans/Democrats] broke legislative rules to push through the legislation
- The debate that led up to Tuesday's vote was a heated one, as [Republicans/ Democrats] have charged that [Democrats/Republicans] manipulated legislative procedures in order to push through the bill that [opens/closes] state lands to the forestry industry. According to a complaint filed with the state attorney general, open meetings rules were violated when [Republicans/ Democrats] convened secret closed sessions in order to debate several amendments to the bill and schedules two special legislative sessions without sufficient prior notice to the public.

Vignettes for Experiment 3 on Incivility and Compromise
Republican Party Win

Wisconsin Officials Legalize Iron Mining in Northern Counties

Madison, WI (AP)—This week, Republicans in Wisconsin's state legislature passed a controversial measure that will open up land in the northern part of the state to the mining of zinc and iron ore. Under the bill, commercial mining companies will be allowed to move forward with excavations of open-pit iron mines in northern Wisconsin.

According to the sponsors of the bill, introducing opportunities for iron mining will be an economic boom for northern Wisconsin towns, which have some of the highest unemployment rates in the state. "For the people in these towns, mining will bring much-needed jobs and economic growth. By bringing 1000 well-paying jobs to the area, iron mining will change the fortunes of local families for years to come," said Republican Frank Krause, the bill's chief sponsor.

Opponents of the bill worry about the pollution and environmental destruction that mining could bring to the landscape of northern Wisconsin. "It would take only one mistake at the mine to end up with heavy metals polluting our streams. By allowing mining, we risk irreparable damage to the quality of the drinking water as well as walleye and sturgeon fishing operations," said Democrat Matthew Vandervelden, who has been an outspoken opponent of the bill.

Democratic Party Wins

Wisconsin Officials Ban Iron Mining in Northern Counties

Madison, WI (AP)—This week, Democrats in Wisconsin's state legislature passed a controversial measure that will close land in the northern part of the state to the mining of zinc and iron ore. Under the bill, commercial mining companies will be forced to halt all mining exploration and excavation operations in northern Wisconsin.

According to the sponsors of the bill, ending iron mining will help protect northern Wisconsin towns from pollution and environmental damages. "It would take only one mistake at the mine to end up with heavy metals polluting our streams. By ending the era of mining, we will be able to protect the quality of the drinking water and save walleye and sturgeon fishing operations from irreparable damage," said Democrat Frank Krause, the bill's chief sponsor.

Opponents of the bill worry about the economic repercussions of ending mining operations for northern Wisconsin towns, which have some of the highest unemployment rates in the state. "For the people in these towns, mining offers much-needed jobs and economic growth. By taking away 1000 well-paying jobs from this area, the end of iron mining will threaten the fortunes of local families for years to come," said Republican Matthew Vandervelden, who has been an outspoken opponent of the bill.

Incivility Case Adds This Subtitle and This Paragraph

- [Democrats/Republicans] claim [Republicans/Democrats] acted unprofessionally and uncivilly during legislative debate
- The debate leading up to the vote was divisive and often unruly. During debate on floor of the state senate on Monday, [Democratic/Republican] sponsors of the bill quickly became hostile, interrupting members of the other party and openly heckling [Democratic/Republican] opponents as they tried to present their concerns about the bill. [Democratic/Republican] Senate President Cal Schuster now faces possible disciplinary action after telling another state senator in the course of a shouting match to, "[Expletive] yourself."

Civility Case Adds This Subtitle and This Paragraph

- [Democrats/Republicans] acknowledge [Republicans/Democrats] managed legislative debate in a professional and civil way.
- The debate leading up to the vote was orderly and respectful even given strong views on both sides. During debate on floor of the state senate on Monday, [Democratic/Republican] sponsors of the bill called on legislators to keep cool heads, and debate remained polite and civil even though both Democrats and Republicans were often quite critical of their opponents' claims. [Democratic/Republican] Senate President Cal Schuster was commended by many for maintaining decorum throughout the debate leading up to the vote.

Appendix B

Logit Models

Table A7.1 **Effects of Procedures and Policy Outcomes on Support for Compromise**

	Prefers compromise as an outcome
Unfair procedures	0.351
	(0.285)
Challenging policy outcome	0.504[a]
	(0.276)
Unfair procedures × Challenging policy outcome	−0.827*
	(0.392)

Table A7.1 **Continued**

	Prefers compromise as an outcome
Constant	−0.113
	(0.195)
Marginal effects of procedural violations	
Unfair procedures, preferred outcome	0.087
	(0.071)
Unfair procedures, challenging outcome	−0.118[a]
	(0.066)
N	425

Logit estimates. Standard errors are in parentheses. Baseline condition is a control that does not mention the procedures used.

*p < 0.05.

[a]p < 0.10.

Table A7.2 **Incivility and Willingness to Compromise**

	Prefers compromise outcome
Own party policy win	−0.585*
	(0.294)
Civility	−0.201
	(0.310)
Own party win × Civil procedures	0.187
	(0.422)
Incivility	−0.785*
	(0.295)
Own party win × Uncivil procedures	1.051*
	(0.408)
Constant	0.724*
	(0.215)
Marginal effect of policy win	
Control	−0.139*
	(0.069)

Table A7.2 **Continued**

	Prefers compromise outcome
Civility frame	−0.097
	(0.073)
Incivility frame	0.115[a]
	(0.069)
N	585

Logit estimates. Standard errors are in parentheses.
*$p < 0.05$.
[a]$p < 0.10$.

8

Do People Want Members of Congress to Compromise?

Tea Party Republican Joe Walsh was elected to represent Illinois's eighth district in Congress in 2010, reclaiming a seat won by a Democrat in 2008. He entered office ready to stand up against President Obama, promising to resist compromises and concessions to fight for the concerns of his constituents. As he explained to a reporter, "I came here ready to go to war. The political powers will always try to get you to compromise your beliefs for the good of the team. The people didn't send me here to compromise" (Altman 2011). But by the fall of 2012, Representative Walsh said that his views on bipartisan cooperation had evolved. On the campaign trail in his re-election bid, he acknowledged, "There has to be (compromise). All great pieces of transformative legislation in this country have been bipartisan" (Lester 2012).[1] Walsh went on to lose his re-election bid. Did Representative Walsh disappoint his constituents when he conceded his hardline position against compromise? Or did his new commitment to compromise come too late to change the minds of voters eager to elect a representative willing to reach across the aisle?

Members of Congress are elected to represent the policy interests of their constituents, to cast votes in line with the views and interests of the folks back home in the district. This is how we have traditionally evaluated the quality of representation that members of Congress provide—by considering the match between the direction of their legislative votes and the preferences of their constituents (Miller and Stokes 1963). But if representation occurs through matching policy preferences, it limits the leeway that legislators have to consider compromise outcomes in Congress. To compromise can often mean moving away from the views of the district—to offer policy concessions in exchange for

---

[1] His opponent, Tammy Duckworth, campaigned on a platform of bipartisan cooperation in 2012, commenting, "I want to work. I want to reach across the aisle. That is what my district wants" (Lester 2012).

Compromise in an Age of Party Polarization. Jennifer Wolak, Oxford University Press (2020). © Oxford University Press.
DOI: 10.1093/oso/9780197510490.001.0001

making progress and avoiding stalemate. What do citizens really want then? Do people want their elected representatives to stand up for the interests of the district, or do they want legislators to make concessions and consider compromises for the sake of policy progress?

Given the design of Congress, compromise is usually necessary for policy progress—in forging agreements that can clear divided committees, in crafting legislation that will draw bipartisan votes, and in resolving differences in bills across chambers. But for Gutmann and Thompson (2012), legislators may betray their constituents when they consider compromise. They assert that campaigns press candidates to take strong positions on issues and lead legislators to make commitments to the electorate that make it difficult to later embrace compromises within Congress. Citizens expect legislators to deliver on their campaign promises and not sacrifice these policy goals to the demands of the opposing party.

In a 2010 interview, incoming Speaker of the House John Boehner also raised doubts about whether citizens hope to see compromises in politics.[2] "I made it clear I am not going to compromise on my principles, nor am I going to compromise the will of the American people. . . . When you say the word 'compromise,' a lot of Americans look up and go, 'Uh oh, they're gonna sell me out.' " This expectation is echoed in studies of congressional decision-making, where it is argued that representatives who support compromises risk electoral retribution in the next election (Binder 2016; Gilmour 1995; Lee 2016). If true, it implies that citizens themselves lie partly to blame for the prevalence of stalemate in Congress. If citizens deliver electoral rewards to legislators who stand firm to their convictions, then politicians will have little reason to make concessions to the other side simply for the sake of getting legislation passed.

I challenge this account and argue that people want more than just ideological correspondence from their representatives in Congress. While those with strong preferences may hold reservations about bipartisanship and compromise within Congress (Harbridge and Malhotra 2011; Harbridge, Malhotra, and Harrison 2014; Hibbing and Theiss-Morse 2002), I show that a majority of citizens say they prefer legislators who compromise to those who hold steadfast to their convictions. Because people value both their policy goals and the principle of compromise, it means that members of Congress may have greater flexibility than we thought in terms of considering legislative compromises.

In this chapter, I explore the electoral consequences of compromise for lawmakers. Even as people report support for compromises in politics, is it something they demand from lawmakers in practice? Beyond understanding the

[2] Interview on *60 Minutes*, December 12, 2010.

bounds of people's support for compromise in policy agreements, it is important to show that these preferences are consequential for the demands people place on their members of Congress. Are members of Congress who vow to compromise punished by their districts or rewarded at the polls? I focus on how people balance their desires for compromise against their goals of policy representation. To test this, I rely on experiments, varying the promises that members of Congress make to their district to see how people punish or reward lawmakers for their willingness to consider policy compromises. In the chapter that follows, I consider the electoral consequences of legislators' specific support of compromise bills that come before Congress, evaluating how impressions of compromise bills shape people's evaluations of legislators and the institution of Congress.

The Importance of Policy Representation

Elected officials are charged with the task of representing the interests of their constituents. Within this mandate, members of Congress can represent their district in a number of different ways. They can cast votes that align with the preferences of their constituents, bring programs and federal money back to the district, and help constituents navigate the federal bureaucracy. Representatives can stand up for group interests through symbolic and descriptive representation as well (Pitkin 1967; Eulau and Karp 1977). But while representation can take many forms, substantive policy representation is usually considered to be at the heart of the connection between constituents and their legislators. When we assess whether members of Congress are acting in the interests of their constituents, we focus on the correspondence of the ideological leanings of the electorate and the votes cast by representatives (e.g., Ansolabehere and Jones 2010; Erikson, Stimson, and MacKuen 2002; Miller and Stokes 1963). Members of Congress are thought to be acting in the interests of their constituents when they vote in ways that align with the stated policy preferences of the majority of the constituents in the district. Citizens are thought to be pursuing representation when they hold legislators accountable for their decisions and vote out representatives who supported policies counter to their preferences.

Just as scholars have focused their attention on substantive policy congruence in particular, citizens also prioritize policy representation among the various ways that legislators can act on the behalf of their constituents. When asked to rank order what kinds of representation they value most from their members of Congress, policy representation tops the list in terms of its importance, and often by a sizable margin (Grant and Rudolph 2004; Griffin and Flavin 2011; Krasno 1994). While people like politicians who perform casework and bring benefits back to the district, policy goals are commonly seen as most important (Lapinski et al. 2016). Fundamentally, people want their elected representatives in Congress to promote the interests of the district and vote in line with the demands of constituents. This sentiment is echoed in Grill's (2007) interviews with average Americans about their expectations of members of Congress. As one interview participant described it, a good legislator is one who will "go after the things I hold dear . . . that, if he was presented with a problem he would react to that problem similarly to what I would do for the problem. You know, just act in a fashion that would represent what my thinking is" (p. 25).

If citizens prioritize policy representation, it should deter members of Congress from being willing to consider legislative compromises. If legislators are expected to vote in line with the ideological preferences of the district, a willingness to make concessions and cede ground can result in policy choices misaligned with district preferences. By agreeing to make compromises while in office, lawmakers risk electoral punishment at the next election from voters who fear the incumbent is not focused on the concerns of the district. If constituents expect their representatives to head to Washington and stand up for the interests of the district, then elected officials may not be keen to stray from their campaign promises and strike compromises (Gutmann and Thompson 2012). When representatives choose to break the pledges that they made to voters, they run the risk of electoral retribution (Tomz and Van Houweling 2012).

We have reason to believe that the importance of ideological congruence has only increased in a time of party polarization. Incumbency is less important to explaining congressional election outcomes than it once was, and the importance of partisanship has increased (Jacobson 2015). Given the partisan sorting of the electorate, people hold increasingly ideologically consistent issue beliefs (Levundusky 2009). Add in the partisan homogeneity of congressional districts due to gerrymandering, and we may well expect that members of Congress are facing growing constituency pressures for party-line voting.

Among strong partisans, we see that party fidelity is valued (Dancey and Sheagley 2018; Harbridge and Malhotra 2011; Harbridge, Malhotra, and Harrison 2014). Yet even as we see the rise of ideological thinking among activists in the electorate, other evidence demonstrates that voters generally do not wish for more partisan voting patterns from lawmakers. Across many studies, we see that party-line voting can hurt legislators' standing with voters (Canes-Wrone, Brady, and Cogan 2002; Carson et al. 2010; Koger and Lebo 2012, 2017; Paris 2017; Sulkin, Testa, and Usry 2015). Even as citizens value congruent policy outcomes, they hold reservations about the persistent partisanship that defines votes in Congress. As a result, this suggests citizens may be open to the possibility of compromise and bipartisan collaboration—even if it results in the dilution of partisan campaign promises.

We also know that constituents care about more than the ideological tenor of congressional voting. Even as the votes cast by members of Congress leave their imprint on how people evaluate their representative (Ansolabehere and Jones 2010), this is not the only metric by which members of Congress are evaluated (Lapinski et al. 2016; Sulkin, Testa, and Usry 2015). Congruent votes are important, but this may not always be at the center of people's desires from their member of Congress. In the words of one legislative staffer in the U.S. Senate, "most people are not very ideological. People just want to see some level of competency" (Lee 2016, p. 47).

As we learn from interviews and focus groups, people have nuanced expectations about their representatives that go beyond just the delivery of congruent policy outcomes (Doherty 2013; Hibbing and Theiss-Morse 1995, 2002; Grill 2007). While we have often focused on people's expectations of congruent outcomes as the primary criterion for how people evaluate their legislators, people imagine a wider role for their representative. When Grill (2007) asks people to explain how they think about the responsibilities of Congress, most of his interview participants accept that legislators cannot always simply vote as the district wishes, and that they can be pulled in other directions by things like what they perceive is best for the country. During the course of his interviews, Grill offers participants a scenario where a representative is torn between what he thinks is the best policy and what the people of his district prefer. When faced with this dilemma, the interview participants acknowledge the difficulty of the decision. While most believe that the preferences of the district should prevail, they appreciate that legislators and their constituents can disagree on what is the best path forward. These interviews suggest that people are capable of nuanced thinking about the tradeoffs that members of Congress face. While people want legislators to fight for the interests of the district, they accept that legislators face forces that pull them in other directions. This suggests that people are not so focused on their policy goals that they cannot appreciate the challenges of lawmaking in a system of checks and balances.

As further evidence that citizens are not in single-minded pursuit of congruent policy outcomes, we also know that people have preferences about how politics should be practiced. People have expectations about how Congress should work and how government should function. When people are asked about what they like and dislike about Congress, they discuss not just what the institution does, but also *how* it works. They question whether government runs as efficiently, honestly, and productively as it could (Hibbing and Theiss-Morse 2002). They dislike contentious politics and gridlock and react negatively to political discussions marked by incivility and conflict (Funk 2001; Hibbing and Theiss-Morse 1995, 2002; Mutz 2015; Mutz and Reeves 2005). They value democratic principles like majority rule, equal protection, minority rights, as well as the resolution of disagreements through compromise (Prothro and Grigg 1960; Sullivan, Piereson, and Marcus 1982). They expect that lawmakers should listen to the public, make policy progress, and serve the national interest (Grill 2007; Hibbing and Theiss-Morse 1995, 2002).

These expectations about how legislators should make decisions have the potential to serve as a check on the choices made by legislators. If people value not just ideologically congruent votes but also compromise and policy progress, then it carves out space for legislators to sacrifice some of their campaign promises, to pursue compromises and not face electoral retribution. I argue that many citizens prefer legislators who are willing to make compromises and that voters are willing to electorally reward politicians who are willing to pursue legislative compromises.

What Do People Want from Their Members of Congress?

To better understand people's expectations of their representatives in Congress, I first consider the preferences that people express in surveys. When asked about how members of Congress should approach the task of legislating, do people prefer legislators who stick to their convictions? In Table 8.1, I report the results from seven surveys that asked respondents about their preferences about how representatives in Congress should approach legislation. Across the different items, a majority of respondents prefer legislators who are willing to make compromises over those who stick to their convictions. When a member of Congress has strong views and the public is divided, only 32% said that members of Congress should vote their conscience, while 55% said that legislators should give in a little and compromise. In a 2013 survey, 67% said that they would rather see members of Congress collaborate and compromise more in legislating— even if it resulted in laws that the respondent did not like. When asked about their general preferences how representatives should approach their job, two-thirds of Americans say they prefer a representative who compromises to get things done over one who sticks to his or her principles. In a 2019 survey, 70% said they preferred a member of Congress who compromises to get things done. Just as people desire a president who is willing to compromise, they also prefer legislators who are open to finding policy compromises.

Do people's demands for politicians who make compromises depend on whether they share the same policy leanings as the person who represents them in Congress? If people are guided by partisan thinking, we might expect less enthusiasm for compromise among those who are represented by co-partisan

Table 8.1 Desired Traits for Members of Congress

	Prefers members of Congress who will	
	Be willing to compromise (%)	Stand firm to their principles (%)
When a U.S. Senator or Member of Congress feels strongly about a major issue and that issue is dividing the nation, what do you think they should do? Stick to their principles and vote their conscience or give in a little and try to find a compromise.[a]	55	32
Would you prefer a representative in the U.S. Congress who compromises to get things done or who sticks to his or her principles no matter what?[b]	66	33
Which of the following two statements come closest to your own opinion? I would rather members of Congress work together and compromise more, even if I do not like the resulting laws. I would rather have partisan gridlock blocking legislation in Congress than for them to pass laws I do not like.[c]	67	28
Which of the following would you prefer that leaders from your party in Congress do? Compromise with the other side to pass legislation, or stick to their principles even if that makes it more difficult to pass legislation.[d]	60	37
If you had to choose, would you rather have a member of Congress who compromises to get things done or sticks to their principles, no matter what.[e]	70	30
Which of the following roles would you like to see your elected representative play? Work in a bipartisan way and be willing to compromise with others to make progress on important problems, or stand firm with their party on issues and stick to their principles without compromise?[f]	76	20
When it comes to government, would you like your representatives in DC to stand by their principles or would you like your representatives in Washington to work with others to get things done?[g]	76	21

[a]Conducted by Fox News from March 16–17, 2010, with a sample of 900 registered voters interviewed by telephone.

[b]Evaluations of Government and Society Study (ANES EGSS-4). Conducted February 18–23, 2012, based on online interviews of a national probability sample of 1,314 respondents.

[c]Conducted by Princeton Survey Research Associates International, September 4–8, 2013 and based on 1,013 telephone interviews (landline and cell).

[d]Associated Press/GfK Knowledge Networks. October 15–19, 2015; 1,027 online interviews.

e. The Economist/YouGov Poll. Based on online interviews of 1,500 respondents conducted January 6–8, 2019.

[f]Council for Excellence in Government survey, May 5–7, 2006, based on 600 telephone interviews.

[g]2012 NORC Presidential Election Study, conducted September 24–October 18, 2012 of 2,136 respondents interviewed by telephone (landline and cell).

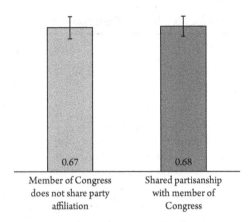

Figure 8.1 Partisan congruence and people's expectations of legislators.

lawmakers. The fourth item in Table 8.1 suggests that people are just as likely to favor legislators who compromise even when asked specifically how leaders from their own party should approach the job. Sixty percent of people say they would like to see co-partisans pursuing compromises rather than sticking to their principles, while only 37% say that co-partisan lawmakers should stick their principles. As a second test of this, I also consider the second item in Table 8.1 and distinguish the preferences of those represented by a member of Congress who shares their party affiliation and those who do not. As shown in Figure 8.1, I find that people's preferences of legislator style are independent of the partisan leanings of their representative. Those who share the same partisanship of their representative are equally likely to desire a representative open to compromise as those represented by a legislator from the opposing party.[3]

Another possibility is that people's expectations of their own member of Congress diverge from the standards they apply to others who serve in Congress. Even as they broadly call on members of Congress to be ready to make compromise, their enthusiasm may wane when asked about the approach that their own member of Congress should take. We know that people think about their own representative in Congress differently than they do the rest of the congressional membership. Most people report high trust and approval of their own representative, as seen in the high reelection rates of incumbents in Congress. But when asked about Congress as an institution or the other membership of the legislature, people are far more pessimistic (Fenno 1975; Hibbing and Theiss-Morse 1995; Mutz and Flemming 1999). Even as people perceive members of

[3] This holds true when considering both subsets of Democratic respondents and Republican respondents.

Congress as corrupt, obstructionist, or ill-intentioned, they see their own representative as serving the interests of the district. They expect their member of Congress to fight for the district, but expect Congress as a whole to tackle the policy challenges of the nation (Fenno 1975). As a result, we have reason to believe that people apply double standards—expecting that their legislator to fight for the district even as they believe that other members of Congress should concede and accept compromises.

To see if this is the case, I draw on both survey evidence and a question wording experiment. Considering first the survey data, the last two questions (see Table 8.1) asked people what traits they want to see from their own member of Congress. While we might suspect that people are less likely to demand compromise from their own representative than from other legislators in Congress, if anything, support for compromise is *higher* when people are asked to think about their own representative. Fully 76% say that they want to see their elected official compromise to make progress on important legislation, and only 20% wanted their representatives to stand loyal to the party. Likewise, in a 2012 survey, only 21% said they would rather their representatives to stay by their principles rather than collaborate with other members of Congress, while 76% said they want their representatives in Washington to work with others to get things done.

As an additional test of whether people hold different expectations of their own representative in Congress versus other members of Congress, I turn to experimental evidence. Using a question-wording experiment, I present participants with the same tradeoff between a legislator who pledges to compromise versus stand firm. Half read a version of the question that asked about members of Congress generally, while the other half were asked about what they wanted to see from their own member of Congress.[4] Participants were drawn from a national sample of 1,045 respondents recruited using Qualtrics.[5] Details of the sample are reported in Appendix A of this chapter. Results are shown in Figure 8.2.

Of those asked about what people wanted to see from members of Congress, 78% said they prefer to see legislators who are willing to compromise, and only

---

[4] The versions of the question asked, "Turning to another topic, members of Congress can approach congressional legislation in different ways. Which of the following statements comes closer to your views? [Members of Congress/My member of Congress] should be willing to compromise some of [their/his or her] positions in order to get things done. [Members of Congress/My member of Congress] should stand up for [their/his or her] principles even if it means not getting as much done."

[5] It is a sample that is more nationally representative than convenience samples of participants but less representative than an experiment placed on a nationally representative survey.

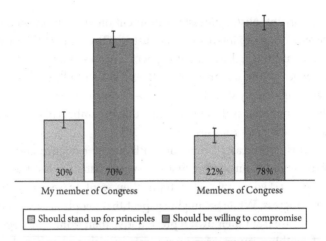

Figure 8.2 Preferences for representatives who are willing to compromise.

22% said they would rather see members of Congress stand firm to their principles. For those asked to think about their own member of Congress, 70% say that they would like to see their own legislator compromise, compared to 30% who think their own member of Congress should stand up for his or her principles. While the effect size is modest, the difference is statistically significant ($t = 2.91$, $p < 0.01$). People hold different expectations of their own representative than they do of members of Congress generally—where compromise sounds like a better plan for other members of Congress rather than one's own representative. Yet while people are more likely to expect compromise from other members of Congress, it is also important to note that most people still prefer that their own member of Congress is willing to consider compromise, by a ratio of 2 to 1. Even if people are less keen to see their own representative compromise than other legislators, a strong majority nonetheless prefers a strategy of compromise even from their own representatives.

The Consequences of a Compromising Mindset

These surveys describe people's expectations for how members of Congress should think about compromise. They show that when people are asked to choose between legislators who stick to their convictions versus those who make concessions, they prefer representatives who are willing to cede ground for the sake of compromise. Are these stated expectations consistent with the standards people use to evaluate members of Congress? We know that what people support in the abstract is not always the same as the options they choose in specific instances (McClosky 1964; Prothro and Grigg 1960). While people might signal support for the principle of compromise, does this inform their behavior in practice? To explore whether people like members of Congress who are willing to compromise in practice, I next turn to experiments. By using experiments, I can consider whether people give warmer evaluations to legislators who are keen to compromise than those who pledge to fight for their convictions. In the survey questions, participants are must choose between the two alternatives, and social desirability pressures may lead them to feel that they should choose the principled option of compromise. In an experiment, I can use random assignment to see if those who read about legislators who compromise give warmer evaluations of the representative than those who read about legislators who pledge to stand for their principles. Because people are not asked to choose between compromise and standing firm as legislative styles, these results should be less influenced by social desirability cues.

In the experiment, I present participants with a vignette about a candidate who has just been elected to Congress. In one version, the representative vows to approach his term with an openness to compromise—where he is willing to look for common ground for the sake of making policy progress. In the other version, he promises to stand up for what he believes in in Congress and not give in to the demands of the other party. I expect that people prefer legislators who compromise to those who vow to stick to their principles and that legislators receive electoral rewards rather than penalties for adopting a compromising mindset.

To better contextualize how people evaluate a legislator's approach to compromise, I also provide the partisanship of the member of Congress to the experimental participants. While people may say that they want legislators to be willing to compromise, one might expect that people's partisan goals impede the translation of their principled support of compromise into supporting candidates who make concessions in practice. If I am represented by a member of Congress who shares my party allegiances, compromise is potentially a threat. It may be much harder for people to support compromise when it means that one's own party objectives may get sacrificed. Likewise, we might also expect compromise to be of greater appeal when thinking about what a legislator from the opposing party should do. If I am represented by a legislator from the rival party, compromise offers a chance to secure policy outcomes that are better aligned with my own policy leanings. By varying the legislator's partisanship as well as his approach to compromise, I can explore the people's expectations for how co-partisan and opposing partisan lawmakers should govern.

In the control condition, the partisanship of the representative is not mentioned. In the partisan versions of the vignette, the legislator is described as either a Democrat or as a Republican. Using the party identification of the experimental participant, I then identify the politician as either in-party or a member of the opposing party.[6] I expect that the rewards for compromise will be greatest from those who read about a candidate from the opposing party and smallest from those who read about a politician from their own party. If compromise instead has more to do with policy content over perspectives about how politics should be practiced, we should see this in the use of double standards—where people call on their own party representative to stand firm while expecting all opposing party legislators to make concessions.

The experiment was conducted online with a sample of 818 participants drawn from a post-election module of the 2012 Cooperative Congressional Election Study. After reading the vignette about the member of Congress, participants were asked to rate him on a 101-point feeling thermometer scale. In a second question, respondents were asked to offer their impression of how well the legislator represented the interests of his district. In Appendix B of this chapter, I report the text of the vignettes as well as results of the regression analysis (Appendix C, Table A8.1). In Figure 8.3, I plot feeling thermometer ratings across conditions. In Figure 8.4, I plot people's assessments of how well the legislator represents the district, averaged across experimental conditions.

When the partisanship of the legislator is not mentioned, I confirm that people give higher ratings to a congressman who supports compromise than one who pledges to fight for his convictions. The average feeling thermometer score for the representative who promises to compromise is 69, which is significantly higher than the average rating of 50 offered for the representative who will fight for his principles. For members of Congress, promises to compromise offer greater dividends than pledges to stand loyal to one's principles, increasing favorability ratings by nineteen points, or about two-thirds of a standard deviation increase.

When the legislator is described as sharing the same partisanship as the member of Congress, people remain just as enthusiastic about the legislator's promises to reach across the aisle to broker compromises with the opposing side. Among those who read about a legislator who shares their same party loyalties, the average feeling thermometer rating is 67—statistically indistinguishable from how people rate the legislator when his party affiliation is not mentioned. People do not penalize co-partisan lawmakers for their willingness to compromise. When considering how people evaluate a co-partisan representative who vows to stand loyal to the interests of the party, I find that people give slightly warmer evaluations of a principled co-partisan than was seen in the

---

[6] For pure independents, I code in-partisans versus out-partisans based on their preferred candidate in the 2012 presidential election.

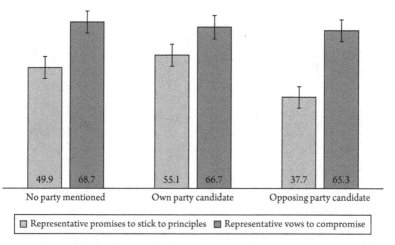

| 49.9 | 68.7 | 55.1 | 66.7 | 37.7 | 65.3 |
| No party mentioned | | Own party candidate | | Opposing party candidate | |

☐ Representative promises to stick to principles ■ Representative vows to compromise

Figure 8.3 Support for legislator who compromises, by party congruence and decision to compromise.

control condition, with an average feeling thermometer rating of 55.[7] Even so, a clear preference for compromise remains, as a co-partisan lawmaker who is keen to find compromises enjoys a twelve point advantage in favorability over a legislator who vows to stand by the party's platform. People like promises to consider compromises even when offered by co-partisans in Congress.

I observe greater partisan differences when considering how people evaluate a legislator from the opposing party. For those who read about an out-party representative who vows to fight for what he believes in, the average feeling thermometer rating is 38. This is significantly lower than the rating offered in the control condition. People are particularly critical of members of the opposing party who are resistant to the prospect of compromise. A promise to consider compromise earn a significantly more enthusiastic reaction, where an out-party representative earns an average rating of 65 on the feeling thermometer measure. In the case of a representative who does not share the same party affiliation, being open to compromise improves the lawmaker's favorability rating by 28 points, which is equivalent to a standard deviation's increase on the measure. Regardless of the partisanship of the legislator, people give warm ratings of a lawmaker who pledges to make compromises.

The same pattern emerges when people are asked to evaluate how well the member of Congress will represent the district, as shown in Figure 8.4. Absent knowledge of the party loyalties of the legislator, people are more likely to say that a member of Congress who is keen to compromise will do a good job representing

---

[7] The difference in ratings of a principled lawmaker between the control condition and the co-partisan condition is not statistically significant ($p < 0.11$).

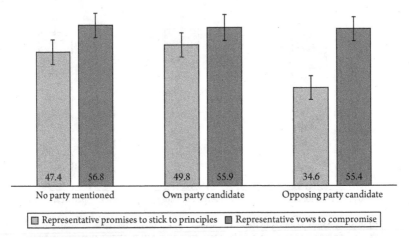

| 47.4 | 56.8 | 49.8 | 55.9 | 34.6 | 55.4 |

No party mentioned   Own party candidate   Opposing party candidate

☐ Representative promises to stick to principles ■ Representative vows to compromise

Figure 8.4 Assessments of quality of legislator representation, by party congruence and decision to compromise.

his district. Among those reading about a member of Congress of their own party, people offer favorable ratings of the representative regardless of his approach to legislation, and the difference between evaluations of two legislative styles is not statistically significant. An in-party representative represents the district equally well whether he pursues compromises or fights for his convictions. However, when the representative is of the other party, people are much more likely to see the compromising legislator as representing the interests of his constituents relative to the one who sticks to his convictions. Particularly when the representative is from the opposing party, people are nervous that the legislator will not effectively represent the district when he vows to stand firm on the issues. But if that legislator is open to compromise, then people feel significantly better about his ability to represent constituents—even though he is a member of the opposing party. A legislator who is willing to compromise is considered equally effective at representing the will of the district whether he is a co-partisan or a member of the opposition.

Together, this evidence suggests that members of Congress have strong incentives to consider compromise in Congress. Gutmann and Thompson (2012) argue that voters dislike legislators who adopt a compromising mindset and prefer those who promise to deliver the legislation they promised during the campaign. I fail to confirm this here. People do not punish a legislator who enters his term promising to compromise with the other side. Even when that representative is fighting for the same partisan interests as the respondent holds dear, people still support a strategy of compromise. Moreover, a willingness to compromise is a way for legislators to curry support among constituents who do not share the same partisanship. Out-party candidates can make significant improvements in their feeling thermometer ratings by being open to legislative compromises. From surveys described in Chapter 4 of this volume, we know that people see value in politicians who stick to their positions as well as elected officials who are willing to make compromises. When asked to choose between those approaches, more people favor politicians who are willing to compromise on policy issues. This experiment provides additional evidence in support of this finding, as people give warmer ratings of politicians who vow to collaborate than those who promise to stick to their convictions.

Compromise and Electoral Retribution

During the course of campaigns, candidates take positions on the issues and make promises to voters. Having won the election, the task of governing begins. Compromises seem necessary to shepherd bills through the legislative process—but those compromises have the potential to contradict the promises that members of Congress have made to their constituents. If citizens strongly value those promised policies, legislators face potential electoral retribution. The last experiment highlights that Americans favor members of Congress who promise to support compromises over legislators who dig in their heels to fight for their causes. Yet even if citizens give warm evaluations to legislators who vow to make the compromises necessary to get the job done, the concessions of compromise may still be used against incumbent candidates in the next election. In the words of one lawmaker, "compromise is seen as weakness by many of your constituents, and by all of your potential opponents in the next primary" (Hoagland 2005). Even if voters support the promise of compromise, they might be more critical of the approach when it is framed in negative terms by opponents in the next election.

I next consider whether the negative framing of a legislator's willingness to compromise by his or her election opponent undermines people's enthusiasm for legislators with a compromising mindset. I focus on the case of primary elections. It is here that the penalties for compromise will likely be the greatest, as lawmakers who consider policy compromises may be perceived as disloyal to the ideological tenets of the party. The electorate in primary elections manifest greater ideological constraint and more polarized policy preferences (Fiorina, Abrams, and Pope 2010; Levendusky 2009), such that ideologically distinctive candidates are advantaged over moderate candidates in primary elections (Brady, Han, and Pope 2007). For a candidate hoping to unseat the incumbent, a track record of policy concessions and legislative compromises provides an opportunity to undermine the incumbent's hopes for re-election. While a pledge to compromise might sound keen to voters at the beginning of a legislative term, what if those compromises are framed in a negative light at the next election?

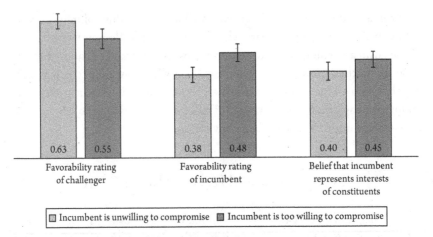

Figure 8.5 Negative framing of compromise and incumbent evaluations.

To explore this, I conducted an experiment in the fall of 2013 with a convenience sample of 227 adults recruited online recruited via the Amazon Mechanical Turk.[8] Participants in the experiment read one of two news stories about a candidate announcing his plans to challenge the incumbent in the primary election. In both experimental vignettes, the challenger candidate says that he is entering the race due to the incumbent's legislative track record. In one version, the challenger claims that the incumbent has shown himself to be too willing to sacrifice his principles and policy priorities to make concessions to the other side. In the other version, the challenger argues that the incumbent is too stubborn to work with the other side and too reluctant to strike compromises. After reading the vignette, I ask people to provide their reactions to both the challenger candidate and the incumbent representative, using seven-point scales of likeability. I also asked respondents to offer their impressions of how well the incumbent represents the interests of constituents in the district on a 101 point scale.[9] Results are presented in Figure 8.5.

I find that the challenger wins greater support when he criticizes the incumbent as being unwilling to compromise than when critiquing the incumbent for not sticking to his convictions ($t = 2.85$, $p < 0.01$). Likewise, respondents are

---

[8] Details of the sample are included in the Appendix A, as well as the full text of the experimental vignettes (Appendix B).

[9] Respondents were asked, "How much do you like the challenger Sam Neville as a candidate for Congress?" and "How much do you like the incumbent John Rooney as a candidate for Congress?" with a seven-point response scale ranging from *dislike very much* to *like very much*. It is rescaled to the range zero to 1. Respondents were also given a feeling thermometer scale for the question, "How well do you feel that the incumbent, Representative Rooney represents the interests of the constituents in this district?" with endpoints labeled *not at all* and *very well*.

less fond of the incumbent when he has been criticized for being too resistant to compromise than when he has been challenged as being too willing to compromise ($t = 3.71, p < 0.01$). This means that a challenger candidate has more to gain for critiquing an incumbent for sticking to his convictions than from arguing that he has been too willing to cede ground on policy issues.

Another way to consider these results is to evaluate how people evaluate the incumbent relative to the challenger in each election frame. In the vignette where the incumbent has been described as resistant to compromise, the challenger earns a likeability rating of 0.63, which is significantly higher than the rating of 0.38 that is earned by the incumbent ($t = 8.36, p < 0.01$). An incumbent who is attacked for his resistance to compromise polls lower than the challenger in the primary race. Turning to the vignette where the incumbent is criticized for his tendency to be willing to cede ground, the challenger's average likeability score (0.55) is not significantly distinguishable from people's rating of the incumbent (0.48; $t = 1.79, p < 0.08$). For a primary challenger contemplating attack ads, calling out an incumbent's resistance to compromise offers greater dividends than criticizing the incumbent's willingness to consider compromises.[10]

People also see the incumbent who compromises as better representing the concerns of the district than the incumbent who stands by his principles, although the difference is only near significant at conventional levels ($t = 1.92, p < 0.06$). While we might worry that a track record of legislative compromise might undermine an incumbent's chances for re-election, I fail to find evidence that people punish members of Congress for a record of compromise and conceding policy ground to the other party. Even when a willingness to compromise is framed negatively as a flaw of a representative, people do not seem keen to punish an incumbent for being willing to compromise.

Compromise and District Preferences

I have shown that people like legislators who are willing to compromise and confirm that politicians' pledges to cooperate with the other side gain higher voter support from citizens than politicians who vow to fight for their convictions. All of this suggests that citizens value more than just policy representation from their legislators. They also care about processes and procedures. How a member of Congress chooses to approach legislation affects how he or she is evaluated by citizens. As a final test of the degree to which people value compromise,

---

[10] In exploring heterogeneous treatment effects, I find no evidence that strong ideologues are any different than moderates in their evaluations of the candidates across treatments.

I consider how people's desires for policy representation intersect with goals of policy compromise.

For some of the bills that come before Congress, it may be easy for representatives to sign on to compromise, as the legislation may nicely align with the will of the district. In other cases, compromise is more challenging—as members of Congress are asked to support a compromise bill that is not necessarily well aligned with the policy preferences of those who live in the district. When these conflicts arise, are people willing to accept a legislator who votes in support of the compromise? Given the importance of policy representation in people's expectations of how legislators should vote on bills (Griffin and Flavin 2011; Grill 2007), I expect that people generally prefer that their representatives vote in ways that follow from the preferences of the district. Yet I expect that people will be more willing to accept a legislator's decision to stray from the will of district when that vote is cast in support a legislative compromise.

I test this with a question wording experiment placed on a module of the 2014 Cooperative Congressional Election Study. A nationally representative sample of 1477 participants read one of four question wordings. The basic form of the question presented a tradeoff between the competing goals of a member of Congress and his constituency. In the first wording, people were asked, "If a member of Congress thinks a bill is in the best interest of the country, but a majority of the people he or she represents are against it, how should the member of Congress vote?" The second wording flipped the preferences of each, such that the legislator opposed the bill despite the support of his constituents. The other two versions of the question mirrored these, but described the legislation as a "compromise bill" rather than just a bill. Respondents reported whether the representative should vote in support of the bill or against the bill.

Results are shown in Figure 8.6. I find that most people think that the preferences of the district should prevail in shaping the vote of the legislator. When the district supports the bill, 65% say that the member of Congress should vote in support of the bill. But when the bill is additionally described as a compromise, people are even more likely to ask the member of Congress to set aside his own preferences and vote in support of the legislation, with 74% preferring the member vote in favor of the bill ($t = 2.68$, $p < 0.01$). Likewise, when the district opposes the bill, 71% say that he should vote against the bill. However, when that bill is described as a compromise, people are significantly more likely to say that the legislator should vote against the district and in support of the compromise bill ($t = 2.40$, $p < 0.02$).

Most people report that members of Congress should vote in ways that are congruent with the demands of constituents. However, people are less likely to demand that legislators follow the desires of the district when the bill in question is described as a legislative compromise. In the case of compromise

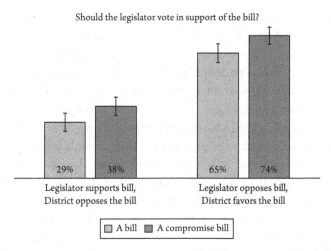

Should the legislator vote in support of the bill?

29%	38%		65%	74%
Legislator supports bill, District opposes the bill			Legislator opposes bill, District favors the bill	

☐ A bill   ■ A compromise bill

Figure 8.6 District preferences, compromises, and legislator support of the bill.

legislation, people are more willing to say that legislators can stray from the mandate of constituents to pursue collaboration with the rival party in Congress. Even though people value policy representation, they are less likely to demand it when members of Congress are considering compromise legislation. For members of Congress debating about the potential electoral costs of signing on to a compromise that might not perfectly match the demands of the district, the penalties of this choice will likely be reduced if voters understand the vote came in support of a compromise agreement.

Conclusions

In elections, the goal for campaign strategists and politicians is persuasion. Elites hope to change opinions, moving voters from uncertainty to certainty, from ambivalent to resolved, and from supporting opponents to endorsing the challenger. But when the campaign ends, elected officials take up the task of policymaking. Here, politicians cannot simply persuade—they must also negotiate and compromise, to work with others to achieve policy ends. Many have thought that voters accustomed to the partisan debates and conflict common to campaign seasons would be unlikely to abandon their partisan camps to endorse collaboration once these campaign debates move to the setting of Congress. But in these experiments, I find that voters are willing to endorse compromise and collaboration and hold legislators who consider compromise in high regard. While there are other pressures via parties, interest groups, and the media that likely make a compromising mindset challenging in Congress, these results suggest that most voters will be quite happy to see representatives move outside their partisan camps and consider middle ground outcomes.

Representatives follow the party line in Congress in part out of a desire to win elections, given an expectation that the legislative successes of the party will cultivate constituent support at the next election (Koger and Lebo 2017). These findings, however, highlight the electoral virtues of support for compromise over party fidelity. In a time where compromise in Congress seems uncommon, politicians should consider the potential electoral rewards for being bipartisan and open to compromise. While citizens no doubt like representatives who share their interests, they also care about how legislators approach the job and are willing to reward politicians who can make concessions for the sake of policy progress. There are incentives for legislators to consider something other than steadfast partisan position taking. Legislators who vote in strictly partisan ways face electoral costs (Carson et al. 2010; Koger and Lebo 2017). The institution of Congress loses support as well when levels of partisan conflict are high (Harbridge and Malhotra 2011; Ramirez 2009). Even as some segments of the electorate become more partisan and ideologically constrained, there are still electoral risks to legislators who engage in too much partisan bickering.

Understanding why people are willing to compromise tells us how political differences can be bridged. Given recent trends toward greater party polarization among both political elites and the electorate, it is important to know how people decide they are willing to look for common ground. Democracy can tolerate disagreement on core principles and values so long as people are willing to follow the rules of the game and are open to political compromise (Prothro and Grigg 1960). If citizens are unwilling to tolerate compromise from their legislators, then party polarization and stalemate in Congress seem inevitable.

A central part of representation for a member of Congress is in explaining what she stands for and how she has served the district during his time in office (Fenno 1978; Grill 2007). How members of Congress explain their votes to the district is important for how citizens evaluate their representatives (Fenno 1978; Grimmer 2013; Grose, Malhotra, and Van Houweling 2015). In shaping this narrative, are members of Congress better served by highlighting how they steadfastly pushed back against the pursuits of their opponents, or by emphasizing the ways in which they pursued compromises and sacrificed some objectives for the sake of policy progress? The evidence here suggests that members of Congress receive electoral rewards for a compromising mindset. This challenges some conventional wisdom about the importance of compromise to voters. In the words of one member of Congress, "compromise has a very small constituency. Very small" (Helderman and Fahrenthold 2012). These results suggest that compromise has a much larger constituency that we may have imagined.

These findings suggest that members of Congress may reap constituency rewards for highlighting their willingness to pursue legislative compromises. Members of Congress may choose to downplay their support for legislative compromises in their reelection bids, out of fears of voter retribution. Yet voters are not single-minded in their desires for policy representation. They can also be sold on the promise of legislative compromise. Setting aside questions of what those compromises were and what they represent, I establish here that there is value to invoking the language of compromise. For legislators debating about whether they should make concessions to the other side, this evidence shows that there are ways to successfully frame those compromises so as to minimize potential repercussions in the next election.

Appendix A
Description of the Experimental Participants

Experiment 1: Own Representative versus Members of Congress

The experiment included 1,050 participants recruited as a national sample of adults in the fall of 2013. Participants completed the experiment as part of a larger questionnaire administered and completed over the internet. The sample was recruited through Qualtrics using their online panel. From their pool of around two million volunteers (recruited from Web ads and permission-based e-mail lists), Qualtrics sent my questionnaire to a sample of 2091 respondents that was representative of the U.S. population in terms of age, race, and gender based on Census data. The response rate was 50% of those who received invitations to participate. The sample is 65% female and 19% nonwhite. In terms of partisanship, 36% identifies as Democratic, 23% as Republican, and 41% as independent or other. Ages range from 18 to 86 with an average age of 48 years.

Experiment 2: Partisan Congruence

The experiment was included in a module of the 2012 Cooperative Congressional Election Study. The experiment was included in the postelection wave, where 823 people participated.

Experiment 3: Negative Framing of Compromise

The experiment included 227 participants recruited through the Amazon Mechanical Turk in September 2013. In the sample, 31% were nonwhite and 32% were female. In terms of education, 48% had a high school degree or less, 8% completed some college, 35% were college educated, and 8% had advanced degrees. In terms of partisanship, 48% identify as Democrats, 11% identify as Republicans, and 41% identify as independents or with another party. The ages of participants range from 18 to 81, with an average age of 30 and a median age of 27.

Experiment 4: Compromise and District Preferences

The experiment was included in a module of the 2014 Cooperative Congressional Election Study. The experiment was included in the pre-election wave of the survey with a nationally-representative sample of 1,477 participants.

Appendix B
Wording of the Experimental Vignettes

Question Wording in Experiment 1

Turning to another topic, members of Congress can approach congressional legislation in different ways. Which of the following statements comes closer to your views? [Members of Congress/ My member of Congress] should be willing to compromise some of [their/his or her] positions in order to get things done. [Members of Congress/ My member of Congress] should stand up for [their/his or her] principles even if it means not getting as much done."

Wording of Vignette in Experiment 2
Legislator Is Willing to Compromise

After winning the race to represent the constituents of the state's 11th congressional district, [Democrat/Republican] Sam Archer used his election night speech to call on politicians in Washington to commit to compromise in the next session of Congress. "In politics, we need to work together with those with opposing viewpoints to find common ground," said Archer. He vowed that during his time in office, he will be willing to make the kinds of compromises necessary to get the job done in Congress.

Legislator Opposes Compromise

After winning the race to represent the constituents of the state's 11th congressional district, [Democrat/Republican] Sam Archer used his election night speech to call on politicians in Washington to stand up for their principles in the next session of Congress. "In politics, people want you to stand for something, not give in to the demands of the opposing side." said Archer. He vowed that during his time in office, he will stand firm for what he believes, even if it means that less gets done in Congress.

Wording of Vignettes in Experiment 3
Incumbent Is Too Willing to Compromise

Today, Sam Neville announced his candidacy for the state's 4th congressional district, where he will face incumbent Representative John Rooney in the next primary election. In his announcement, Neville said that he decided to enter the race because of Representative Rooney's votes over the last congressional session. According to Neville, "John Rooney has proven to be too willing to compromise on the issues important to this country. Rather than sticking to his convictions, he has ceded ground to the other side and sacrificed his policy priorities simply for the expediency of getting bills passed in Congress. The people of this district deserve a representative who will stand up for his principles and not give in to the other side."

Incumbent Is Unwilling to Compromise

Today, Sam Neville announced his candidacy for the state's 4th congressional district, where he will face incumbent Representative John Rooney in the next primary election. In his announcement, Neville said that he decided to enter the race because of Representative Rooney's votes over the last congressional session. According to Neville, "John Rooney has proven to be too unwilling to work with the other side on the issues important to this country. Rather than collaborating with opponents to pass legislation, he has refused to budge from his commitments or make any concessions to the other side. The people of this district deserve a representative who is willing to make the kinds of compromises necessary to get the job done in Congress."

Question Wording in Experiment 4

Version 1

If a member of Congress thinks a bill is in the best interest of the country, but a majority of the people he or she represents are against it, how should the member of Congress vote?

Version 2

If a member of Congress thinks a bill is not in the best interest of the country, but a majority of the people he or she represents are in favor of it, how should the member of Congress vote?

Version 3

If a member of Congress thinks a compromise bill is in the best interest of the country, but a majority of the people he or she represents are against the compromise, how should the member of Congress vote?

Version 4

If a member of Congress thinks a compromise bill is not in the best interest of the country, but a majority of the people he or she represents are in favor of the compromise, how should the member of Congress vote?

Response Options

Vote for the bill.
Vote against the bill.

Appendix C

Regression Results

Table A8.1 **Effects of Promises to Compromise on Legislator Support**

	Feeling thermometer rating of legislator	How well legislator represents the district
Legislator supports compromise	18.809*	9.447*
	(3.289)	(3.125)
Own-party legislator	5.195	2.459
	(3.270)	(3.107)
Legislator supports compromise × Own-party legislator	−7.244	−3.340
	(4.715)	(4.476)
Opposing-party legislator	−12.206*	−12.739*
	(3.240)	(3.090)
Legislator supports compromise × Opposing-party legislator	8.780[a]	11.355*
	(4.599)	(4.365)
Marginal effects of compromise manipulation		
Marginal effect for compromise, own-party legislator	11.565*	6.107[a]
	(3.379)	(3.205)
Marginal effect for compromise, opposing-party legislator	27.589*	20.802*
	(3.214)	(3.048)
Constant	49.937*	47.381*
	(2.321)	(2.218)
R^2	0.15	0.09
N	759	764

Regression estimates, standard errors in parentheses.
*$p < 0.05$.
[a]$p < 0.10$.

9

Support for Compromise in Principle and in Practice

When asked how their member of Congress should serve the district, most people say they want their representatives to be willing to make compromises. Yet even as people say that they like compromise as a way to resolve political disagreements, are they truly willing to accept their legislators' support of the specific compromises that come before Congress? Some suspect that voters are less likely to call on their legislators to compromise once they realize the concessions, trade-offs, sacrifices, and negotiations that policy compromises require. In the words of one editorial, "People want Congress to compromise. Except that they really don't. . . . Everyone likes the *idea* of compromise. . . . But, our desire for compromise goes out the window when it's an issue that matters to us" (Cillizza and Sullivan 2013).

Compromises represent the pursuit of what is feasible and better over the insistence on what is optimal and best. By their nature, compromises will feel less rewarding than a win. When we achieve our policy goals in politics, we can feel certain that we have accomplished what we set out to. But compromises can leave us uncertain about whether too much was sacrificed or not enough was gained. When the terms of a compromise are made explicit, partisans may be disappointed about not securing greater advances for the party and resent the policy gains made by their rivals. If people like compromises less once they understand what policy concessions those compromises require, then members of Congress may come to believe that the potential electoral risks of compromise outweigh the pragmatic rewards of legislative progress.

In this chapter, I consider the consequences of policy compromises for how people evaluate their representatives as well as the institution of Congress. Using a set of experiments based on legislative compromises that emerged from Congress, I explore how feelings about compromise bills shape people's evaluations of lawmakers and the institution. I consider how people evaluate Congress after learning about its success or failure to reach compromise, as well

Compromise in an Age of Party Polarization. Jennifer Wolak, Oxford University Press (2020). © Oxford University Press.
DOI: 10.1093/oso/9780197510490.001.0001

as people's ratings of their representatives after learning of their support or opposition to a legislative compromise. I also consider whether people evaluate laws differently when they are reminded of the concessions that compromises require, as well as people's perceptions of the legitimacy of political outcomes founded on compromise.

Explaining People's Support for Specific Compromises

To assess how people evaluate policy compromises in practice, I rely on a set of experiments. With surveys, we can ask people about how much they like a piece of compromise legislation, but it is difficult to know whether those reactions are driven primarily by the policy content of the legislation or by its character as a product of legislative compromise. Among those giving negative evaluations, are they disappointed with the ideological content of the policy, or do they dislike seeing party goals compromised through concessions to the other side? By using experiments, I can isolate people's reactions to the process of compromise. By holding the policy content constant and varying only the characterization of the process that generated the outcome, I can assess the specific effects of the policy process, apart from the provisions within any piece of legislation.[1] I then consider whether people are wary of agreements described as compromises and whether reminders of the concessions made by their own party serve to undermine people's favorability toward policy outcomes.

In my experiments, I focus on policy debates where Democrats and Republicans in Congress were able to successfully forge compromise legislation. To ensure that these policies represent compromise agreements, I focus on bills that not only drew bipartisan support in Congress, but specifically those cases where journalists and political elites described the policy using the language of compromise. Because calling a piece of legislation a compromise remains a bit subjective, I checked both news coverage of the bills and the floor speeches, interviews, and press releases of members of Congress to confirm that many viewed the legislation as an example of compromise. By considering several

---

[1] I do not manipulate the content of the policy to better isolate any distinctive effects associated with people's perceptions of compromises. Manipulating both policy and process could risk the validity of the compromise manipulation. To take an ideologically extreme policy and label it as a compromise would be to present a policy that might not be credibly perceived as a compromise. To see if policy congruence conditions the effects of compromise frames, I instead check for heterogeneous treatment effects among supporters and opponents of the presented legislation.

policy issues, I can also mitigate concerns that the observed effects are unique to any particular policy domain.

By focusing on recent policy debates in Congress, I select cases where compromise is feasible in a time of polarized politics. In politics, there is a sense that some domains are off limits to compromise—where principles are so important that no concessions would be tolerable. In other cases, the parties just seem too far apart to find agreement. If the two sides of a disagreement truly have nothing in common, then it is hard to find a foundation on which to build a compromise. By focusing on recent policy conflicts, I focus on a subset of policy domains where compromise is possible in politics. There is pessimism at times about whether there are places where compromise is possible, but even as congressional productivity has waned, bills still get passed under divided government in a polarized Congress. I focus on these cases as illustrations of the kinds of compromises that are possible in a time of party polarization.

If I instead asked people to evaluate constructed vignettes about hypothetical compromises, the proposed compromise might not be realistic or viable in politics, and readers might disagree about whether the concessions made by each side truly represent the features of legislative compromise. By selecting cases of recent compromises in Congress, it ensures that the policy outcomes are truly representative of the subset of possible compromises that would be mutually agreeable to Democrats and Republicans in Washington. Focusing on contemporary policy debates also contributes to the realism and external validity of the experiments. Rather than asking people to consider hypothetical legislation or possible future bills, I draw on the details of specific policy examples that inform how people see Congress and their elected representatives. How people evaluate these compromises in the experiments should be representative of how they evaluate these pieces of legislation in practice.

I focus on three issues: the reauthorization of the Violence Against Women Act, the education reforms in the Every Student Succeed Acts, and the Medicare reforms passed in the Medicare Access and Children's Health Insurance Program (CHIP) Reauthorization Act. The policy content within each is distinctive, as were the fault lines of party disagreements. Yet the three pieces of legislation share several commonalities. All three represent significant pieces of legislation that are important to many in the electorate. All three were passed in periods of divided government, and all three were discussed as examples of legislative compromise in both press accounts and the comments of members of Congress.

I consider first people's support for the policy outcome itself, to see if people like legislation less when they are told that the bill represents a compromise between their party and the rival party. If people like compromises only in principle and not in practice, then policy compromises may not win as warm of evaluations as legislation that does not highlight the concessions that compromise agreements require. Partisan heuristics are a guiding force for how people form their evaluations in politics, where people make inferences about what policies they support and what candidates they prefer based on the party cues they are given (Bartels 2002; Conover and Feldman 1989; Nicholson 2012). If people's evaluations of the outcome are guided by their partisan biases, then agreements brokered in cooperation with rivals in the opposing party are open to suspicion.

Second, I consider the effects of passing compromise legislation for how people evaluate Congress as an institution. People's preferences about how they want to see political disagreements settled are consequential, as the public's approval of Congress rests not just what Congress does, but also how it works (Hibbing and Theiss-Morse 2002). When asked about why they disapprove of Congress, the complaints people offer about Congress are tied to how the institution works and how much legislators accomplish, rather than necessarily the bills it considers or the direction of policy outcomes. When levels of legislative productivity are low and levels of partisan discord are high, Congress faces greater public disapproval (Durr, Gilmour, and Wolbrecht 1997; Ramirez 2009).

People like Congress the most when it is productive, efficient, civil, and performing without partisan acrimony (Funk 2001; Hibbing and Theiss-Morse 2002; Ramirez 2009). When members of Congress engage in contentious debates, many perceive that legislators are not doing their jobs well. Rather than acting on the issues that the country cares about, they are caught up in partisan squabbling. As a result, Hibbing and Theiss-Morse (2002) propose that Americans see compromises are an undesirable manifestation of Congress's deliberative process. In their account, Congress is, "the institution that the people believe most publicly displays the processes most reprehensible to them: bickering, compromise, inefficiency, selling out to special interests" (p. 82). If this is the case, then it may be that compromises hurt people's evaluations of the institution of Congress. However, if people instead think about compromise in terms of its normative virtues rather than its political costs, political compromises will not be damaging to institutional approval, and may instead enhance it.

Third, I consider how casting votes for and against policy compromises affects people's rating of their member of Congress. Even though citizens are not always well-informed by the votes cast by their members of Congress, studies affirm that how legislators vote on specific bills informs how they are evaluated by the electorate (Bovitz and Carson 2006; Canes-Wrone, Minozzi, and Revely 2011; Nyhan et al. 2012). Our typical expectation is that people evaluate their representatives in term of their ideological congruence, preferring legislators who successfully represent constituents' views in their votes (e.g., Ansolabehere and Jones 2010; Fenno 1978, Miller and Stokes 1963). If voters value ideological congruence the most, then it may matter little whether the legislation is described as a product of compromise. Constituents will simply reward legislators who vote in line with their preferences and punish representatives who case incongruent votes.

Yet there are reasons to believe that people care not just about the ends but also the means when thinking about how their members of Congress vote. As I demonstrated in the last chapter, members who made vows to compromise in Congress secured warmer evaluations than those members who promised to stick to their convictions. Does this pattern hold when we consider people's reactions to the specific votes cast by members of Congress? Prior studies suggest that people evaluate the votes cast by their members of Congress not just in terms of their content, but also in terms of how they are explained to constituents (Grose, Malhotra, and Van Houweling 2015; McGraw 1991; McGraw, Best, and Timpone 1995). The negative side effects of incongruent votes may well be mitigated by information about the process behind that vote. While I expect that people value ideological congruence the most when considering the votes of their representatives, the process could be important to contextualizing or interpreting those cases where members of Congress cast incongruent votes.

Finally, I consider how the passage of compromise legislation influences people's perceptions of the legitimacy of the policy outcome. Apart from how much people like a political outcome or how they evaluate those who supported that outcome, they also hold beliefs about the degree to which that outcome represents a fair and legitimate outcome. People's perceptions of the legitimacy of political outcomes are important for the political health of a democracy. We do not always get all of what we want in politics—our candidate loses the election or our side fails to secure enough votes to pass the bill we prefer. When confronted with disliked outcomes, Americans usually accept what they do not prefer, so long as they believe that outcome is the product of a fair, legitimate processes. When people believe that the institutions followed the rules and played fair, citizens are more accepting of disliked political outcomes (Gibson 1989; Gibson, Caldeira, and Spence 2005).

People's views of the legitimacy of a political process often have more to do with their perceptions of how decisions were made rather than the outcome that was received (Hurwitz and Peffley 2005; Tyler 1990; Tyler and Huo 2002). Legitimate processes are characterized by their unbiased nature, where no side had undue influence. Voice and influence are also important, where each side had the chance to express their concerns and be heard in the process (Leventhal 1980; Tyler 2001). To that end, the process of forging political compromises should encourage people to view government decisions as legitimate. When both sides agree to a compromise, it suggests that both Republicans and Democrats had voice in the decision and that the agreement respected the concerns of both sides. As such, I expect that people will perceive congressional policies as more legitimate when they are described as the product of compromise.

Compromise to Pass Domestic Violence Legislation

In March 2013, President Barack Obama signed the Violence Against Women Reauthorization Act into law. The legislation was designed to provide law enforcement and community organizations with more tools to combat crimes of domestic violence and sexual assault. Passed in 1994, the law expired in 2011 and was up for reauthorization in Congress in 2012. As the legislation came up for reconsideration and reauthorization, its legacy was as a generally popular bill that had received little public opposition in the years since its original passage. However, progress on reauthorization stalled in 2012, with the parties unable to find workable compromises on the specific details of the deal.

The debate was revived in 2013 with optimism that a workable compromise could be found. The Senate moved first. Their version of the bill was described as a compromise in at least some press accounts, as Democrats had responded to Republican concerns by removing language about visas for some undocumented victims of domestic violence (Kasperowicz 2013; Serwer 2013). The bill's sponsors also used the language of compromise in press releases on the bill. One of the legislation's authors, Republican Senator Mike Crapo, pledged, "I look forward to working with Senator Leahy and my colleagues on compromise language that can garner the necessary support in both the Senate and House to pass this critical legislation." Similar sentiments were echoed among Republican supporters in the House. A group of nineteen Republicans signed a letter to chamber leadership calling on them to move on the bill, arguing, "Now is the time to seek bipartisan compromise on the reauthorization of these programs."

In February, the Democratic-controlled Senate passed the bill with bipartisan support and a vote of 78–22. In the Republican-controlled House of Representatives, the legislation had a rockier path, as Republican Party leadership remained wary of the Senate's version of the bill. They attempted to push for an alternative version that weakened some of the protections offered in the Senate's version, but the version failed to garner enough votes to pass. A version of the bill closer to the Senate's language was then put to a vote and passed with bipartisan support in the Republican-controlled House of Representatives by a vote of 286–138.

This policy is a useful case to consider how people evaluate policy compromises. First, it is an example of the potential for bipartisan agreement even in times of divided government and polarized parties. The Republican-controlled House and Democratic-controlled Senate were able to pass significant legislation by working together. The reauthorization also represents a significant piece of legislation, making Mayhew's (2015) list of the most important enactments of Congress in 2013. The legislation also represents policy progress in a domain that is salient to constituents. Compared to technical matters such as banking regulations or agricultural price supports, this legislation takes on issues that many Americans care about. In the wake of the 2012 campaign season and its rhetoric around the "war on women," many in Congress saw this vote as one that was very important to constituents back in the district.

To what extent are people's evaluations of the outcome shaped by the process used to pass the bill? I consider whether people feel differently about the legislation when it is described as the product of the parties working together on a compromise. I also consider how the rewards for compromise compare to the penalties for failing to compromise, leveraging the legislation's history as a bill that failed to pass the House before a similar version was ultimately passed.

Within the experiment, I present participants with a short description of the provisions of the bill. I hold the substantive details of the policy constant and vary how I describe the legislative process as well as the outcome of the House's vote. In the policy outcome manipulation, half of the participants were told the legislation passed, while the other half were told that the bill failed to gain enough support to pass. This evokes the bill's own vote history in the House, where alternate versions of the bill failed to pass in 2012 as well as 2013 before being successfully passed later in 2013. In the policy process manipulation, I varied whether the outcome was described as a product of political compromise or not. Those in the control condition received no explanation of the process that led to the bill's outcome. In the treatment groups, participants were told that the bill's success or failure rested on the willingness of members of Congress to strike compromise. The wording reflected the outcome of the bill. Those who read about the bill's successful passage were told that the legislation represented a compromise between Democrats and Republicans, where both parties ceded ground to find a mutually acceptable bill. In the case where the legislation failed to pass, participants were told that it was the result of Democrats and Republicans digging in their heels and refusing to make concessions and consider compromises. The text of the vignettes can be found in the Appendix B of this chapter.

The experiment was administered in the fall of 2013 to a national sample of 1,050 participants recruited through Qualtrics.[2] After participants read the

---

[2] The details of the sample are included in Appendix A.

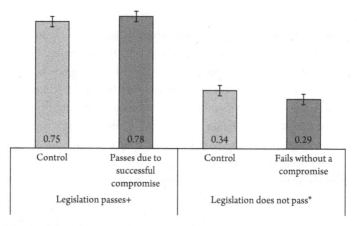

Figure 9.1 People's evaluations of outcome under successful and unsuccessful compromises.

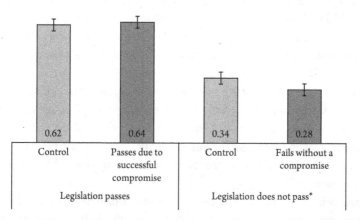

Figure 9.2 Congressional approval under successful and unsuccessful compromises.

vignette, they were asked about their satisfaction with the outcome in light of the information they had just read, on a five-point scale from *very unsatisfied* to *very satisfied*. I also asked participants whether they approve or disapprove of how the House of Representatives handles its job in light of what they just read, on a feeling thermometer rating scale ranging from *strongly disapprove* to *strongly approve*. I rescale both measures to range from zero to 1, and report average levels of satisfaction with the outcome in Figure 9.1 and congressional approval in Figure 9.2.

I consider first the case where the legislation is described as successfully passing the House of Representatives. Do people feel more satisfied with the policy outcome when it is described as the product of partisan compromise? I find that those who read about a compromise are slightly more satisfied with the outcome (0.78) than those were not told that the legislation was the product of compromise (0.75), although the difference is substantively small and only approaches statistical significance ($t = 1.64, p < 0.10$). This small boost in public approval does not carry over to people's evaluations of Congress however. I find that approval of the House of Representatives is the same whether the bill's successful passage was described as a product of political compromise or not ($t = 0.68, p < 0.50$).[3] While Americans report in surveys that they want to see members of Congress striking compromises, they offer no specific rewards to Congress when it delivers compromise legislation. It may be that compromise is valued more in principle than it is in practice. It may also be that people simply expect compromise from members of Congress as part of the nature of the job, such that when compromises are struck, Congress is simply meeting, and not exceeding, the public's expectations.

I next consider the case where the Violence Against Women Reauthorization Act fails to win support in the House of Representatives. I find that people are far less satisfied with the policy outcome when the bill fails to pass and that feelings of disappointment increase when this is attributed to Congress's failure to reach a compromise. In the case of the control condition of the bill's failure to pass, the average level of satisfaction with the outcome is 0.34. This falls to 0.29 when the bill's demise is attributed to the sides refusing to compromise. This represents a statistically significant difference ($t = 2.03, p < 0.05$). People's satisfaction with congressional outcomes rests not simply on whether legislation passes or fails, but also the reasons for those successes and failures. Bills that fail due to an unwillingness of the parties to compromise result in heightened levels of public dissatisfaction.

Moreover, the same pattern emerges when considering levels of congressional approval. People are significantly more negative in their evaluations of the House of Representatives when the bill's failure to pass is attributed to a failure to compromise ($p = 2.64, p < 0.01$). When the bill fails, the average rating of Congress in the control condition is 34 on the one hundred-point scale, which falls to 28 when the bill's demise is attributed to a failure to compromise. While Congress may not receive any particular dividend for producing compromise legislation, it loses public support when its failure to pass legislation is described as due to an unwillingness of legislators to cooperate.

I also considered whether political compromises were appraised differently among those with stronger preferences, given that biased reasoning will likely be greatest among those with the strongest prior attitudes. However, I find little

---

[3] I also tested whether those who strongly cared about the issue respond any differently to the treatment and found no evidence that this was the case.

evidence that people evaluated the compromise outcomes differently as a result of the strength of their prior preferences, as shown in Table A9.1 in Appendix C of this chapter.[4] Strong partisans and independents respond similarly to the treatment, indicating that those with strong prior attitudes are not any more critical of party compromises in Congress. Likewise, when considering heterogeneous treatment effects across levels of issue importance, I find similar reactions to the compromise manipulation among those who seek more government action on the issue versus those who would be content with less government action. People view compromise outcomes similarly regardless of the intensity of their prior preferences.

Overall, I find that people's self-reported satisfaction with the policy result is most strongly shaped by the outcome of the vote, where people report greater satisfaction with the policy result in the case where the bill passes rather than when it fails to pass. Yet the process used also shapes how people assess the policy result. A bill that is the product of a successful compromise is seen a bit more warmly than one where the process was not mentioned, indicating that people like to see compromises from Congress. I also find that people are significantly unhappier about the bill's failure to pass when it is attributed to a failure to compromise, again reinforcing the finding that people's evaluations of policy outcomes reflect both the policy result and the policy process used. When it comes to people's evaluations of the institution of Congress, I find that there are no specific rewards attached to passing the bill when it is described as a compromise. However, the punishment for failing to pass the bill is significantly greater when people are told that the outcome reflected the parties' reticence to find compromise.

Compromise on Education Reforms

I next consider how people respond to a compromise on education policy, focusing on the case of the Every Student Succeeds Act. Signed into law in December 2015, the Every Student Succeeds Act was designed as a significant education reform to the No Child Left Behind Act that was enacted in 2002. It maintained standardized testing and accountability standards imposed by No

---

[4] I considered heterogeneous treatment effects for the compromise manipulation within both the bill passage and bill failure conditions to see if Democrats, strong partisans, or those with strong prior attitudes responded different to the treatment. I found no significant interaction effects. To measure people's prior attitudes, I relied on an item in the pretest questionnaire that asked participants, "Do you think the U.S. government is doing too much, too little, or about the right amount to assist women who are victims of domestic and sexual violence?" Eleven percent said the right amount, 18% said too much, and the remainder answered too little.

Child Left Behind, but shifted responsibility for these standards to the states. While both houses of Congress were under Republican leadership, the bill was supported by many Democrats in Congress, clearing the House by a vote of 359–64 and passing the Senate by a vote of 85–12. It was covered in the press as an example of a legislative compromise, one achieved under a Republican-controlled Congress and Democratic president. One of the leaders on the bill in the House, Democratic Representative Bobby Scott, lauded the legislation on the House floor as, "the embodiment of what we can do when we work together in Washington—a workable compromise that does not force either side to desert its core beliefs."

Democrats and Republicans had agreed that changes were needed to the No Child Left Behind Act, with both sides supporting more influence for the states in setting standards. Points of disagreement included the need to retain standardized testing as well as the scope of federal influence in education. In press coverage of the legislation in the *Washington Post*, it was described as, "a true compromise in that everyone got at least some of what they were hoping for, but no one is completely satisfied" (Brown 2015). Republicans won ground in dialing back national involvement in education, but had hoped to go farther. Democrats were able to add federal funding for prekindergarten education, but had hoped to retain wider national authority to intervene to help low-income and disadvantaged students. As expressed by Democratic Senator Patty Murray, one of the legislative leaders on the bill, "It's not the bill I would have written on my own. And I know this isn't the bill Republicans would have written on their own. That's the nature of compromise. But we put partisanship aside and proved that Congress can get results for the American people. And that kind of bipartisanship is what we need more of here in Congress."

This is a useful case to explore how citizens evaluate the legislation as a policy compromise. The Every Student Succeeds Act represents a major policy change, one that Mayhew (2017) includes among the most important policy enactments of 2015. Members of Congress were keen to make reforms to the policy, and it covers a policy domain of interest and importance to many in the electorate. The legislation's predecessor, the No Child Left Behind Act, was a law that many Americans knew by name—97% of respondents in a May 2013 Gallup survey said that they had heard of it. It is also legislation that many Americans wanted to see reformed. In a January 2011 Gallup poll, most Americans favored major revisions to the No Child Left Behind law.

As such, it is useful to understand how people feel about those reforms when they know that they are a product of compromise. As a policy case, it resembles the case of the Violence Against Women Reauthorization Act in that it also involves significant legislation in a domain salient to many Americans. But while the Violence Against Women Reauthorization Act could be described as largely an extension of popular existing legislation on a valence issue, the Every Student Succeeds Act covers more politically divisive terrain, representing a substantive reform of existing education policy rather than a continuation of generally popular legislation.

In this experiment, participants read a vignette that described the bill and some of its major features. The description emphasized both the left-leaning parts of the legislation—expanding government's role in provided access to prekindergarten programs and ensuring education funding for poor districts, as well as right-leaning provisions, like limiting federal influence on education and affording more discretion to states. Those in the control condition only read this summary, while those in the experimental condition read a longer version that included a passage in the middle of the vignette that explicitly described the legislation as a compromise between Democrats and Republicans. I further strengthened the manipulation by not just describing the bill as a compromise, but also emphasizing the nature of compromise by adding, "Both Democrats and Republicans made key gains, but the final law is not exactly what either side would have hoped for." By using a more contentious piece of legislation and mentioning the potential negatives of compromise, this experiment arguably represents a tougher test of whether citizens tolerate compromises in politics.

The experiment was administered to a group of 990 nationally representative Americans, as part of a module of the 2016 Cooperative Congressional Election Study. After reading either the control or experimental vignette, I asked participants to offer their evaluation of the legislation and whether they support or oppose the Every Student Succeeds Act. In Figure 9.3, I report the percentage that give supportive ratings of the bill among all respondents, by condition. Overall, the legislation was highly rated in the sample, with three-quarters of respondents reporting that they support the policy outcome. While those who read that it was a compromise were slightly less likely to support the legislation, the difference between the conditions is not statistically significant ($t = 1.36, p < 0.18$). People like the policy compromise that Democrats and Republicans were able to put together on education reform, and they are not any more critical of the legislation when reminded that the parties had to make concessions to make it possible. That said, I fail to find evidence that people give warmer evaluations of the policy when it is described as a compromise, as was suggested in the case in the Violence Against Women Reauthorization Act.[5]

Do people punish or reward their members of Congress for supporting compromises? In the experiment, I next informed the participants how their

[5] I also explored whether strong partisans or strong ideologues were less approving of the legislation when it was described as a compromise, and I find no evidence that this is the case. Republican respondents are less likely to report favorable reactions to the bill but do not react to the compromise treatment differently than Democrats do.

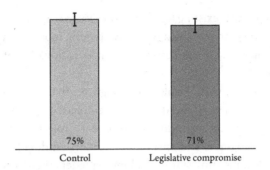

Figure 9.3 Support for the education bill.

own representative in Congress voted on the bill. Those in the control condition were told, "The representative from your district, {*name of current house representative*}, voted [in favor of/against] the bill," while those in the compromise condition read the same except the word "bill" was replaced by the word "compromise." All were then asked, "In light of this information, do you approve or disapprove of your member of Congress?" and given a feeling thermometer rating scale to register their reaction.[6] Based on the respondents' reported preferences in the prior question, I classify the representative's vote as either congruent or incongruent with the respondent's preferences.[7] Given the importance of partisanship to how people evaluate their member of Congress, it is also important to see if there are dividends or punishments for compromise that are uniquely rewarded to those legislators who share the same party affiliation as the respondent. As such, I further subdivide responses based on whether one is represented in Congress by someone who shares the partisanship or does not.[8]

In Figure 9.4, I show people's ratings of their representative in Congress, conditioned on support for the bill, shared partisanship, and whether the legislation was described as a compromise or not. I also report regression results in Appendix C (see Table A9.2, including the marginal effects of the compromise treatment within the conditions. I find that when members of Congress vote congruently with the preferences of their constituents, it matters little whether the bill was described as a compromise or not. This is true whether one is

---

[6] Ten members of Congress failed to vote on the bill. Eighteen respondents in the sample lived in districts represented by those members of Congress. They read a version highlighting that their representative did not vote on the bill but are excluded from the analyses of people's evaluations of their legislator.

[7] I am able to do so given that the treatment is not associated with support for the legislation.

[8] Partisan identifiers and party leaners are coded 1 when they share the same partisanship as their representative and zero when they do not. Independents are coded zero.

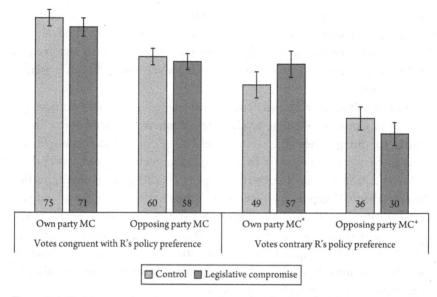

75	71	60	58	49	57	36	30

Own party MC	Opposing party MC	Own party MC*	Opposing party MC+
Votes congruent with R's policy preference		Votes contrary R's policy preference	

☐ Control ■ Legislative compromise

Figure 9.4 Position on education compromise and evaluation of one's representative.

represented by a legislator from their own party or one from the opposing party. Members of Congress earn warmer evaluations when they vote in ways that are congruent with the preferences of their constituents, and it does not matter if that policy outcome was a product of political compromise or not. Given a congruent policy vote, respondents do not seem to care if that bill represented a political compromise.

However, when one's member of Congress votes in ways contrary to the preferences of the respondent, it matters whether the legislation was described as a compromise or not. The effects of compromise are conditional on the partisanship of one's member of Congress. Consider the first the case of a constituent who learns that their co-partisan representative in Congress has decided to vote contrary to the policy outcome that the constituent wanted. In the control condition, the co-partisan representative earns a low rating, just below neutral with an average of 49 on the one hundred-point scale. Even a co-partisan faces consequences for a failure to vote congruent to the constituent's interests, given that a same-party representative who votes with constituents' preferences earns a rating of 75 (in the control condition). However, respondents are less punishing of an incongruent vote from their co-partisan representative when informed that the contrary vote concerned a legislative compromise. Constituents prefer that their representatives vote with their preferences, but when they do not, those disliked votes hurt incumbent approval less when the legislation was a compromise. When one learns that their co-partisan member of Congress has voted against their preferences, they are more forgiving in the case where the bill has been described as a compromise between Democrats and Republicans. Even as people desire ideologically congruent votes, they seem less likely to punish co-partisans for contrary votes when those votes were cast on legislative compromises.

In contrast, the reverse holds in the case of an incongruent vote from an out-partisan in Congress. Baseline levels of representative approval is low in the control condition, where the incongruent-voting out-partisan representative earns an average rating of 36 on the feeling thermometer scale. However, these evaluations drop even further, to an average rating of 30, when one learns that their member of Congress voted contrary to their wishes on a piece of compromise legislation, a difference that approaches statistical significance ($p < 0.07$). While a co-partisan representative is less likely to be punished for a contrary vote in the case of a compromise, a representative from the opposing side seems more likely to incur the disappointment of constituents when that contrary vote concerned compromise legislation.

Compromise on Health Care

As a third case, I consider whether people react differently to health care legislation when the policy change is framed as a compromise, focusing on Medicare reforms passed under a Republican Congress and Democratic president. In April 2015, Congress passed the Medicare Access and CHIP Reauthorization Act. Ushered through the House of Representatives through the collaborative efforts of Speaker of the House John Boehner and House Democratic leader Nancy Pelosi, the legislation altered the way that physicians were paid for treating Medicare patients and corrected a spending gap in how Medicare was funded. Additional provisions of the bill limited Medicare spending and extended health-care benefits for children in need. Substantively, it represented arguably the most significant health care reform since the passage of the Affordable Care Act, winning a spot on Mayhew's (2017) list of important laws passed during the 114th Congress.

The legislation passed with wide bipartisan support, by a vote of 392–37 in the House and 92–8 in the Senate. In the wake of the bill's passage, both members of Congress and journalists described the bill as a significant legislative compromise. In a speech to the floor of the House on March 26, John Boehner pronounced, "This is what we can accomplish when we focus on finding common ground." These sentiments were echoed by other Republicans, including Paul Ryan, who commented, "When we see opportunities to find common ground, we are moving forward on big things" (Steinhauer and Pear 2015b).

Republicans gained ground in achieving Medicare reforms without raising taxes, while Democrats were pleased to be able to protect spending for the Children's Health Insurance Program. But as press coverage in the *New York Times* noted, "The compromise between Mr. Boehner and Ms. Pelosi had something for everyone to dislike" (Steinhauer and Pear 2015a). Democrats had hoped for greater expansion of health care benefits for children, while Republicans had wanted greater efforts to close funding gaps that remained. In this way, the legislation represented a policy compromise. Both sides achieved some key goals, but Democrats and Republicans both ended up making some concessions from what their ideal version of the legislation would have been. As was the case for the Every Student Succeeds Act, the legislation also shows that compromise is possible under divided government and polarized parties. While Republicans controlled Congress and could have gambled with a bill passed solely on partisan lines, they instead chose to work with Democrats.

Was a strategy of compromise the right move in the eyes of the electorate? In a third experiment, I explore whether people think differently about the legislation when it is simply described in terms of its content versus the case where the character of the compromise is also described. All participants first read a paragraph describing the Medicare Access and CHIP Reauthorization Act and its key provisions related to extension of children's health care, cuts to Medicare spending, and increased premiums for some wealthier recipients. Those in the experimental condition were also given a second paragraph that described the terms of the compromise.

In the first experiment on the domestic violence legislation, the frame was simple: the bill was described as the product of a compromise between Democrats and Republicans. The second experiment described the education policy as a compromise as well, and I further emphasized this by mentioning that both parties made gains but that neither side got exactly what they wanted in the policy reform. In this third experiment, I provide even greater specificity about the terms of the compromise. The text first acknowledges the policy as a compromise between Republicans and Democrats, one where both sides made gains by being willing to make some concessions. Successive text then described the details of those parts of the agreement. Democrats were able to extend health-care benefits for children in need, but not for as long of a period as hoped. Republicans succeeded at achieving spending cuts for Medicare, but the reforms were not as encompassing as they had hoped.[9] This experiment represents a tough test of whether people like policy compromises not just in principle, but also in practice. By detailing both the concessions made by one's own party as

---

[9] The text of the vignettes can be found in Appendix B.

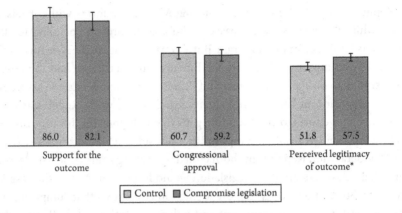

Figure 9.5 Health-care legislation and policy compromise.

well as the gains made by the opposing party, this frame gives readers explicit reasons to dislike the compromise policy.

I test whether this is the case using a web-based experiment conducted in September 2015 with a convenience sample of 331 adults recruited through Amazon's Mechanical Turk. After reading the vignette, I asked participants how satisfied they were with the outcome. In Figure 9.5, I present the percentage who reported being satisfied by each experimental condition. Overall, most respondents were satisfied with the policy outcome. In the control condition, 86% of respondents said that they were satisfied with the outcome. Support is slightly lower in the case where the vignette emphasized the details of the compromise, with 82% expressing satisfaction, but this difference is not statistically significant ($t = 0.95$, $p < 0.35$). Even when they are reminded that compromises come with concessions from one's own side, people are not markedly less enthusiastic about policy outcomes that are the product of political compromises.

I next asked people to assess whether they approve or disapprove of how Congress handles its job, taking into consideration the outcome of the vote on this bill. The scale ranges from zero (*strongly disapprove*) to 100 (*strongly approve*) with average levels of congressional approval within the conditions shown in Figure 9.5. In the control condition, average rating of congressional approval was 61, while the average rating in the compromise condition was 59, a difference that is not statistically significant ($t = 0.57$, $p < 0.57$). I fail to find any penalty for compromise in the feeling thermometer ratings people offer about Congress. While there are no particular dividends for accomplishing policy compromise, Congress faces no drop in approval when people are reminded that policy cooperation can come with concessions from their own side and gains for the opposing side.

Finally, I ask respondents about their perceptions about the legitimacy of the process. The public's perceptions of legitimacy are important to the stability of the democratic system. When people are dealt losing hands in politics, it is their belief in the legitimacy of the political system that encourages acceptance of disliked outcomes (Gibson 1989; Gibson, Caldeira, and Spence 2005). To assess people's appraisals of the legitimacy of the outcome, I asked three questions about their perceptions of the policy process. First, I asked participants about their perceptions of political voice, and whether members of Congress who share their views had a say in shaping the legislation. Second, I asked about their perceptions of unbiasedness, and whether any point of view had undue influence in producing this outcome. Finally, I asked about the quality of decision-making, and whether members of Congress can be trusted to make decisions that are good for the country as a whole.[10] I sum responses to create a scale and present averages within each experimental condition in Figure 9.5. I find that people are significantly more likely to perceive the policy process as legitimate when it is described as a political compromise ($t = 3.19, p < 0.01$). In the control condition, the mean legitimacy rating is 52 on the one hundred-point scale. This climbs to just over 57 when the policy is described as the product of political compromise. People are more likely to perceive policy outcomes as legitimate when they are built on legislative compromises.[11]

Moreover, these effects are most pronounced among those whose prior policy preferences are the most out-of-step with the final policy outcome. In a pretest questionnaire, experimental participants were asked about their prior attitudes about health care, including their support for Medicare reform and their desire for government investment in children's health care.[12] Using these items, I determine those who have prior policy preferences that are most aligned (and

---

[10] The specific items included, "Members of Congress who share my views were given a say in this decision-making process," "Members of Congress can be trusted to make decisions that are good for the country as a whole," and "No one interest or point of view seemed to have more input and consideration than others in producing this outcome in Congress." Response options fell on a seven-point Likert scale ranging from *strongly agree* to *strongly disagree*. Responses were summed to make a scale. The associated Cronbach's alpha is 0.61.

[11] As in the first two experiments, I find no evidence of heterogeneous treatment effects associated with the compromise frame and policy support and congressional approval for those with congruent policy preferences or strong partisan preferences.

[12] Before reading the vignettes, participants were asked to rate their agreement with some of the main platforms of the legislation on a six point scale, including taking steps to make the Medicare system financially sound, ensuring that low-income and middle-income children have access to health care, subsidies to help some low income groups afford health care, and protecting Medicare from rate increases or cuts to services. From those items, I create a scale of how well the final compromise aligns with people's preferences on the major parts of the legislation.

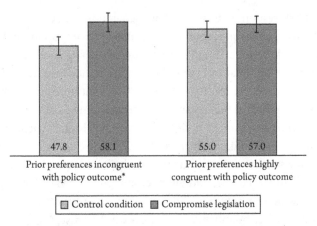

Figure 9.6 Perceived legitimacy, compromise, and policy congruence.

least congruent) with the specific terms of the compromise struck by Congress. I then look for heterogeneous effects of the compromise treatment across levels of policy congruence to see if describing legislation as a compromise uniquely boosts perceptions of outcome legitimacy among those who find the policy most incongruent with their prior preferences. In Table A9.3 in Appendix C, I present regression results and marginal effects, while in Figure 9.6, I show the levels of perceived legitimacy by experimental condition for those at the 10th percentile of policy congruence and those at the 90th percentile. For those at low levels of policy congruence, describing the legislation as the product of congressional compromise substantially increases one's likelihood of perceiving the process as legitimate, from a score of 48 in the control condition to a score of 58 in the compromise condition, nearly two-thirds of a standard deviation increase on the scale of the measure. As the level of policy congruence between one's prior preferences and the final legislation increases, the effects of the compromise treatment diminish in magnitude. When faced with a policy outcome well-aligned with one's preferences, the legitimacy of the outcome is rated similarly whether it was a product of legislative compromise or not.[13]

Stated another way, when we look at those in the control condition, we find that those whose prior preferences are poorly aligned with the outcome are far more pessimistic about the legitimacy of the process and are less likely to perceive the process as affording them voice and influence compared to those whose prior attitudes align nicely with the outcome. However, when the same policy outcome is described as the product of a legislative compromise where both

---

[13] For those above the 75th percentile of policy congruence, the effects of policy compromise on feelings of legitimacy are no longer statistically significant.

sides made concessions to reach an agreement, this legitimacy gap disappears. A person confronted with an incongruent policy outcome described as a compromise is as likely to see the policy progress as legitimate as a person who finds the outcome highly congruent with their own preferences. This suggests that when members of Congress strike compromises, it helps people accept outcomes that may not be terribly well-aligned with their interests.

Conclusions

Surveys show that Americans are strongly supportive of the principle of compromise in politics. Yet we worry that the principles they support in the abstract might not be the same as what they demand in specific situations. Compromises might be a good idea only up until they come at the cost of policy goals that one cares about. I find that when a policy's failure to pass is attributed to an unwillingness of the parties to find compromise, people are significantly more negative in their evaluations of Congress. Consistent with prior studies that show at party conflict is damaging to people's approval of the institution of Congress (Durr, Gilmour, and Wolbrecht 1997; Ramirez 2009), people punish Congress for failing to reach compromises.

Yet I find little evidence that Congress gains in public standing as a result of successfully reaching compromise agreements in politics. This might be a reflection of people's expectations. If people believe legislators should compromise, then successful compromise agreements might be just evidence of Congress doing what people expect. Because people overestimate the level of consensus on issues and underestimate the challenges of finding compromise (Hibbing and Theiss-Morse 2002), there may not be any intrinsic rewards for reaching those ends through compromise, at least in the minds of voters. However, in the face of policy failure, where a bill does not pass and blame needs to be assigned, the associated explanations may become more important (McGraw 1991). Negative outcomes generally are of greater concern than policy successes, so the failure of the bill to pass arguably draws greater scrutiny and elevates the importance of blame-placing. This could explain why voters punish Congress for a failure to compromise, even though they do not reward the institution for successful collaboration. This pattern also helps us understand why congressional approval remains so low—legislative compromises fail to boost approval, while any failures to reach agreements serve to drive approval down.

I find a similar pattern in people's evaluations of the members of Congress, where the nature of the process matters more in the face of undesirable outcomes rather than when people's aspirations are met. When people learn that their member of Congress has voted congruent with their policy interests, it matters little whether that policy outcome is described as a compromise or not. There is no punishment (or reward) for members of Congress when people are told that that vote came as the product of party concessions to the rival party in government. When constituents are told that their representative voted with them on the issue, they receive similarly positive evaluations regardless of the process used. However, the process is more important in cases where respondents learn that their member of Congress voted against the interests on the legislation. In these cases, people are less likely to punish their co-partisan member of Congress if they are told that incongruent vote was part of a legislative compromise. If a representative votes contrary to the wishes of constituents in his or her party, the penalties for that vote are mitigated when the bill is described as a compromise.

While the last chapter shows legislators' pledges to compromise boost their support among constituents, legislators' advocacy of specific policy compromises in Congress does not translate into the same increases in public support. In this way, I confirm that there is at least some slippage in the values people desire in the abstract and the degree to which those values inform evaluations of specific policies. Yet while people do not give warmer evaluations of policy outcomes and Congress when told that those policies are the product of political compromise, there is little evidence that people are any more negative about compromises in politics. We might worry that people are wary of compromise, as it can suggest an outcome that is less than optimal—one where concessions were made to the rival party, and one where not all of one's policy goals are achieved. But those details do not undermine people's support for policy compromises in Congress. While party fidelity has electoral costs (Carson et al. 2010; Koger and Lebo 2017), supporting compromises seems unlikely to lead to electoral retribution. This suggests that members of Congress have incentives to advertise their support for compromises to their constituents, rather than obscure their support for compromise bills.

Finally, these findings highlight the importance of policy compromise for people's perceptions of the legitimacy of government decisions. When policy outcomes are described as the product of legislative compromise, people are more likely to grant legitimacy to the process that produced the outcome. The legitimacy gains associated with the compromise frame are the greatest among those who find the policy outcome most incongruent with their prior preferences among the issue. When dealt a disliked hand in politics, people are more likely to accept the outcome as legitimate when it is described as the outcome of party collaboration and compromise in Congress. While others have raised worries about Americans' cynicism about compromise as a process (Hibbing and Theiss-Morse 2002), these results highlight the virtues of compromise for people's opinions of how government works. When legislators choose to compromise, it affects how people evaluate the legitimacy of government outcomes. In a time of polarized politics, heightened partisan passions, and a cynical, mistrustful electorate (Hetherington and Rudolph 2015), legitimacy is a valuable resource.

Appendix A

Description of the Experimental Participants

Experiment 1: Evaluations of Congress

The experiment included 1,050 participants recruited as a national sample of adults in the fall of 2013. Participants completed the experiment as part of a larger questionnaire administered and completed over the internet. The sample was recruited through Qualtrics using their online panel. From their pool of around two million volunteers (recruited from Web ads and permission-based e-mail lists), Qualtrics sent my questionnaire to a sample of 2091 respondents that was representative of the U.S. population in terms of age, race, and gender based on Census data. The response rate was 50% of those who received invitations to participate. The sample is 65% female and 19% nonwhite. In terms of partisanship, 36% identifies as Democratic, 23% as Republican, and 41% as independent or other. Ages range from 18 to 86 with an average age of 48 years.

Experiment 2: Evaluations of One's Representative

The experiment was included in a module of the 2016 Cooperative Congressional Election Study. It was placed in the pre-election survey with a nationally-representative sample of 990 participants.

Experiment 3: Evaluations of Legitimacy

The experiment was conducted in the fall of 2015 with a sample of 331 respondents recruited through Amazon's Mechanical Turk. The Mechanical Turk offers interested adults the opportunity to complete small tasks online for small sums of money. The convenience sample in this experiment is 36% female and 25% nonwhite. Forty-three percent of the sample identifies as Democrats,

18% identify as Republicans, and 39% identify as political independents or not affiliated with the major parties. Respondents range in age from 18 to 69 with an average age of 34 and a median age of 30.

Appendix B
Experimental Stimuli: Wording of the Vignettes

Experiment 1
Bill Passes—Control Condition

On Monday, the House of Representatives voted in support of the Violence Against Women Act, a measure that assists victims of domestic and sexual violence. The provisions of the bill expand federal programs to help local communities with the investigation and prosecution of violent crimes against women as well as aid to victims of abuse.

The sponsors of the bill will have a press conference later today to discuss the outcome and the reasons why the bill passed.

Bill Passes—Due to Congressional Compromise

On Monday, the House of Representatives voted in support of the Violence Against Women Act, a measure that assists victims of domestic and sexual violence. The provisions of the bill expand federal programs to help local communities with the investigation and prosecution of violent crimes against women as well as aid to victims of abuse.

The sponsors of the bill credit House efforts at bipartisanship as the key reason why the bill passed. The legislation drew nearly equal support from Democrats and Republicans, reflecting their success in hammering out a compromise bill. Both sides ceded ground from their original proposals to find a solution that each side could support.

Bill Does Not Pass—Control Condition

On Monday, the House of Representatives failed to secure enough votes to pass the Violence Against Women Act, a measure aimed at assisting victims of domestic and sexual violence. Had the bill garnered more support, it would have expanded federal programs meant to help local communities with the investigation and prosecution of violent crimes against women as well as aid to victims of abuse.

The sponsors of the bill will have a press conference later today to discuss the outcome and the reasons why the bill did not pass.

Bill Does Not Pass—Failure to Compromise

On Monday, the House of Representatives failed to secure enough votes to pass the Violence Against Women Act, a measure aimed at assisting victims of domestic and sexual violence. Had the bill garnered more support, it would have expanded federal programs meant to help local communities with the investigation and prosecution of violent crimes against women as well as aid to victims of abuse.

The sponsors of the bill blame rigid partisanship as the key reason why the bill failed. Democrats dug in their heels to resist key parts of the Republican proposal, while Republicans were reluctant to consider a compromise or make concessions to the other side. Each side blamed the other for failing to find a common-ground solution on the legislation.

Experiment 2

Control Condition

Last fall, Congress passed the Every Student Succeeds Act, a major education reform that replaces the No Child Left Behind Act. The new law limits federal influence over education policy, granting states greater discretion to set their own academic goals. The legislation also expands the government's role in providing access to high-quality preschools, while ensuring educational funding for the poorest school districts.

Compromise Frame

Last fall, Congress passed the Every Student Succeeds Act, a major education reform that replaces the No Child Left Behind Act. Members of Congress struck a compromise to reach an agreement. Both Democrats and Republicans made key gains, but the final law is not exactly what either side would have hoped for. The law limits federal influence over education policy, granting states greater discretion to set their own academic goals. The legislation also expands the government's role in providing access to high-quality preschools, while ensuring educational funding for the poorest school districts.

Experiment 3

Control Condition

Congress Passes Legislation to Extend Children's Health Care Benefits and Fix Medicare Funding

Earlier this year, Congress passed the Medicare Access and CHIP Reauthorization Act of 2015. The bill grants a two-year extension to CHIP, a government program that provides health insurance to over eight million children from low-to-moderate income families who would not otherwise be able to afford it. The legislation also helps close a funding gap in Medicare by imposing spending cuts and requiring higher premiums for some wealthier recipients.

Compromise (Order of Last two Sentences Was Randomly Assigned)

Congress Passes Legislation to Extend Children's Health Care Benefits and Fix Medicare Funding

Democrats and Republicans Make Concessions to Find a Compromise That Benefits Both Sides
Earlier this year, Congress passed the Medicare Access and CHIP Reauthorization Act of 2015. The bill grants a two-year extension to CHIP, a government program that provides health insurance to over eight million children from low-to-moderate income families who would not otherwise be able to afford it. The legislation also helps close a funding gap in Medicare by imposing spending cuts and requiring higher premiums for some wealthier recipients.

The legislation represents a compromise between Democrats and Republicans, who both achieved key policy goals by making some concessions. Democrats met their goal of extending current health care benefits for millions of poor children, while members of the GOP were successful in adding provisions that will close existing funding gaps in Medicare through long-term spending cuts. However, Republicans accepted less substantial reforms to Medicare than they would have liked, while Democrats who had hoped to reauthorize the program for four more years had to settle for two.

Appendix C

Regression Results

Table A9.1 **Satisfaction with Policy Outcome, Domestic Violence Experiment**

	Legislation passes			Legislation does not pass		
Compromise frame	0.033	0.036	0.012	−0.051	−0.025	−0.046
	(0.024)	(0.032)	(0.038)	(0.028)	(0.040)	(0.055)
Preference for government action on domestic violence	0.001*			−0.006*		
	(0.001)			(0.001)		
Compromise × prior preference	0.000			0.000		
	(0.001)			(0.001)		
Strength of prior preference		0.000			−0.003*	
		(0.001)			(0.001)	
Compromise × strength of preference		0.000			−0.001	
		(0.001)			(0.001)	
Strength of partisanship			−0.003			0.027
			(0.013)			(0.019)
Compromise × strength of partisanship			0.016			0.001
			(0.018)			(0.025)
Constant	0.726*	0.747*	0.759*	0.443*	0.415*	0.287*
	(0.017)	(0.022)	(0.027)	(0.020)	(0.028)	(0.040)
R²	0.028	0.007	0.01	0.21	0.057	0.016
N	517	517	471	509	509	474

Notes: Regression estimates. Standard errors are in parentheses.
*p < 0.05.

Table A9.2 **Evaluation of Member of Congress, Education Vote**

	Evaluation of MC
Legislation framed as compromise	−5.933[a]
	(3.169)
Member of Congress casts congruent vote	23.576*
	(2.769)
Own-party member of Congress	12.865*
	(3.405)
Compromise × Congruent vote	4.063
	(3.893)
Compromise × Own-party MC	13.830*
	(4.815)
Congruent vote × Own-party MC	1.977
	(4.116)
Compromise × Congruent vote × Own-party MC	−15.466*
	(5.852)
Constant	36.371*
	(2.241)
Marginal effects of compromise manipulation	
Own-party representative, congruent vote	−3.505
	(2.439)
Representative not of same party, congruent vote	−1.869
	(2.261)
Own-party representative, incongruent vote	7.897*
	(3.625)
Representative not of same party, incongruent vote	−5.933[a]
	(3.169)
R^2	0.303
N	967

Notes: Regression results. MC, member of Congress. Standard errors are in parentheses.
*$p < 0.05$.
[a]$p < 0.10$.

Table A9.3 **Heterogeneous Effects of Compromise Treatment, Study 3**

	Perceived legitimacy
Compromise frame	26.962*
	(10.731)
Congruence between prior preferences and outcome	28.986*
	(11.502)
Compromise frame × policy congruence	-33.271*
	(16.571)
Constant	33.265*
	(7.445)
Marginal effects of compromise treatment	
At minimum policy congruence	18.644*
	(6.681)
At 10th percentile	10.326*
	(2.908)
At median policy congruence	5.336*
	(1.796)
At 90th percentile	2.009
	(2.569)
At maximum policy congruence	-1.318
	(3.933)
R^2	0.05
N	322

Notes: Regression estimates. Standard errors in parentheses. *$p<0.05$.

10

Conclusions

There are many reasons to worry about the public's willingness to support the compromises made by elected officials. In a time of party polarization, compromise agreements force members of Congress to make concessions and collaborate even as the shared policy terrain between them dwindles. Even as most citizens hold policy views arrayed around a moderate center, their manner of thinking is often deeply partisan. Co-partisans are viewed as virtuous allies while those on the opposing side are cast as villains and scoundrels. Citizens and politicians are invited to take sides and wage partisan battles in a political system that encourages the adversarial practice of politics.

Even despite these pressures, most Americans say they want their elected officials to try to reach compromise agreements in politics. They do so not because it suits their partisan agendas or satisfies self-interested ends. Instead, they accept compromise as a part of politics because they learn that they should do so. In schools and in their engagement in civic life, they learn about how democracy works—about the importance of following the rules, the rights and responsibilities of citizens, and the norms that govern democratic life. Among these lessons, they learn about how compromise is a virtuous way to find agreements in the presence of deep political divisions. These early lessons on the value of compromise are carried into adulthood, shaping people's expectations of how the president and members of Congress should approach the work of policymaking. People see compromise as a principled way of resolving policy disputes and prefer politicians who are willing to work with the other side. They reward legislators who vow to make compromises and punish Congress for its failures to reach compromises. Compromise is not something that only moderates and independents demand, as even strong partisans voice support for the principle of compromise in politics.

In a sense, it might not be surprising to see that people feel a socialized pressure to support policy compromise—even when it is contrary to their partisan goals and policy aspirations. After all, we know that people often act on such socialized motives in political life. People turn out to vote not just out of a desire

Compromise in an Age of Party Polarization. Jennifer Wolak, Oxford University Press (2020). © Oxford University Press.
DOI: 10.1093/oso/9780197510490.001.0001

to influence the election, but out of a sense of obligation that they should fulfill their civic duty (Riker and Ordeshook 1968). When they choose to participate in neighborhood organizations and as volunteers, they often do so out of a sense of concern and connectedness with others in their community (Putnam 2000). When engaged in experiments of economic games like the dictator game or ultimatum game, most choose an equitable distribution over one that serves their self-interest (Fehr and Fischbacher 2003). When asked to extend civil rights and liberties to groups that seem threatening, they do so out of a socialized obligation to respect democratic principles (Sullivan, Piereson, and Marcus 1982).

But what is distinctive here in the case of socialized support for the principle of compromise is that these attitudes are not just guiding our engagement in politics or motivating some course of action. Instead, these beliefs constrain the demands we make of politicians. Our socialization about what kind of citizen we should be influences the kind of policy outcomes we are willing to accept. This is important as we have generally understood policy space as strictly ideological terrain. Some hold moderate views, while others are ideologues. Some hold nonattitudes, and others feel the conflict of attitudinal ambivalence. In thinking about what kind of policies people want to see in politics, we have focused on their issue beliefs and the variations in the intensity, extremity, and consistency of these policy preferences. But when we are asked to recommend how a political disagreement should be settled or to define what political outcome is best, we do not draw solely on these partisan and ideological considerations. We also lean on what we learned in school about how disagreements should be resolved. Our preferences about how elected officials should approach their jobs and what policy outcomes we would like to see reflect our partisan policy goals as well as our principled views about how politics should be practiced.

Because people think about compromise in principled ways, it means that people are not guided by their policy beliefs alone in politics. If partisans are unwilling to work with the other side and are fundamentally opposed to compromise, the prospects for congressional compromise dim. But if people care about both policy outcomes as well as the processes by which government works, then it suggests that our principled thinking about compromise can constrain some of our most partisan instincts. Even if we value candidates who promise party fidelity, this does not require that people will reject candidates who vow to be open to compromise. Even if we value seeing our party win in politics, it does not mean we will enthusiastically back our party at the cost of the principle of compromise.

This has several important implications for how we think about politics. First, this highlights that Americans value more than just ideological policy representation from their representatives in Congress. Many have raised fears that the demands of the electorate restrain members of Congress from signing on to compromises. If voters want legislators to deliver on their campaign promises and cast ideologically congruent votes above all else, then it will be difficult for legislators to support compromises that fall short of those ideals. Yet even as citizens are guided by their policy aspirations, they acknowledge the need for policy compromise. When one's co-partisan representative in Congress casts a ballot contrary to the preferences of the constituent, they are less likely to punish the legislator for that vote when told it was compromise legislation. They respond favorably to candidates who vow to compromise and support incumbents even when they are criticized for straying from their principles and being too willing to compromise.

Second, people care about the processes by which political disputes are resolved, and this informs the kinds of outcomes they want to see in politics. We know from prior studies that people care a good deal about how government works and the processes by which policy are made (Hibbing and Theiss-Morse 1995, 2002). These process considerations are frequently linked to the things people dislike about government, where pessimism about how government works can lead to the erosion of public confidence in government and cynicism about the responsiveness of politicians. When people look to Washington, they are discouraged by a system they see as guided by selfish politicians, special interests, and partisan bickering. However, these results highlight a normatively positive note about Americans' concerns about political processes—as our desire for compromise also finds its origins in our expectations about how government should work. While Hibbing and Theiss-Morse (2002) are pessimistic that people will tolerate compromise in politics, I find that people's views about political processes matter beyond their role in explaining people's dissatisfaction with government. These process considerations can guide their views of policy outcomes and demands of elected officials. Even though we dislike many aspects about how government works, we still care about compromise as a way of settling political disputes.

Third, these findings demonstrate that Americans maintain important points of agreement even during a time of deep political divisions. Even as news stories often focus on the forces that pull people apart in politics, Americans are brought together by shared support of compromise. In surveys, Americans voice widespread support for the principle of compromise. They believe in the value of compromise as a political norm, and apply this principle to how they evaluate politicians and policy outcomes. Even though some have worried about the erosion of democratic norms in recent years (Foa and Mounk 2015; Howe 2017), I find little evidence of this here. High levels of support of compromise persists across multiple surveys over time. People engage in principled thinking about how political disagreements should be settled. Even though the angry voices of the ideologues seem to drive political dialogues, the realities of public opinion reveal that Americans want to see ways forward past these divisions. They want the left and the right to work together to find compromises that address the nation's problems.

Fourth, these results highlight an important limit to partisan thinking in the electorate. Accumulating evidence highlights the pervasive effects of partisan bias, where party allegiance shapes not just vote choices, but also how we evaluate the news, assess political facts, rate the opposing party, and choose dating partners (Huber and Malhotra 2017; Iyengar, Sood, and Lelkes 2012; Mason 2018; Taber and Lodge 2006). Yet there are limits to partisanship's influence. Even as our priors shape how we view candidates and evaluate the news, they seem have little influence on our general support for the principle of compromise. Both strong partisans and independents value compromise as a way to settle disputes. Moreover, those who are the most prone to rely on their partisan biases are among the most supportive of compromise. This is important, because even if a majority of Americans favored policy compromises, politicians might still avoid compromises if party activists and primary voters in the district were fundamentally opposed to the concessions of compromise.

We have reasons to fear that these most engaged citizens will be the most prone to rely on partisan modes of citizenship (Mutz 2006). The most educated and the most partisan lean on their partisan biases in approaching new information (Taber and Lodge 2005) and organize their views in ideological ways (Abramowitz 2011). Yet these individuals are also among the strongest supporters of democratic principles (Bobo and Licari 1989; McClosky and Brill 1983). This provides an important countervailing pressure. If those who have the strongest partisan demands of politicians are also the most likely to believe in compromise as a process of resolving differences, then this kind of principled thinking can check the partisan tendencies of political sophisticates. This is possible because the origins of people's beliefs in compromise are socialized through education and engagement in civic life, and distinct from partisanship and the desire for moderate policy. Compromise is not just something desired by political moderates or the less politically engaged. Demand for political compromise comes from independents and strong partisans alike.

When our partisan goals come into conflict with our principled thinking about democratic processes, partisan goals will sometimes prevail. People do like to be on the winning side of policy battles. But in many cases and for many voters, principled thinking about compromise can check the pursuit of a partisan win. The desirability of compromise in principle still informs our practical demands in politics. As such, these findings offer another corrective about the potency of partisanship in the electorate. While much attention has been devoted to the stark rise of partisan thinking in the electorate, there are still bounds to partisanship's importance. Even as the share of ideological activists is on the rise, moderates make up the largest share of the electorate (Fiorina, Abrams, and Pope 2010). Even as some are drawn to partisan life, others choose to identify as independents in order to separate themselves from the partisan battles of political life (Klar and Krupnikov 2016). Even as many hold passionate views about political issues, not all do (Fiorina and Abrams 2009). Even as some political views are so closely held so as to make compromise unpalatable (Ryan 2016), not all policy issues animate similar intensity of feelings. Even as people desire ideologically congruent policy outcomes, these tendencies are checked by the countervailing desire for politicians who are willing to find compromises.

Fifth, I demonstrate the importance of acknowledging the multiple considerations that guide people's desires about political outcomes. People value policy outcomes as well as political processes, and both influence their preferences about how disputes should be settled. This is important to recognize as we often tend to assume that Americans are single-minded in their pursuit of policy goals. I show instead that people draw on both principled thinking about compromise and partisan thinking about policy goals in deciding what political outcomes to endorse. This means that even though people are often guided by partisan bias, there are bounds to partisanship's influence. Even though we like to win policy debates, winning is not all that we care about. Even as we want our representatives to vote with the district, we can still make allowances for compromise. The fact that people's policy desires are checked by principled thinking further suggests that principled thinking could be cultivated or encouraged— that politicians could use the language of compromise to explain their positions or that candidates could campaign with promises to consider compromises.

When considering the prospects for compromise in Washington, there remain steep challenges to negotiating successful compromise agreements. Given the rising party polarization in Congress, the amount of shared policy space between the parties has declined. As the ideological distance between the parties grows, it is harder work to find places of common agreement, and successful compromises may require greater concessions from the parties. But if most Americans want to see legislators strike compromises, why does policy compromise seems so uncommon in Washington? I believe several forces may be at work.

First, we likely underestimate how often members of Congress are engaged in the pursuit of policy compromise. Even as members work on finding acceptable compromises, these negotiations take place away from the public eye and are unlikely to land on the nightly news (Atkinson 2017). When Congress does make the news, it is more likely to be due to failures to find agreement than those cases where members of Congress forge successful compromises on budget proposals and policy reforms. Congress's failures to find agreement, manifest in government shutdowns, gridlock, filibusters, and partisan arguments, can seem more newsworthy and attention-grabbing than legislative efforts to craft successful compromises. People are much more nimble at naming cases where Congress has failed to act than enumerating policy domains where Congress and the president have successfully brokered compromise agreements. Even in times of gridlock and partisan acrimony, Congress has continued to craft compromise laws. But only a small share of Americans follow the news closely enough to be able to name those cases. This likely leads to an underestimation of legislators' willingness to make compromises.

As people tend to underestimate the feasibility of policy compromise in Washington, they also tend to overestimate how difficult it might be for Democrats and Republicans to work together. People misperceive the distance between themselves and those on the other partisan side (Ahler and Sood 2018; Westfall et al. 2015). We overestimate levels of party polarization, which can make us pessimistic about the degree to which workable agreements can be found on policy issues. These misperceptions are greatest among those with strong beliefs, political activists and political sophisticates (Van Boven, Judd, and Sherman 2012; Westfall et al. 2015). This means that campaign donors and party activists as well as Washington pundits and editorial writers are among the most likely to see significant ideological gulfs between Democrats and Republicans. To the degree to which these groups inform both perceptions about public preferences among both elites as well as other Americans, we may end up overly pessimistic about the prospects for political compromise under party polarization.

It may also be the case that members of Congress are underestimating the level of support for compromise within the electorate. Legislators are not always accurate in knowing the preferences of their constituents (Hedlund and Friesema 1972). While they look to their districts for cues on how to vote (Bergen and Cole 2015; Butler and Nickerson 2011), the constituents that legislators hear from are often not representative of the district at large, but instead disproportionately weighted toward activists, donors, and co-partisans (Broockman and Ryan 2016; Miler 2010). To the degree to which ideologues are overrepresented among those in contact with their representative, legislators may overestimate popular opposition to policy compromise in their districts. Legislators might also choose to not advertise those cases where they sign on to compromise agreements out of fears that it will make their re-election campaigns more challenging. Even though strong partisans and engaged citizens are supportive of compromise in politics, talk of policy concessions and bipartisan cooperation may do little to mobilize activists to give their time to the reelection effort. To encourage donors to contribute to the campaign, politicians may be better served by emphasizing their ideological goals over their willingness to seek workable compromises.

When explaining the challenges of finding compromise in Congress, the evidence overall suggests that voters' demands are not a major obstacle to the pursuit of compromise. Instead, the pressures that inhibit policy compromise may well find their origins outside the electorate. Even if Americans express a desire for compromise in Congress, the pressures of congressional parties may lead legislators to put partisan agendas ahead of public preferences (Koger and Lebo 2017). Interest groups—and their ability to call attention to compromise votes, fund attack ads, and rally opposition—may also serve as a deterrent from signing on to legislative compromises. Legislators may fear that they will be unable to convince constituents of the virtues of the legislative compromises they supported. These forces compound the challenges of finding compromise in a time of growing ideological distance between Democrats and Republicans in Congress.

In explaining her decision to leave the Senate after seventeen years of service, Olympia Snowe called for both citizens and politicians to be open to compromise. "Our leaders must understand that there is not only strength in compromise, courage in conciliation and honor in consensus-building—but also a political reward for following these tenets. That reward will be real only if the people demonstrate their desire for politicians to come together" (Snowe 2012). In a time of party polarization, compromise is difficult but needed. Even as we worry about the challenges of policy progress in times of ideological division, the public is willing to support the sacrifices demanded by policy compromise.

REFERENCES

Abramowitz, Alan I. 2011. *The Disappearing Center: Engaged Citizens, Polarization, and American Democracy*. New Haven, CT: Yale University Press.

Ahler, Douglas J., and Gaurav Sood. 2018. "The Parties in Our Heads: Misperceptions about Party Composition and Their Consequences." *Journal of Politics* 80(3): 964–981.

Altman, Alex. 2011. "Conflict vs. Compromise: A Tale of Two Freshmen in Congress." *Time* 177(10).

Anderson, Christopher J., André Blais, Shaun Bowler, Todd Donovan, and Ola Listhaug. 2005. *Losers' Consent: Elections and Democratic Legitimacy*. Oxford: Oxford University Press.

Anderson, Christopher J., and Andrew J. LoTempio. 2002. "Winning, Losing and Political Trust in America." *British Journal of Political Science* 32: 335–351.

Ansolabehere, Stephen, and Philip Edward Jones. 2010. "Constituents' Responses to Congressional Roll-Call Voting." *American Journal of Political Science* 54: 583–597.

Atkinson, Mary Layton. 2017. *Combative Politics: The Media and Public Perceptions of Lawmaking*. Chicago: University of Chicago Press.

Avery, Patricia G., John L. Sullivan, and Sandra L. Wood. 1997. "Teaching for Tolerance of Diverse Beliefs." *Theory Into Practice* 36: 32–38.

Bafumi, Joseph, and Robert Y. Shapiro. 2009. "A New Partisan Voter." *The Journal of Politics* 71: 1–24.

Baker, Ross K. 2015. *Is Bipartisanship Dead? A Report from the Senate*. Boulder, CO: Paradigm.

Banducci, Susan, and Jeffrey Karp. 2003. "How Elections Change the Way Citizens View the Political System: Campaigns, Media Effects, and Electoral Outcomes in Comparative Perspective." *British Journal of Political Science* 33: 443–467.

Barker, David C., and Christopher J. Carman. 2012. *Representing Red and Blue: How the Culture Wars Change the Way Citizens Speak and Politicians Listen*. Oxford: Oxford University Press.

Bartels, Larry M. 2002. "Beyond the Running Tally: Partisan Bias in Political Perceptions." *Political Behavior* 24: 117–150.

Bayh, Evan. 2010. "Why I'm Leaving the Senate." *The New York Times*, February 20. www.nytimes.com/2010/02/21/opinion/21bayh.html

Berelson, Bernard. 1952. "Democratic Theory and Public Opinion." *Public Opinion Quarterly* 16: 313–330.

Bergan, Daniel E., and Richard T. Cole. 2015. "Call Your Legislator: A Field Experimental Study of the Impact of Citizen Contacts on Legislative Voting." *Political Behavior* 37: 27–42.

Binder, Sarah A. 2016. "Polarized We Govern?" In Alan S. Gerber and Eric Schickler, eds., *Governing in a Polarized Age: Elections, Parties, and Political Representation in America*. New York: Cambridge University Press, 223–242.

Bobo, Lawrence, and Frederick C. Licari. 1989. "Education and Political Tolerance." *Public Opinion Quarterly* 53: 283–308.

Bovitz, Gregory L., and Jamie L. Carson. 2006. "Position-Taking and Electoral Accountability in the U.S. House of Representatives." *Political Research Quarterly* 59: 297–312.

Brady, David W., Hahrie Han, and Jeremy C. Pope. 2007. "Primary Elections and Candidate Ideology: Out of Step with the Primary Electorate?" *Legislative Studies Quarterly* 32: 79–105.

Broockman, David E., and Timothy J. Ryan. 2016. "Preaching to the Choir: Americans Prefer Communicating to Copartisan Elected Officials." *American Journal of Political Science* 60: 1093–107.

Brunell, Thomas. 2008. *Redistricting and Representation: Why Competitive Elections are Bad for America*. New York: Routledge.

Butler, Daniel M., and David W. Nickerson. 2011. "Can Learning Constituency Opinion Affect How Legislators Vote? Results from a Field Experiment." *Quarterly Journal of Political Science* 6: 55–83.

Campbell, David E. 2006. *Why We Vote: How Schools and Communities Shape Our Civic Life*. Princeton, NJ: Princeton University Press.

Canes-Wrone, Brandice, David W. Brady, and John F. Cogan. 2002. "Out of Step, Out of Office: Electoral Accountability and House Members' Voting." *American Political Science Review* 96(1): 127–140.

Canes-Wrone, Brandice, William Minozzi, and Jessica Bonney Reveley. 2011. "Issue Accountability and the Mass Public." *Legislative Studies Quarterly* 36: 5–35.

Cappella, Joseph N., and Kathleen Hall Jamieson. 1997. *Spiral of Cynicism: The Press and the Public Good*. New York: Oxford University Press.

Carson, Jamie L., Gregory Koger, G., Matthew J. Lebo, M. J., and Everett Young. 2010. "The Electoral Costs of Party Loyalty in Congress." *American Journal of Political Science* 54: 598–616.

Center for Civic Education. 1994. *National Standards for Civics and Government*. Washington, DC: National Center for Civic Education and the Pew Charitable Trusts.

Chong, Dennis, Herbert McClosky, and John Zaller. 1983. "Patterns of Support for Democratic and Capitalist Values in the United States." *British Journal of Political Science* 13: 401–440.

Cillizza, Chris, and Sean Sullivan. 2013. "People want Congress to compromise. Except that they really don't." *The Washington Post*, June 13. www.washingtonpost.com/news/the-fix/wp/2013/06/13/people-want-congress-to-compromise-except-that-they-really-dont/

Clarke, Harold D., and Alan C. Acock. 1989. "National Elections and Political Attitudes: The Case of Political Efficacy." *British Journal of Political Science* 19(4): 551–562.

Cohen, Jeffrey E. 2015. *Presidential Leadership in Public Opinion: Causes and Consequences*. Cambridge, UK: Cambridge University Press.

Coleman, John J., and Paul F. Manna. 2000. "Congressional Campaign Spending and the Quality of Democracy." *Journal of Politics* 62: 757–789.

Conover, Pamela Johnston, and Stanley Feldman. 1982. "Projection and the Perception of Candidates' Issue Positions." *Western Political Quarterly* 35(2):228–244.

Conover, Pamela Johnston, and Stanley Feldman. 1989. "Candidate Perception in an Ambiguous World: Campaigns, Cues, and Inference Processes." *American Journal of Political Science* 33(4): 912–940.

Craig, Stephen C., Michael D. Martinez, Jason Gainous, and James G. Kane. 2006. "Winners, Losers, and Election Context: Voter Responses to the 2000 Presidential Election." *Political Research Quarterly* 59: 579–592.

Dancey, Logan, and Geoffrey Sheagley. 2018. "Partisanship and Perceptions of Party-Line Voting in Congress." *Political Research Quarterly* 71: 32–45.

Davis, Darren W. 2007. *Negative Liberty: Public Opinion and the Terrorist Attacks on America*. New York: Russell Sage Foundation.

Davis, Darren W., and Brian D. Silver. 2004. "Civil Liberties vs. Security: Public Opinion in the Context of the Terrorist Attacks on America." *American Journal of Political Science* 48: 28–46.

Delli Carpini, Michael X., and Scott Keeter. 1996. *What Americans Know about Politics and Why It Matters*. New Haven, CT: Yale University Press.

Dobel, J. Patrick. 1990. *Compromise and Political Action: Political Morality in Liberal and Democratic Life*. Savage, MD: Rowman & Littlefield.

Doherty, David. 2013. "To Whom Do People Think Representatives Should Respond: Their District or the Country?" *Public Opinion Quarterly* 77: 237–255.

Druckman, James N., Erik Peterson, and Rune Slothuus. 2013. "How Elite Partisan Polarization Affects Public Opinion Formation." *American Political Science Review* 107: 57–79.

Dryzek. John S. 2000. *Deliberative Democracy and Beyond: Liberals, Critics, Contestations*. Oxford: Oxford University Press.

Durr, Robert H., John B. Gilmour, and Christina Wolbrecht. 1997. "Explaining Congressional Approval." *American Journal of Political Science* 41(1): 175–207.

Easton, David, and Jack Dennis. 1969. *Children in the Political System: Origins of Political Legitimacy*. New York: McGraw-Hill.

Erikson, Robert S., Michael B. MacKuen, and James A. Stimson. 2002. *The Macro Polity*. New York: Cambridge University Press.

Eulau, Heinz, and Paul D. Karps. 1977. "The Puzzle of Representation: Specifying Components of Responsiveness." *Legislative Studies Quarterly* 2: 233–254.

Evans, Heather K. 2014. *Competitive Elections and Democracy in America: The Good, the Bad, and the Ugly*. New York: Routledge.

Evans, Ronald W. 2004. *The Social Studies Wars: What Should We Teach the Children?* New York: Teachers College Press.

Fehr, Ernst, and Urs Fischbacher. 2003. "The Nature of Human Altruism." *Nature* 425: 785–791.

Fenno, Richard F. 1975. "If As Ralph Nader Says, Congress Is 'The Broken Branch,' How Come We Love Our Congressman So Much?" In Norman J. Ornstein, ed., *Congress in Change: Evolution and Reform*, 277–287. New York: Praeger.

Fenno, Richard. 1978. *Homestyle: House Members in Their Districts*. Boston: Little Brown.

Fiorina, Morris P., and Samuel J. Abrams. 2008. "Political Polarization in the American Public." *Annual Review of Political Science* 11: 563–588.

Fiorina, Morris P., with Samuel J. Abrams. 2009. *Disconnect: The Breakdown of Representation in American Politics*. Norman: University of Oklahoma Press.

Fiorina, Morris P., Samuel J. Abrams, and Jeremy C. Pope. 2010. *Culture War? The Myth of a Polarized America*. 3d ed. New York: Longman.

Foa, Roberto, and Yascha Mounk. 2015. "Are Americans Losing Faith in Democracy?" *Vox*, December 18. https://www.vox.com/polyarchy/2015/12/18/9360663/is-democracy-in-trouble

Funk, Carolyn L. 2001. "Process Performance: Public Reaction to Legislative Policy Debate." In John R. Hibbing and Elizabeth Theiss-Morse, eds. *What Is It about Government That Americans Dislike?* Cambridge, UK: Cambridge University Press.

Gangl, Amy. 2003. "Procedural Justice Theory and Evaluations of the Lawmaking Process." *Political Behavior* 25: 119–149.

Gibson, James L. 1987. "Homosexuals and the Ku Klux Klan: A Contextual Analysis of Political Tolerance." *Western Political Quarterly* 40: 427–448.

Gibson, James L. 1989. "Understandings of Justice: Institutional Legitimacy, Procedural Justice, and Political Tolerance." *Law and Society Review* 23(3): 469–496.

Gibson, James L. 1991. "Institutional Legitimacy, Procedural Justice, and Compliance with Supreme Court Decisions." *Law and Society Review* 25: 631–636.

Gibson, James L., and Richard D. Bingham. 1983. "Elite Tolerance of Nazi Rights." *American Politics Research* 11: 403–428.

Gibson, James L., Gregory A. Caldeira, and Lester K. Spence. 2005. "Why Do People Accept Public Policies They Oppose? Testing Legitimacy Theory with a Survey-Based Experiment." *Political Research Quarterly* 58(2): 187–201.

Gilmour, John B. 1995. *Strategic Disagreement: Stalemate in American Politics*. Pittsburgh: University of Pittsburgh Press.

Ginsberg, Benjamin, and Robert Weissberg. 1978. "Elections and the Mobilization of Popular Support." *American Journal of Political Science* 22: 31–55.

Granberg, Donald. 1993. "Political Perception." In Shanto Iyengar and William J. McGuire, eds., *Explorations in Political Psychology*. Durham, NC: Duke University Press.

Grant, J. Tobin, and Thomas J. Rudolph. 2004. "The Job of Representation in Congress: Public Expectations and Representative Approval." *Legislative Studies Quarterly* 29: 431–445.

Green, Donald Philip, Bradley Palmquist, and Eric Schickler. 2002. *Partisan Hearts and Minds: Political Parties and the Social Identity of Voters*. New Haven, CT: Yale University Press.

Greene, Steven. 1999. "Understanding Party Identification: A Social Identity Approach." *Political Psychology* 20: 393–403.

Greene, Steven. 2004. "Social Identity Theory and Political Identification." *Social Science Quarterly* 85(1): 138–153.

Greenstein, Fred. 1965. *Children and Politics*. New Haven, CT: Yale University Press.

Griffin, John D., and Patrick Flavin. 2011. "How Citizens and Their Legislators Prioritize Spheres of Representation." *Political Research Quarterly* 64: 520–533.

Grill, Christopher J. 2007. *The Public Side of Representation: A Study of Citizens' Views about Representatives and the Representative Process*. Albany: State University of New York Press.

Grimmer, Justin. 2013. *Representational Style in Congress: What Legislators Say and Why It Matters*. New York: Cambridge University Press.

Grose, Christian R., Neil Malhotra, and Robert Van Houweling. 2015. "Explaining Explanations: How Legislators Explain their Policy Positions and How Citizens React." *American Journal of Political Science* 59: 724–743.

Grossmann, Matt, and David A. Hopkins. 2016. *Asymmetric Politics: Ideological Republicans and Group Interest Democrats*. New York: Oxford University Press.

Gutmann, Amy, and Dennis Thompson. 2012. *The Spirit of Compromise: Why Governing Demands It and Campaigning Undermines It*. Princeton, NJ: Princeton University Press.

Habermas, Jürgen. 1989. *The Structural Transformation of the Public Sphere: An Inquiry into a Category of Bourgeois Society*. Cambridge, MA: MIT Press.

Harbridge, Laurel, and Neil Malhotra. 2011. "Electoral Incentives and Partisan Conflict in Congress: Evidence from Survey Experiments." *American Journal of Political Science* 55: 494–510.

Harbridge, Laurel, Neil Malhotra, and Brian F. Harrison. 2014. "Public Preferences for Bipartisanship in the Policymaking Process." *Legislative Studies Quarterly* 39: 327–355.

Hedlund, Ronald D., and H. Paul Friesema. 1972. "Representatives' Perceptions of Constituency Opinion." *Journal of Politics* 34: 730–752.

Helderman, Rosalind S., and David A. Fahrenthold. 2012. "In 'Fiscal Cliff' Talks, Boehner Must Deal with Tough GOP Caucus as well as Obama." *The Washington Post*, November 15. www.washingtonpost.com/politics/in-fiscal-cliff-talks-boehner-must-deal-with-tough-gop-caucus-as-well-as-obama/2012/11/15/056896fe-2e90-11e2-89d4-040c9330702a_story.html

Hetherington, Marc J., Meri T. Long, and Thomas J. Rudolph. 2016. "Revisiting the Myth: New Evidence of a Polarized Electorate." *Public Opinion Quarterly* 80: 321–350.

Hetherington, Marc J., and Thomas J. Rudolph. 2015. *Why Washington Won't Work: Polarization, Political Trust, and the Governing Crisis*. Chicago: University of Chicago Press.

Hibbing, John R., and Elizabeth Theiss-Morse. 1995. *Congress as Public Enemy: Public Attitudes toward American Political Institutions*. Cambridge, UK: Cambridge University Press.

Hibbing, John R., and Elizabeth Theiss-Morse. 2002. *Stealth Democracy: Americans' Beliefs about How Government Should Work*. New York: Cambridge University Press.

Hibbing, John R., Elizabeth Theiss-Morse, and Eric Whitaker. 2009. "Americans' Perceptions of the Nature of Governing." In Jeffery J. Mondak and Dona-Gene Mitchell, eds. *Fault Lines: Why the Republicans Lost Congress*. New York: Routledge.

Hoagland, Jim. 2005. "The Price of Polarization." *The Washington Post*, May 5. www.washingtonpost.
  com/wp-dyn/content/article/2005/05/04/AR2005050402049.html

Holian, David B., and Charles L. Prysby. 2015. *Candidate Character Traits in Presidential Elections.*
  New York: Routledge.

Howe, Paul. 2017. "Eroding Norms and Democratic Deconsolidation." *Journal of Democracy*
  28: 15–29.

Huber, Gregory A., and Neil Malhotra. 2017. "Political Homophily in Social Relationships:
  Evidence from Online Dating Behavior." *Journal of Politics* 79: 269–283.

Huckfeldt, Robert, and Jeanette Morehouse Mendez. 2008. "Moths, Flames, and Political
  Engagement: Managing Disagreement within Communication Networks." *Journal of Politics*
  70(1): 83–96.

Huddy, Leonie, Lilliana Mason, and Lene Aarøe. 2015. "Expressive Partisanship: Campaign
  Involvement, Political Emotion, and Partisan Identity." *American Political Science Review* 109:
  1–17.

Hurwitz, Jon, and Mark Peffley. 2005. "Explaining the Great Racial Divide: Perceptions of Fairness
  in the U.S. Criminal Justice System." *Journal of Politics* 67(3): 762–783.

Inskeep, Steve, and Shankar Vendantam. 2012. "Why Compromise Is a Bad Word in Politics."
  NPR News, March 13. www.npr.org/2012/03/13/148499310/why-compromise-is-terrible-
  politics

Iyengar, Shanto, Yphtach Lelkes, Matthew Levendusky, Neil Malhotra, and Sean J. Westwood.
  2019. "The Origins and Consequences of Affective Polarization in the United States." *Annual
  Review of Political Science* 22: 129–146.

Iyengar, Shanto, Gaurav Sood, and Yphtach Lelkes. 2012. "Affect, Not Ideology: A Social Identity
  Perspective on Polarization." *Public Opinion Quarterly* 76(3): 405–431.

Iyengar, Shanto, and Sean J. Westwood. 2015. "Fear and Loathing across Party Lines: New
  Evidence on Group Polarization." *American Journal of Political Science* 59: 690–707.

Jacobson, Gary. 2015. "It's Nothing Personal: The Decline of the Incumbency Advantage in U.S.
  House Elections." *Journal of Politics* 77: 861–73.

Jacobson, Gary C. 2016. "No Compromise: The Electoral Origins of Legislative Gridlock."
  In Samuel Kernell and Steven Smith, eds. *Principles and Practice in American Politics.*
  Washington, DC: CQ Press.

Jacobson, Gary C., and Jamie L. Carson. 2016. *The Politics of Congressional Elections.* Lanham,
  MD: Rowman and Littlefield.

Jewitt, Caitlin E., and Paul Goren. 2015. "Ideological Structure and Consistency in the Age of
  Polarization." *American Politics Research* 44(1): 81–105.

Kasperowicz, Pete. 2013. "House Easily Passes Senate's Violence against Women Bill." *The Hill*,
  February 28. thehill.com/blogs/floor-action/house/285499-house-passes-senates-violence-
  against-women-bill

Kinder, Donald R., Mark D. Peters, Robert P. Abelson, and Susan T. Fiske. 1980. "Presidential
  Prototypes." *Political Behavior* 2: 315–337.

Klar, Samara, and Yanna Krupnikov. 2016. *Independent Politics: How American Disdain for Parties
  Leads to Political Inaction.* Cambridge, UK: Cambridge University Press.

Koger, Gregory, and Matthew J. Lebo. 2012. "Strategic Party Government and the 2010 Elections."
  American Politics Research 40: 927–945.

Koger, Gregory, and Matthew J. Lebo. 2017. *Strategic Party Government: Why Winning Trumps
  Ideology.* Chicago: University of Chicago Press.

Krasno, Jonathan S. 1994. *Challengers, Competition, and Reelection: Comparing Senate and House
  Elections.* New Haven, CT: Yale University Press.

Krehbiel, Keith. 1998. *Pivotal Politics: A Theory of U.S. Lawmaking.* Chicago: University of Chicago
  Press.

Kurtzleben, Danielle. 2015. "People Say They Want Compromise But Not Really." *National Public
  Radio*, May 21. www.npr.org/sections/itsallpolitics/2015/05/21/408550005/people-say-
  they-want-compromise-but-not-really

Lapinski, John, Matt Levendusky, Ken Winneg, and Kathleen Hall Jamieson. 2016. "What Do Citizens Want from Their Member of Congress." *Political Research Quarterly* 69(3): 535–545.

Lawrence, David G. 1976. "Procedural Norms and Tolerance: A Reassessment." *American Political Science Review* 70: 80–100.

Lawrence, Regina G. 2000. "Game-Framing the Issues: Tracking the Strategy Frame in Public Policy News." *Political Communication* 17: 93–114.

Layman, Geoffrey C., Thomas M. Carsey, and Juliana Menasce Horowitz. 2006. "Party Polarization in American Politics: Characteristics, Causes, and Consequences." *Annual Review of Political Science* 9: 83–110.

Lee, Frances E. 2016. *Insecure Majorities: Congress and the Perpetual Campaign*. Chicago: Chicago University Press.

Lelkes, Yphtach. 2016. "Mass Polarization: Manifestations and Measurements." *Public Opinion Quarterly* 80: 392–410.

Lester, Kerry. 2012. "Walsh Says He'd Compromise More in a Second Term." *Chicago Daily Herald*, September 29.

Levendusky, Matthew. 2009. *The Partisan Sort: How Liberals Became Democrats and Conservatives Became Republicans*. Chicago: University of Chicago Press.

Leventhal, Gerald S. 1980. "What Should Be Done with Equity Theory? New Approaches to the Study of Fairness in Social Relationships." In K. Gergen, M. Greenberg, and R. Willis, eds., *Social Exchange*, 27–55. New York: Plenum.

Lindner, Nicole M., and Brian A. Nosek. 2009. "Alienable Speech: Ideological Variations in the Application of Free-Speech Principles." *Political Psychology* 30: 67–92.

Lipsitz, Keena. 2011. *Competitive Elections and the American Voter*. Philadelphia: University of Pennsylvania Press.

Lodge, Milton, and Charles S. Taber. 2013. *The Rationalizing Voter*. Cambridge, UK: Cambridge University Press.

Mansbridge, Jane. 1980. *Beyond Adversary Democracy*. New York: Basic Books.

Marcus, George E., John L. Sullivan, Elizabeth Theiss-Morse, and Sandra L. Wood. 1995. *With Malice Toward Some: How People Make Civil Liberties Judgments*. New York: Cambridge University Press.

Maestro, Betsy, and Giulio Maestro. 2008. *A More Perfect Union: The Story of Our Constitution*. New York: Lothrop, Lee & Shepard Books.

Margalit, Avishai. 2010. *On Compromise and Rotten Compromises*. Princeton, NJ: Princeton University Press.

Marks, Gary, and Norman Miller. 1987. "Ten Years of Research on the False-Consensus Effect: An Empirical and Theoretical Review." *Psychological Bulletin* 102(1): 72–90.

Mason, Lilliana. 2015. "'I Disrespectfully Agree': The Differential Effects of Partisan Sorting on Social and Issue Polarization." *American Journal of Political Science* 59: 128–145.

Mason, Lilliana. 2018. *Uncivil Agreement: How Politics Became Our Identity*. Chicago: University of Chicago Press.

Mayhew, David R. 2005. *Divided We Govern: Party Control, Lawmaking, and Investigations, 1946–2002*. New Haven, CT: Yale University Press.

Mayhew, David. 2015. "List of Important Enactments, 2013–2014." campuspress.yale.edu/davidmayhew/files/2015/05/dataset-DWG-laws-2013-14.pdf

Mayhew, David. 2017. "List of Important Enactments, 2015–2016." campuspress.yale.edu/davidmayhew/files/2017/04/dataset-DWG-laws-2015-16-2ba0cwe.docx

McCarty, Nolan, Keith T. Poole, and Howard Rosenthal. 2016. *Polarized America: The Dance of Ideology and Unequal Riches*. Boston: MIT Press.

McClosky, Herbert. 1964. "Consensus and Ideology in American Politics." *American Political Science Review* 58: 361–382.

McClosky, Herbert, and Alida Brill. 1983. *Dimensions of Tolerance: What Americans Believe about Civil Liberties*. New York: Russell Sage Foundation.

McClosky, Herbert, and John Zaller. 1984. *The American Ethos: Public Attitudes toward Capitalism and Democracy*. Cambridge, MA: Harvard University Press.

McGraw, Kathleen M. 1991. "Managing Blame: An Experimental Investigation into the Effectiveness of Political Accounts." *American Political Science Review* 85: 1133–1158.

McGraw, Kathleen M., Samuel Best, and Richard Timpone. 1995. ""What They Say or What They Do?" The Impact of Elite Explanation and Policy Outcomes on Public Opinion." American *Journal of Political Science* 39: 53–74.

Miler, Kristina C. 2010. *Constituency Representation in Congress: The View from Capitol Hill*. New York: Cambridge University Press.

Mill, John Stuart. 1910. *Representative Government*. London: Dent and Sons.

Miller, Steven D., and David O. Sears. 1986. "Stability and Change in Social Tolerance: A Test of the Persistence Hypothesis." *American Journal of Political Science* 30: 214–236.

Miller, Warren E., and Donald E. Stokes. 1963. "Constituency Influence in Congress." *American Political Science Review* 57: 45–56.

Mondak, Jeffery. 2012. *Personality and the Foundations of Political Behavior*. New York: Cambridge University Press.

Mullen, Brian, Jennifer L. Atkins, Debbie S. Champion, Cecelia Edwards, Dana Hardy, John E. Story, and Mary Vanderklok. 1985. "The False Consensus Effect: A Meta-analysis of 155 Hypothesis Tests." *Journal of Experimental Social Psychology* 21: 262–83.

Muste, Christopher P. 2014. "Reframing Polarization: Social Groups and 'Culture Wars.'" *PS: Political Science & Politics* 47: 432–442.

Mutz, Diana C. 1998. *Impersonal Influence: How Perceptions of Mass Collectives Affect Political Attitudes*. New York: Cambridge University Press.

Mutz, Diana C. 2006. *Hearing the Other Side: Deliberative versus Participatory Democracy*. New York: Cambridge University Press.

Mutz, Diana C. 2015. *In-Your-Face Politics: The Consequences of Uncivil Media*. Princeton: Princeton University Press.

Mutz, Diana C., and Gregory Flemming. 1999. "How Good People Make Bad Collectives: A Social-Psychological Perspective on Public Attitudes Toward Congress." In Joseph Cooper, ed., *Congress and the Decline of Public Trust*, 79–99. Boulder, CO: Westview Press.

Mutz, Diana C., and Byron Reeves. 2005. "The New Videomalaise: Effects of Televised Incivility on Political Trust." *American Political Science Review* 99: 1–15.

National Council for the Social Studies. 1994. *Expectations of Excellence: Curriculum Standards for the Social Studies*. Washington, DC: National Council for the Social Studies.

Neblo, Michael A., Kevin M. Esterling, Ryan P. Kennedy, David M.J. Lazer, and Anand Sokhey. 2010. "Who Wants To Deliberate—And Why?" *American Political Science Review* 104: 566–583.

Newhauser, Daniel. 2012. "Steven LaTourette: Congress Doesn't Function." *Roll Call*, August 1. www.rollcall.com/news/Steven-LaTourette-Says-Congress-Does-Not-Function-216623-1.html

Nicholson, Stephen P. 2012. "Polarizing Cues." *American Journal of Political Science* 56: 52–66.

Nicholson, Stephen P., Chelsea M. Coe, Jason Emory, and Anna V. Song. 2016. "The Politics of Beauty: The Effects of Partisan Bias on Physical Attractiveness." *Political Behavior* 38: 883–898.

Nie, Norman H., Jane Junn, and Kenneth Stehlik-Barry. 1996. *Education and Democratic Citizenship in America*. Chicago: University of Chicago Press.

Nowicki, Dan. 2018. "Flake, Kyl Denounce Dysfunctional Congress' Hyper-Partisanship, Blame the Media." *The Arizona Republic*. April 1. www.azcentral.com/story/news/politics/arizona/2018/04/01/flake-kyl-denounce-dysfunctional-congress-hyper-partisanship-blame-media/468045002/

Nyhan, Brendan, Eric McGhee, John Sides, Seth Masket, and Steven Greene. 2012. "One Vote Out of Step? The Effects of Salient Roll Call Votes in the 2010 Election." *American Politics Research* 40: 844–879.

Ornstein, Norman. 2011. "Worst. Congress. Ever." *Foreign Policy*, July 19. foreignpolicy.com/2011/07/19/worst-congress-ever/

Ornstein, Norm. 2016. "Is This the Worst Congress Ever?" *The Atlantic*, May 17. www.theatlantic.com/politics/archive/2016/05/is-this-the-worst-congress-ever/483075/

Owen, Diana, and Jack Dennis. 1987. "Preadult Development of Political Tolerance." *Political Psychology* 8: 547–561.

Paris, Celia. 2017. "Breaking Down Bipartisanship: When and Why Citizens React to Cooperation across Party Lines." *Public Opinion Quarterly* 81: 473–494.

Patterson, Thomas E. 1994. *Out of Order*. New York: Vintage.

Patterson, Thomas E. 2003. *The Vanishing Voter: Public Involvement in an Age of Uncertainty*. New York: Alfred A. Knopf.

Peffley, Mark, Pia Knigge, and Jon Hurwitz. 2001. "A Multiple Values Model of Political Tolerance." *Political Research Quarterly* 54: 379–406.

Pitkin, Hanna F. 1967. *The Concept of Representation*. Berkeley: University of California Press.

Popkin, Samuel L. 1994. *The Reasoning Voter: Communication and Persuasion in Presidential Campaigns*. Chicago: University of Chicago Press.

Prothro, James W., and Charles M. Grigg. 1960. "Fundamental Principles of Democracy: Bases of Agreement and Disagreement." *Journal of Politics* 22: 276–294.

Putnam, Robert D. 1993. *Making Democracy Work: Civic Traditions in Modern Italy*. Princeton, NJ: Princeton University Press.

Putnam, Robert D. 2000. *Bowling Alone: The Collapse and Revival of American Community*. New York: Simon & Schuster.

Rahn, Wendy M., John Brehm, and Neil Carlson. 1999. "National Elections as Institutions for Generating Social Capital." In Theda Skocpol and Morris P. Fiorina, eds., *Civic Engagement in American Democracy*, 111–160. Washington, DC: Brookings Institution Press.

Ramirez, Mark D. 2009. "The Dynamics of Partisan Conflict on Congressional Approval." *American Journal of Political Science* 53(3): 681–94.

Riker, William, and Peter Ordeshook. 1968. "A Theory of the Calculus of Voting." *American Political Science Review* 62: 25–43.

Rokeach, Milton. 1960. *The Open and Closed Mind: Investigations into the Nature of Belief Systems and Personality Systems*. New York: Basic Books.

Ross, Lee, David Greene, and Pamela House. 1977. "The 'False Consensus Effect': An Egocentric Bias in Social Perception and Attribution Processes." *Experimental Social Psychology* 13: 279–301.

Rostbøll, Christian F. 2017. "Democratic Respect and Compromise." *Critical Review of International Social and Political Philosophy* 20(5): 619–635.

Ryan, Timothy J. 2017. "No Compromise: Political Consequences of Moralized Attitudes." *American Journal of Political Science* 61(2): 409–423.

Sears, David O., and Christia Brown. 2013. "Childhood and Adult Political Development." In Leonie Huddy, David O. Sears, and Jack S. Levy, eds., *The Oxford Handbook of Political Psychology*, 59–95. 2d ed. New York: Oxford University Press.

Sears, David O., Richard R. Lau, T.R. Tyler and H.J. Allen. 1980. "Self-Interest vs. Symbolic Politics in Policy Attitudes and Voting." *American Political Science Review* 74: 670–684.

Serwer, Adam. 2013. "GOP Caves, Stops Blocking Violence Against Women Act." *Mother Jones*. February 28. www.motherjones.com/politics/2013/02/gop-violence-against-women-act-passes/

Sigel, Roberta S. 1966. "Image of the American Presidency: Part II of an Exploration into Popular Views of Presidential Power." *Midwest Journal of Political Science* 10(1):123–137.

Singh, Shane, Ignacio Lago, and André Blais. 2011. "Winning and Competitiveness as Determinants of Political Support." *Social Science Quarterly* 92: 695–709.

Snowe, Olympia. 2012. "Why I'm Leaving the Senate." *Washington Post*, March 1. www.washingtonpost.com/opinions/olympia-snowe-why-im-leaving-the-senate/2012/03/01/gIQApGYZlR_story.html

Steinhauer, Jennifer, and Robert Pear. 2015. "Bipartisan Deal on Health Care Issues Hits a Snag Among Senate Democrats." *The New York Times*, March 24.

Steinhauer, Jennifer, and Robert Pear. 2015. "House Approves Bill on Changes to Medicare." *The New York Times*, March 26.

Stouffer, Samuel C. 1955. *Communism, Conformity, and Civil Liberties*. New York: Doubleday.

Sulkin, Tracy, Paul Testa, and Kaye Usry. 2015. "What Gets Rewarded? Legislative Activity and Constituency Approval." *Political Research Quarterly* 68(4): 690–702.

Sullivan, John L., George E. Marcus, Stanley Feldman, and James E. Piereson. 1981. "The Sources of Political Tolerance: A Multivariate Analysis." *American Political Science Review* 75: 92–106.

Sullivan, John L., James Piereson, and George E. Marcus. 1982. *Political Tolerance and American Democracy*. Chicago: University of Chicago Press.

Sullivan, John L., Pat Walsh, Michal Shamir, David G. Barnum, and James L. Gibson. 1993. "Why Politicians Are More Tolerant: Selective Recruitment and Socialization among Political Elites in Britain, Israel, New Zealand and the United States." *British Journal of Political Science* 23: 51–76.

Taber, Charles S., and Milton Lodge. 2006. "Motivated Skepticism in the Evaluation of Political Beliefs." *American Journal of Political Science* 50: 755–769.

Terbush, Jon. 2013. "Confirmed: This Is the Worst Congress Ever." *The Week*, December 26. theweek.com/articles/453744/confirmed-worst-congress-ever

Theiss-Morse, Elizabeth, and John R. Hibbing. 2005. "Citizenship and Civic Engagement." *Annual Review of Political Science* 8: 227–249.

Tocqueville, Alexis de. 1969. *Democracy in America*. Garden City, NY: Doubleday Anchor.

Tomz, Michael, and Robert P. Van Houweling. 2012. "Political Pledges as Credible Commitments." Working paper. www.stanford.edu/~tomz/working/TomzVanHouweling-Pledges-2012-03-27.pdf

Torney-Purta, Judith, Rainer Lehmann, Hans Oswald, and Wolfram Schulz. 2001. *Citizenship and Education in Twenty-Eight Countries: Civic Knowledge and Engagement at Age Fourteen.* Amsterdam: International Association for the Evaluation of Educational Achievement.

Tyler, Tom R. 1990. *Why People Obey the Law*. New Haven, CT: Yale University Press.

Tyler, Tom R. 1994. "Governing amid Diversity: The Effect of Fair Decision-making Procedures on the Legitimacy of Government." *Law & Society Review* 28(4): 809–832.

Tyler, Tom R. 2000. "Social Justice: Outcome and Procedure." *International Journal of Psychology* 35: 117–125.

Tyler, Tom R. 2001. "The Psychology of Public Dissatisfaction with Government." In John R. Hibbing and Elizabeth Theiss-Morse, eds. *What Is It about Government That Americans Dislike?* Cambridge, UK: Cambridge University Press.

Tyler, Tom R., and Yuen J. Huo. 2002. *Trust in the Law: Encouraging Public Cooperation with the Police and Courts*. New York: Russell Sage Foundation.

Ulbig, Stacy G. 2008. "Voice Is Not Enough: The Importance of Influence in Political Trust and Policy Assessments." *Public Opinion Quarterly* 72: 523–539.

Van Boven, Leaf, Charles M. Judd, and David K. Sherman. 2012. "Political Polarization Projection: Social Projection of Partisan Attitude Extremity and Attitudinal Processes." *Journal of Personality and Social Psychology* 103: 84–100.

Verba, Sidney, Kay Lehman Schlozman, and Henry E. Brady. 1995. *Voice and Equality: Civic Voluntarism in American Politics*. Cambridge, MA: Harvard University Press.

Weinstock, Daniel. 2013. "On the Possibility of Principled Moral Compromise." *Critical Review of International Social and Political Philosophy* 16: 537–556.

Westfall, Jacob, Leaf Van Boven, John R. Chambers, and Charles M. Judd. 2015. "Perceiving Political Polarization in the United States: Party Identity Strength and Attitude Extremity Exacerbate the Perceived Partisan Divide." *Perspectives on Psychological Science* 10: 145–158.

Wojcieszak, Magdalena, and Vincent Price. 2009. "What Underlies the False Consensus Effect? How Personal Opinion and Disagreement Affect Perception of Public Opinion." *International Journal of Public Opinion Research* 21(1): 25–46.

Wolak, Jennifer. 2006. "The Consequences of Presidential Battleground Strategies for Citizen Engagement." *Political Research Quarterly* 59: 353–361.

Wolak, Jennifer. 2014. "How Campaigns Promote the Legitimacy of Elections." *Electoral Studies* 34: 205–215.

Wolf, Michael R., J. Cherie Strachan, and Daniel M. Shea. 2012. "Forget the Good of the Game: Political Incivility and Lack of Compromise as a Second Layer of Party Polarization." *American Behavioral Scientist* 56: 1677–1695.

Zellman, Gail, and David O. Sears. 1971. "Childhood Origins and Tolerance for Dissent." *Journal of Social Issues* 27: 109–136.

INDEX

Tables and figures are indicated by *t* and *f* following the page number

For the benefit of digital users, indexed terms that span two pages (e.g., 52–53) may, on occasion, appear on only one of those pages.